T0271624

ESTABLISHED
1756

BOROUGH
MARKET

The
Knowledge

ESTABLISHED
1756

BOROUGH MARKET

The Knowledge

WITH ANGELA CLUTTON

PHOTOGRAPHY BY KIM LIGHTBODY

HODDER &
STOUGHTON

First published in Great Britain in 2022 by Hodder & Stoughton
An Hachette UK company

1

Hardback ISBN 978 1 39970062 7
eBook ISBN 978 1 39970063 4

Executive Publisher: Liz Gough
Project Editor: Isabel Gonzalez-Prendergast
Assistant Editor: Olivia Nightingall
Design: Dave Brown at APE
Photography: Kim Lightbody
Food Stylist: Kitty Coles
Props Stylist: Tabitha Hawkins
Production Controller: Matthew Everett

The Borough Market team:
Director of Communications and Engagement: Kate Howell
Project Manager: Claire Ford
Consultant: Mark Riddaway
Trader Knowledge interviews: Clare Finney
Wine Consultant: Jane Parkinson

Colour origination by Born LTD
Printed and bound in Italy by Elcograf

Hodder & Stoughton Ltd
Carmelite House
50 Victoria Embankment
London
EC4Y 0DZ

www.hodder.co.uk

Introduction: Borough Market

First and foremost, Borough Market's traders are here to sell food – amazing food from every corner of the world, produced in ways that place an unusually strong emphasis on quality and sustainability. But food isn't the only thing they offer. They also provide, in abundance and completely free of charge, their knowledge.

While modern retail becomes increasingly remote and impersonal, dominated by digital giants and supermarket self-checkouts, markets provide an echo of a time when shopping was about interaction as well as consumption. It's almost inconceivable that you could pass through Borough Market without buying a hunk of cheese or a bottle of oil, and it's absolutely impossible to leave without having a conversation. That exchange may be little more than a friendly smile and a word about the weather, but it could amount to something altogether more enlightening.

The traders know so much about food. They work with it every day. Many of them produce it themselves. They know where it comes from, what makes it special and how to get the best from it. Most importantly, they genuinely care, and they're desperate for other people to care too.

Some people feel intimidated by the idea of shopping at a place where not everything is pre-portioned and extensively labelled, where unfamiliar vegetables, fish and cuts of meat sit side by side with the carrots, salmon and sausages. The warmth and expertise of the traders is what breaks that down. No one will judge you for not knowing how to prepare a whole crab or choose between four different types of rye bread. They'll just tell you what you need to know.

That's what this book is all about: using the knowledge of the Market's traders to demystify some of the ingredients sold here, allowing you to broaden your horizons, try new foods or get more out of the ones you already enjoy. Angela Clutton is the perfect conduit for all that knowledge: as the host of Borough Market's Cookbook Club and presenter of the Borough Talks podcasts, she knows the place inside out and loves nothing more than to share her enthusiasm. Her brilliant recipes bring together Market ingredients, the traders' tips and her own abundant skill to create dishes that are both inspiring and accessible.

You don't have to come to Borough Market for this cookbook to be relevant. Most of it applies wherever you shop. But if you do visit these historic halls, you'll find the perfect ingredients to bring these recipes to life. And you're also guaranteed a chat.

Introduction: The Knowledge

I can tell you exactly when I fell head-over-heels, no-going-back-from-this in love with Borough Market: Thursday 17th August 2017. I was doing one of the lunchtime cooking demonstrations out in the Market, and talking about the particular fabulous variety of plums I'd bought that morning to use for the ice cream I was making. A lady in the crowd called out to ask me which stall they were from, then beetled off, and returned excitedly waving a brown paper bag of said plums.

That summed up for me so much about the Market experience. How it is all about the connection between produce, traders, shoppers and the Market community. Ultimately, too, about how we choose to feed ourselves, if choice is a luxury we are fortunate enough to have. Those are the fundamentals behind this book.

I really hope each of our chapters gives you insight into food values and the impacts of how our food is produced, and encourages you to think about your own shopping and cooking choices and how vital they are to the sustainability of a positive food system.

More even than that, I hope this book allows you – whether you are a frequent visitor to the Market, an occasional shopper there, or hoping one day to make it along – to feel the Market experience. To get a sense of its energy, its positivity, and that appreciation of good food bounces off its every railway bridge arch and cobbled alleyway.

Each chapter here is packed with trader knowledge, covering everything from filleting a fish, to honey varietals, fixing a martini and so much more. They are like every conversation I've had over the years with the Market traders, with all their years of experience coming together. You will hear the voices of the traders as you read, and then mine too guiding you through the 80 or so recipes that are using the traders' knowledge and produce as launch points for a breadth of home-cooking.

Borough Market is for me – and I know for many others too – a place of inspiration, excitement and comfort. May our book, too, find a way to be those things in your kitchen.

Angela Clutton

London, 2022

How to use this book

Each chapter is packed with trader knowledge, their produce insights and tips.
All can be navigated by using these icons, which should help you to find what's what and where:

Features

Lists

Questions & answers

Skills guides

Stocks

Drink pairings

Then come the recipes – and nestled amongst those you'll find recipe tips and more trader tips. Often the recipes refer back to trader knowledge earlier in the same chapter, or elsewhere amongst these pages. All of which is by way of saying that the trader knowledge and the recipes are intended to work together and complement each other. To get the most out of this book, I urge you to read both.

The chapters very much interlink too. So, for example, The Greengrocers chapter is packed with veg-led recipes but there are also other vegetable dishes to be found in other chapters. At the back of the book you'll find a full list of all the recipes.

And then, sprinkled through the recipes, are 'A few ways with....' squash, dried beans, jointed chicken and more. These are not formal recipes but intended as launch points for your own culinary creativity and how you might shop and cook with certain produce.

Speaking of shopping: we hope you will have a wonderful time armed with shopping lists as you wander the stalls of Borough Market and / or your own local market. Given this book is as much about how food is produced as what you do with it in your kitchen, we hope too that in all your food shopping you will take its philosophy on board and choose (where you can) to shop with local, smaller, ethical, sustainable producers who really care about the produce they sell.

Cooking the recipes

The most useful things when cooking are always your judgement and sense of taste.

Recipes can only ever really be a guide – a good guide, I absolutely hope and intend. But some things will always be determined by the heat you have your hob at, your oven's idiosyncrasies, the size and weights of your pans and dishes... I urge you to think as you cook, not just follow. Doing that will make you – me, all of us – better cooks.

And taste! Then season accordingly.

The ingredients lists for each recipe are your shopping lists. All the basic ingredient prep for each recipe is in its method, and I hope that way of cooking will ease you through the flow of chopping and prepping as the recipe goes along. It should empower you to feel the rhythm of the recipe and dance along with it. However, if you are a cook who prefers to prep ahead your onions and so on, a quick read through of the recipe before you begin should help you work out what needs to be done.

Don't be scared to swap ingredients in or out according to what's in season or personal preferences. These are pages to be scribbled on as the recipes are shaped to fit how you like to cook and eat.

Please think about food waste and how to avoid it; this applies to ingredient preparation as well as using up what you've made. While you prepare ingredients, look out for guides in this book for making stocks from meat, fish or veg 'waste', and think too about finding ways to use your leftovers.

Basic ingredients

Unless the recipe says otherwise:

- Start cooking with your ingredients at room temperature
- Butter can be salted or unsalted
- Eggs are large and always organic
- Milk, yoghurt, etc are full-fat
- Salt is flaked

- All olive oil is extra-virgin. Some recipes suggest a particular type or flavour profile, otherwise the olive oil feature on pages 96–8 will help you shop for what to use when
- When shopping for fish or seafood, for animal produce or their by-products (such as butter or milk) choose the highest quality, most ethically-produced and sustainable versions you can. They'll also be the most delicious versions of themselves

Basic equipment

Here are some of the pieces of equipment that I use a lot in my kitchen and you will find useful as you cook through these pages:

- Probe thermometer – for deep-frying, for meat, for quite a lot really
- Knives: a heavy chef's knife, a filleting knife with a flexible blade, and a small pointed paring knife
- Small and large frying pans – ones that can go in the oven without their handles melting
- Casserole dishes that can be used on top of the stove and in the oven – ideally a few of different shapes and sizes
- Baking dishes
- Digital scales
- Microplane grater – maybe even a couple of different sizes
- Pestle and mortar
- Measuring spoons
- 'Y'-shape vegetable peeler
- Mandoline – not essential, but very handy
- Slotted spoon
- Tongs for turning meat / veg
- Ice-cream machine – this might be less of an investment of time and space than you think
- Sustainable options for wrapping your food: non-PVC clingfilm, beeswax wraps, greaseproof paper...

THE FISHMONGERS

The Haward family have been cultivating oysters in and around the creeks of Mersea Island, Essex, since the 1700s. Now in the hands of an eighth generation of oystermen, their business is as devoted to maintaining the ecosystem of the River Blackwater and the surrounding coastline as it is to the careful harvesting of oysters.

The art of cultivating oysters

Tom Haward, Richard Haward's Oysters

Two thousand years ago, when the Romans founded the city of Colchester, they fell in love with the local oysters. They weren't the first, and they wouldn't be the last. Native oysters were particularly popular between the 17th and 19th centuries, when they were extremely plentiful – and very cheap. People today think of champagne as the drinks pairing for oysters, but it used to be ale or stout. My second great-grandfather had ale and oysters for his wedding breakfast at the local pub with his wife-to-be, Emma. But when harsh winters, pollution and a disease called bonamiosis decimated stocks in the mid-20th century, native oysters became scarce and their availability was largely confined to expensive London restaurants.

Since then, it has been hard to get stocks of native oysters up to a level that is commercially sustainable. The situation is improving, though. For decades, my family has been working to protect and improve Colchester natives. Since 2011 we've been part of the Essex Native Oyster Restoration Initiative (ENORI), a collaboration between oystermen, academics, conservationists and the government, designed to restore stocks in the Blackwater estuary. Today, ours is one of the few oyster fisheries to sell the Colchester native oyster when it's in season.

We also sell rock oysters. Back when native oyster stocks were plummeting, Atlantic rock oysters were introduced to Britain to keep the industry going. They're much more robust and, unlike natives, they thrive as much in summer as they do in winter, so they don't have a season. The idea that you can only eat oysters in the months of the year with an 'r' in them is really a hangover from when people only ate native oysters. It doesn't hold true for rock oysters at all.

We are cultivators rather than farmers. Some oysters spawn on our beds and others we bring in from the deeper waters of the River Blackwater, which is the estuary that feeds into the shallower creeks where our beds are located. While the deeper waters provide excellent initial conditions, the concentration of nutrients isn't high enough to produce the kind of succulent meat we want, so we move the oysters to the shallower, nutrient-rich creeks to finish growing and really plump up.

> " The idea that you can only eat oysters in the months of the year with an 'r' in them is really a hangover from when people only ate native oysters.

> " Oysters taste of the environment they're grown in. Here in Mersea, they develop a really big, punchy flavour, with a long finish.

Oysters taste of the environment they're grown in. Here in Mersea, the marsh grasses capture the mud, and the creek acts like a bottleneck, creating high levels of plankton, salt and magnesium. As a result, the oysters develop a really big, punchy flavour, with a long finish. Down Jersey way, where the sea is sandier and rockier, they have a slightly more mineral taste. Oysters from Ireland, France or America all have a different composition of flavours, just like wines from different regions.

The oysters we cultivate – both native and rock oysters – spend their entire lives in the wild, whereas hatchery oysters are started in a lab, then taken to the sea when they get to a certain size to carry on growing. This also affects the flavour, because wild oysters can take three to four years to get to the size we want. During that time, they are slowly plumping up and absorbing flavour from the sea. Hatchery oysters grow much more quickly. They're less briny in flavour, and to me taste almost appley.

We harvest our oysters using ladder dredges. The word 'dredging' has bad connotations, due to the damage caused in other parts of the fishing industry, but the dredges we use don't carve up the seabed. In fact, they improve the ecosystem by skimming off the top layer of the oyster bed. This prevents the bed from getting so silted up that the remaining oysters suffocate. We've been hand-dredging like this since the 1700s, and it's very sustainable. We also put down more oysters than we harvest. Because oysters – like mussels and clams –

are filter feeders, the more of them there are, the cleaner the water and the healthier the surrounding environment. You should see the water around us: it's crystal clear and the sea life is flourishing.

Of course, the reason oysters clean the surrounding water so well is that they absorb everything they ingest: good and bad. They're like Superman, absorbing the radiation of both kryptonite and the sun. That's why we have to clean them by placing them in seawater that has been purified with UV to kill E. coli, salmonella and other nasties. As they filter this water, any impurities they've ingested are removed. A lot of producers send their oysters to purification centres that use manufactured saltwater, but this changes the flavour profile. By using water from the River Blackwater, we ensure our oysters retain the beautiful flavours associated with their natural habitat

Deep-fried oysters with horseradish sauce, quick-pickled ginger and spring onion, page 36.

HOW TO... shuck oysters

'Ultimately, oyster shucking is about finding your own technique. Everyone I've ever taught to shuck, shucks completely differently to me, including my fiancée. When my mum first taught me, when I was 11 years old, I wasn't allowed to wear a glove – if you work with your bare hands, you're inclined to be more careful. Shucking is not hard, but it does take practice to understand where the biting point is as you run your knife along the outside of the shell. Once you find that, the hinge will just give. That's the hardest part done. Then it's just a case of prising the shell open. With giant oysters that takes some strength, but with the normal ones it's doable without too much effort. Practice makes perfect, as they say. I make it look quick and easy, but I've been shucking oysters every day for over 20 years.'

Tom Haward, Richard Haward's Oysters

Brown shrimp

Character Tiny, sweet and pinkish brown when cooked – which they must be almost as soon as they're caught, to prevent them from sticking together.

Source Caught by day boats in Morecambe Bay, off the coast of Lancashire and Cumbria, where they're often set in spiced butter to create the famous local speciality, potted shrimp.

Langoustines

Character Pale, sunset-coloured crustaceans resembling a cross between a prawn and a lobster, both in appearance and flavour.

Source Over a third of the world's langoustines are landed in Scotland, though the vast majority are exported to other countries.

Five crusta

Carabineros

Character Dazzlingly crimson in colour, with an equally intense flavour, many regard these as peak prawn.

Source A deep-sea species sustainably caught by small family-owned boats off the coast of Spain and Morocco.

ceans

Vannamei (king prawn)

Character Sweet and meaty tropical prawns with grey shells that turn orange-pink with heat.

Source Farmed along the equator in Central America and Asia, where concerns around environmental impacts have led to more sustainable methods being adopted.

Madagascan prawns

Character Large, succulent, grey-pink prawns renowned for their sweet flavour and lean meat.

Source Farmed in the warm waters of Madagascar in accordance with Marine Stewardship Council sustainability standards.

A family business founded by Les Salisbury, whose first foray into fishing was catching Morecambe Bay shrimps as a child, Furness Fish Markets has been at the heart of Borough Market since the 1990s. As well as its famous potted shrimps, the company also sells fresh day-boat fish caught from around the British Isles and delivered each day to the stall, which is managed by Max Tucker.

Max Tucker

Furness Fish Markets

How do wild and farmed fish differ?

Wild fish are always going to taste a little different, on account of what they eat and the fact they swim around more. For example, wild bream tastes a lot earthier and meatier than farmed, which is fattier and a little bit sweeter. There's nothing wrong with that – a bit of fat is quite nice sometimes – but it depends on your preference. It's like game versus poultry: that's the analogy I use. The second big difference is seasonality. Wild mackerel, bass and a few other species migrate to warmer waters once a year – increasingly twice a year, because of climate change – but farmed fish are available all year.

Terrible tales are told of conditions on some fish farms. What should we be looking out for?

Look for sea-reared fish, it's farmed off the coast, where the water is naturally cleansed and refreshed. The sea trout we buy is reared off the coast of the Shetland Islands, so the conditions are as close to the wild as you get. Our farmed Loch Duart salmon is reared in a spacious environment, with natural food, for three months longer than normal farmed salmon. You can really see the difference. The fish I've seen imported from countries where they're raised in tanks often display defects: a missing eye, cramped backs, no dorsal fin. Ultimately, if you want to know about the fish you're eating, the best place you can go is a fishmonger. You won't get that information off a packet on a shelf.

What are the sustainability issues around wild fishing?

The big issue is overfishing by huge industrial trawlers that are clearing out the seas with a lot of bycatch: unwanted fish that are caught in the massive nets and then discarded. These trawlers buy up fishing quotas from small, family-owned day boats, which are being abandoned by the younger generations. Young people don't want to go into the trade because they can't make a living out of it – thanks to the trawlers – or don't fancy the lifestyle. That leaves the family with a fishing quota and no one to fish, so they sell their quota to the trawlers, which can then catch even more. It's a vicious circle.

What are the best indicators for freshness and quality in fish?

Clear glassy eyes, red gills, firm body – and smell. Fresh fish don't smell. That's a fact. If there's a hint of a fish smell around the stall, that's from the boxes. They get sprayed out every day, but after a while you need to replace them. Find a store that's clean inside and doesn't smell too 'fishy'.

How should we store fish?

Take your fish out of the paper, put it on a plate, cover it with cling film, then keep it in the fridge. If it's live produce, do the same but use a damp tea towel to keep it moist. Fresh fish freezes well. There is some truth in it being better when frozen at sea, because they chill the fish down within seconds, but you can have more faith in what you're getting if you buy fresh fish from a trusted fishmonger then freeze it at home.

What is the merit of buying fillets from a fishmonger?

A good fishmonger will buy a whole fish and fillet it on site, so you get much better-quality fillets. Most factories and larger retailers fillet by machine or pay people to fillet to a certain weight so there's more wastage and the fillet is less carefully cut.

What are the more sustainable, locally sourced fish we should be looking out for?

As a replacement for turbot, brill is a good bet. Pollock is a great white fish, that people don't buy enough of, which is a great shame. The flesh is firm, the fish is beautiful. It's just as good as cod, as is coley. People don't realise it, but coley is often used for fish and chips in the UK.

How do we get the most out of a fishmonger?

Be nice to them! Find a fishmonger who enjoys their job. People ask me about our display, saying: 'Do you have to do that every day? Aren't you bored of it?' And I say: 'It takes between two and three hours to set it up and pack it down every day, but if it was boring I wouldn't be doing it.' I'm not creative – give me a pen and paper and I can't draw for toffee. But there aren't many people in London who can do what I do with a fish counter. I love what I do, and that comes across.

^ Lay the cooked crab on its back.

^ Use your thumbs to pop the body section away from the top shell

^ Twist off the legs and claws.

^ Pull away and discard the grey, hairy 'dead man's fingers'.

Preparing a brown crab

There's no getting away from the fact that picking a cooked crab is fiddly, messy, and the absolute best way to get delicious, super-fresh crab meat.

Brown or white crab meat is tucked into its every crevice. Here is how Jed Hall at Shellseekers Fish & Game gets out as much meat as possible.

Set about trying to get as much meat as you can out of the body and where the legs and claws join the body. As you work, put the white and brown meat into separate bowls. Split the body in two and get into every crevice with a teaspoon, fork, lobster pick – whatever helps you get into the tight angles.

^ Now for the legs and claws. Use the back of a heavy knife (or rolling pin) to crack them open. Take care, as fragments of shell will fly off.

^ Again, pick at every bit to get as much white meat out as possible, removing the central cartilage from the claws.

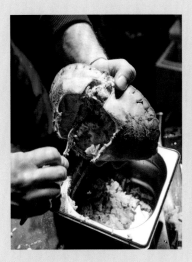

^ Scoop the brown meat out of the shell. Check through your bowls of white and brown meat to make sure no tiny pieces of shell or cartilage have crept in.

^ To serve the crab in the shell – so for dressed crab – season the meat, then spoon the brown meat into the two sides and fill the middle with the white meat.

Add a squeeze of lemon juice and some parsley then serve, or use the meat as your recipe requires.

Crab toasts with crab and vegetable broth, page 34.

Almond clams (dog cockles)

Character The almond clam is so called for its sweet, nutty flavour, which needs little embellishment. Its pretty mottled shell can vary in pattern and colouring, from dusky pink, to yellow, to reddish brown.

Uses Most commonly served raw or lightly fried with garlic, the almond clam quickly turns tough when overcooked.

Five clams

Razor clams

Character Tubular in shape. The sweet, delicate pearlescent flesh of the razor calm resembles that of squid in texture and appearance.

Uses One of the more versatile clams when it comes to flavour: onions, samphire, parmesan, garlic and chilli all pair well with it. As with all clams, it is sensitive to overcooking.

Dorset clams (palourdes)

Character A striking, toast-like black and brown shell with delicate ridges. Salty, fresh and delicately sweet, these are among the most prized of clams.

Uses One of the classic uses of palourde clams is to steam them open in a little olive oil, garlic and wine for a spaghetti vongole.

American hard clams (quahogs, chowder clams)

Character A chunky, triangular shell with a prominent beak. Its fine, tightly spaced bands boast tints of light brown, grey, even violet, and its size varies greatly – some are huge.

Uses The largest of these clams tend to be used, as their name suggests in chowder, being deeply meaty, and too large and tough to serve raw.

Cherrystone clams

Character Smaller than chowder clams, but from the same species, with the same distinctive colouring and bands.

Uses Succulent and meaty, the cherrystones lend themselves to grilling and pasta sauces.

Much of the magic that happens at the fishmongers' is done slightly away from the shopper's gaze, making this glimpse behind the Furness Fish market stand to witness Max Tucker's skill and artistry – hard won over decades of being a fishmonger – all the more special as he sets out the building blocks for filleting round fish.

Scaling and filleting a round fish

^ The fish Max is filleting here is a seabass. Skip to the opposite page if your fish is already scaled and gutted. Work the descaler across the fish in upward strokes towards the head, holding the fish firmly in place as you work, and getting as close to the dorsal fin as possible.

^ Now cut the head off at an angle right behind the gill plate and fin. As the head is moved away, some of the seabass' innards will come away too. To complete the gutting, use the space made by removing the head to scrape away the remaining innards, taking special care to remove the yellow gallbladder.

^ A filleting knife with its flexible blade is the essential tool for the actual filleting – and it needs to be very sharp. Max changes and sharpens which knife he is using as he goes along, to make sure it is just the right tool for getting the fillet cleanly off the bone.

^ Find the line by the fin-edge of the fish and – starting at the tail end and working a couple of millimetres in from the edge – insert the knife blade at a 45-degree angle.

^ Hold the fish firmly in place with one hand as you use the knife to skim closely above the bones. Working with the blade angled slightly upwards helps. Flick the blade over the spine when you reach it. Cut along the fillet to release it.

^ Now for the second fillet. Turn the fish over and this time cut in at the head end, a few millimetres in from the fin-edge, at a 45-degree angle.

^ Try to release the fillet in one long, smooth cut. Flick the blade over the spine and release the fillet.

Bream fillets with buttered cobnuts and mixed beans, page 45.
Charred pineapple and soused mackerel with cucumber and mint, page 183.

^ Trim away any fat and make a neat line along the belly of each fillet. Trim the belly, check for any stray bones that can be removed with tweezers and admire your two fillets before cooking them.

Five unusual fish cuts

Andy Stevenson,
Shellseekers
Fish & Game

Tongue

What we call the 'tongue' of the cod or the hake is actually the chin or throat of the fish, not its tongue. In Spain it's a delicacy. It is often just chargrilled and drizzled with lemon juice and extra-virgin olive oil, or – in the Basque country – cooked in a traditional stew known as kokotxas, and served with salsa verde, a vivid green sauce of lemon, garlic and parsley.

Cheeks

The cheeks of monkfish and cod are a classic cut in many parts of the world. They are very tender – almost like scallops – because there's no bone or sinew and almost no movement in that part of the fish. This texture makes them very versatile: they can be used in stir-fries or curries, or just pan-fried in breadcrumbs or spices. Skate cheeks are particularly fantastic – they taste amazing deep fried. They're often thrown away, so they are relatively cheap.

Liver

Most fish livers aren't worth eating, but when people buy red mullet they almost always say keep the liver in. It has a creamy texture and a rich taste, a bit like chicken liver. Those who like it will set it aside from the rest of the fish and enjoy it blended into a rich sauce or pan-fried with sliced garlic. Monkfish liver is a delicacy in Japan. And, of course, there's cod liver, which doesn't just need to be ingested in capsule form, but can be enjoyed cooked.

Roe

Fish roe are the eggs or spawn of a fish. The best known is caviar, which is sturgeon roe, but there are all sorts of roe, most of which have that salty taste and distinctive popping texture. Many people pan-fry roe and have it on toast, or use it as a garnish. Cod roe can also be whipped with oil to make taramasalata. Scallop roe – also called 'coral', because of its beautiful colour – is really popular with chefs, who dry it out and use it as a seasoning, to bring colour and flavour to a dish.

Skin

Most fish skin is delicious, either fried up in the pan, grilled until crispy, or dehydrated into crisps for snacking. However, I would avoid fish with particularly thick or leathery skins, such as dover sole, halibut or monkfish.

Fishmonger's pie with fish crackling, page 42.

Sardines with fennel, capers and mint

Sardines are for more than just packing into tins – fabulous though tinned sardines can certainly be. Look out for fresh sardines at the fishmongers around the same time as their herring-family cousin, the popular mackerel. In the UK, they are in season in the late summer months. This recipe embraces that seasonality in a light, bright, slightly sweet dish that's best served with buttery new potatoes.

Asking your fishmonger to butterfly and pin bone the fish for you will help ensure you waste as little as possible, and avoids the nuisance of small bones when eating – with the bonus that the sardines will look beautiful to serve.

Serves 4 as a main or 8 as a starter or small plate

1 onion

3 tablespoons olive oil

2 garlic cloves

3 fennel bulbs

2 bay leaves

100ml white wine

1½ tablespoons medium-strength honey (see pages 102–3 for honey styles)

8 sardines (or 4 mackerel), butterflied and pin boned

1 orange

2 tablespoons capers

2 sprigs of mint

Peel the onion and slice into thin half-moons. Heat 2 tablespoons of the olive oil in a large frying pan or shallow casserole dish over a medium heat, add the onion and cook until just softening. Peel then crush or roughly chop the garlic and add to the pan to soften too for a couple of minutes.

Trim the top and bottom of the fennel bulbs, remove the outside layer if it looks damaged, and remember how good fennel trimmings can be for fish stock – page 52. Thinly slice the fennel bulbs, then add them to the pan along with the bay leaves. Season and stir, then pour in the wine, stir again, cover the pan and leave for 10 minutes, stirring halfway through. Take off the lid, mix through the honey and cook for another 5 minutes. The fennel should be completely soft and becoming a lovely golden colour. Spoon the contents of the pan onto a serving plate, discarding the bay leaves.

Add the remaining tablespoon of the olive oil to the same pan over a medium heat. Once hot, sit the sardines in skin-side down (you may need to do this in two batches). Season and cook for 2 minutes, then turn over and cook through for another 2 minutes. Cook each side 2 minutes longer if using larger mackerel. Lift the fish onto the fennel.

Give a squeeze of orange over the top and a couple of grindings of pepper. Rinse and drain the capers, chop with the mint leaves, and scatter over. Serve while still warm.

Bourbon and coriander seed gravadlax

Making gravadlax means getting hold of top-quality salmon (or indeed trout). It is well worth taking the time to source salmon that's been reared responsibly, and the best way to know is to just ask the fishmonger.

This recipe layers up the classic gravadlax cure of salt, sugar and dill with extra depth of flavour from bourbon, coriander seeds and orange zest. A couple of days of curing give delicious, silky slices of salmon that are so versatile – whether on rye bread that has been spread with a little mustard or with some tarragon mayonnaise spooned on top, as a canape or starter, with scrambled eggs... You'll think of plenty more.

Serves 10-12 as a starter or small plate; or 6 as a main

1.2kg very fresh salmon fillet,
   as symmetrical a piece as possible
   and of even thickness

1 tablespoon mixed peppercorns

1 tablespoon coriander seeds

70g coarse sea salt

70g unrefined caster sugar

40g dill

1 orange

50ml bourbon

You will need 4 cans of food as weights

Run your hand over the salmon to check for any remaining bones and use tweezers to remove any. Trim off any very thin ends on the fish as they will over-cure and be inedible. Cut the salmon in half and sit the pieces side-by-side skin-side down on a large piece of foil.

Use a pestle and mortar to crush the peppercorns and coriander seeds, then mix them in a large bowl with the salt and sugar. Roughly chop the dill and stir through. Pare 6 broad strips of peel off the orange, taking as little white pith as possible. Pour the bourbon over the salmon, rubbing it in gently, then sit three strips of orange peel on each piece of salmon, giving the peel a squeeze to get its oils going.

Smear the cure mixture all over one piece of the salmon. Lift up the other piece and sit it on top of the cure, skin-side up. The cure is effectively being sandwiched between the two flesh sides of the fish. Make sure any exposed bits of salmon get some cure over them.

Wrap it up tightly in the foil and sit in a baking dish with a chopping board or plate on top, then add the food tins on top of that to weigh it down. Put it in the fridge for 2-3 days (at the lower end of the time if it's a thin tail piece). Turn the parcel over occasionally to ensure even distribution of the cure.

Unwrap the parcel and scrape off the cure. Your gravadlax is now ready to slice and serve in any way that you would smoked salmon.

With the cure removed, and the fish unsliced and wrapped up, your gravadlax will keep for up to a week in the fridge and it also freezes very well.

Don't waste any of the thin ends you cut off before curing – they'll be great for fishcakes, linguine, or for adding to a fish pie...

Borough Market – The Knowledge

Arbroath smokie croquetas

At Oak & Smoke you'll find smokies: haddock that has been salted and hot-smoked over an open fire. They're what the small town of Arbroath on the east coast of Scotland is world-renowned for. Here, their deep flavour is wrapped in creamy sauce and deep-fried into crunchy croquetas.

Smokies come in string-tied pairs. This recipe uses just a single smokie, but its partner will happily freeze to become a useful stand-by for fish pies, soups and more. You could swap the smokie for undyed smoked haddock– see tip below.

Makes 16–20 croquetas, depending on size

1 Arbroath smokie

1 banana shallot

2 tablespoons olive oil

70g unsalted butter

200g plain flour

600ml whole milk

1 tablespoon finely chopped dill or freshly grated horseradish

2 eggs

150g panko breadcrumbs

1 litre rapeseed or sunflower oil

Flake the flesh from the Arboath smokie skin and skeleton, watching for small bones. There should be about 200g meat.

Peel and finely chop the shallot. Heat the olive oil and butter in a medium saucepan over a low heat, then add the chopped shallot and cook until softening but not colouring. Add 100g of the plain flour and stir for 3 minutes, then slowly add the milk, stirring after every addition. Season, then cook this gently for 15–20 minutes, stirring all the time. It is done when the sauce is thick enough to come away from the sides of the pan.

Mix the flaked fish into the sauce along with the dill or horseradish. Pour into a shallow dish, sit a piece of non-PVC cling film directly on its surface to prevent skin forming, then leave to cool. Chill for at least 2 hours or overnight.

Prepare to roll the croquetas: put into separate shallow bowls the remaining 100g of flour, the eggs and the panko breadcrumbs. Beat the eggs. Lightly coat your hands with a little of the flour and tear off golf-ball-size pieces of the croqueta mixture. Shape into rounds or sausage-shapes. One at a time, roll each piece in flour, egg and then the breadcrumbs. Sit them on a plate as you finish them and the croquetas are now ready to deep-fry or can be chilled for several hours until needed.

To deep-fry: heat the rapeseed (or sunflower) oil in a large saucepan to 180C, or until a small piece of bread dropped in sizzles and browns. Carefully transfer each croqueta into the hot oil in batches of 3 or 4. Cook for a couple of minutes until golden brown, then lift out with a slotted spoon and drain on kitchen paper. Serve straight away. Repeat for the rest of the croquetas, using the slotted spoon to remove any breadcrumbs from the oil.

If using undyed smoked haddock, you need to cook it first: replace the Arbroath smokie with 200g of smoked haddock. Poach it in the 600ml milk for 8–10 minutes until it can be flaked. Then set aside and continue with the rest of the recipe.

The whole crab: crab toasts
with crab and vegetable broth

The whole crab comes together in this combination of light fragrant broth served with earthily delicious toasts. Note too, though, that you can hop in or out of the recipe at any point. Go only as far as the stock and keep for using in risottos, bisques and more. One step further and you have the broth. Or get yourself some crab meat and join in only for the toasts.

The guide by Shellseekers Fish & Game on page 22 shows how to wrestle the meat out of the crab. When making stock, I think it doesn't matter if you don't necessarily get it all out – anything left in the crevices of the shell, legs and claws only enhances the stock or broth.

Serves 4 as a light main

For the crab stock

1 cooked brown crab (about 800g)

1 banana shallot

1 garlic clove

1 tablespoon black peppercorns

1 teaspoon fennel seeds

1 teaspoon coriander seeds

1 teaspoon green cardamom pods

1 orange

For the crab broth

1 onion

1 tablespoon vegetable or rapeseed oil

2 garlic cloves

2cm piece of fresh ginger

½ red chilli

Small handful of fresh coriander

1.2 litres crab stock

75g shiitake mushrooms

1 small pak choi

Tamari sauce, to taste

1 spring onion

For the crab toasts

About 200g crab meat
  (mix of white and brown)

1½ teaspoons Dijon mustard

¼ teaspoon cayenne

1 tablespoon creme fraiche
  or 1 egg white

4 small slices of bread

1 teaspoon white sesame seeds

Pick the meat from the crab (see page 22) and set aside.

To make the stock, transfer the picked crab shell, legs and claws to a large saucepan or stockpot.

Peel and roughly chop the shallot and garlic. Add to the pan along with the peppercorns and fennel seeds. Lightly crush and add the coriander seeds and cardamom pods. Use a vegetable peeler to pare the peel from half the orange and add it to the pan as well. Cover with water, put a lid on, and gently simmer for 1 hour, skimming the scum from the surface as needed. Strain, and that's your crab stock.

Now make the crab broth. Peel and finely chop the onion. Heat the oil in a large saucepan over a medium heat, add the onion and saute until softening but not colouring. Use that time to peel and crush the garlic cloves, grate the ginger (no need to peel), thinly slice the chilli, and finely chop the coriander stalks. Add all those to the onion and cook for 5 minutes, then add the crab stock. Bring to the boil, then turn down to a simmer. Thinly slice the mushrooms and pak choi, add to the broth and let them simmer gently for 5 minutes. Add tamari sauce to taste and finish by thinly slicing the spring onions and coriander leaves and adding those just before serving.

To make the crab toasts, mix together the crab meat, mustard, cayenne and creme fraiche (or egg white). Season. Toast the bread under a grill, making sure one side is only lightly toasted. Spread the crab over each lightly toasted side, then scatter over the sesame seeds, gently pressing them in. Return to the grill for 3–5 minutes.

Serve the toasts straight away with bowls of the broth (reheated if necessary).

Deep-fried oysters with horseradish sauce, quick-pickled ginger and spring onion

Raw oysters never lose their appeal (certainly not gauging by the queues for them at Borough Market) but I'd like to make the case here for cooked oysters. I can't help but feel cooking brings out their flavour, and the texture becomes meltingly soft. Deep-frying is perhaps best of all for the contrast the crunch brings. And this recipe adds to that a balance of flavours – with salty, tangy, sour and even a little sweetness all working together.

Head to page 17 for oyster-shucking guidance, and 14 to find out from Tom Haward (of Richard Haward's Oysters) about oyster seasons, varieties, history and sourcing.

Serves 4, with 3 oysters each

1 spring onion

12 oysters

1 litre rapeseed or sunflower oil

75g plain flour

For the batter

150g plain flour

250ml cold sparkling water

1 teaspoon salt

For the horseradish sauce

3 tablespoons creme fraiche

1½ tablespoons freshly grated horseradish

½ teaspoon lemon juice

For the quick-pickled ginger

20g piece of fresh ginger

50ml rice vinegar or moscatel white wine vinegar

1 teaspoon caster sugar

½ teaspoon salt

Make the batter first. Whisk the flour in a bowl with the water and salt. Cover and chill for up to 2 hours if you have the time, or use straight away.

For the horseradish sauce, mix the creme fraiche, grated horseradish and lemon juice in a bowl and season to taste. Set aside and keep in the fridge if making ahead.

Quick-pickle the ginger just before you are going to start shucking and frying your oysters. Peel the ginger with the side edge of a spoon and cut into neat matchsticks. Pour the vinegar into a small bowl along with 50ml hot water, the sugar and salt. Stir to dissolve the sugar and salt, then add the ginger matchsticks. Set aside.

Trim your spring onion and slice into long thin strips.

Now you are ready to shuck your oysters – see page 17. As you shuck each one, drain off the liquid and sit the oysters on a plate. Keep the rounded shell of each oyster for serving them in.

Pour the oil into a large deep saucepan to come about a third of the way up the pan. Heat to 175C/350F and, while it's getting hot, carefully dry the oysters by sitting them on kitchen paper. Season the flour with salt and pepper and roll the oysters in it to lightly cover.

When the oil has reached its temperature, use a fork to – one at a time – dip an oyster in the batter and then slide it into the hot oil. Depending on the size of your pan, you should be able to fry six at a time. Give the oysters just a couple of minutes to turn golden brown. Use a slotted spoon to lift them out of the oil and onto kitchen paper to drain. Repeat with the rest of the oysters.

Working quickly while the oysters are still hot, spoon horseradish sauce into each oyster shell. Sit a deep-fried oyster on top and lay a couple of strips of quick-pickled ginger and spring onion over. Serve straight away.

Keep the quick-pickle juice
to use as a drinking vinegar
shrub or in a salad dressing.

Borough Market – The Knowledge

Mussels in lemongrass, galangal and turmeric broth

British mussels return to the fishmonger after their breeding season in the warmer waters of summer, so look out for them in the colder months from September to March. That is when they will be at their most abundant, sustainable and delicious. I think especially delicious when cooked in this aromatic broth, thickened by the breadcrumbs, which also give some lovely flavour contrast and crunch.

De-bearding mussels simply means pulling away the wiry bits that may be where the bivalve's shells join together. Give the threads a good tug as you go through the mussels checking for which ones are (or, more importantly, aren't) closed.

Serves 2 as a main or 6 as a starter or small plate

1kg mussels

1 banana shallot

2 tablespoons ghee or rapeseed oil

1 lemongrass stalk

2 garlic cloves

5cm piece of turmeric root

5cm piece of galangal

50g coriander

1 x 400ml tin coconut milk

30g panko breadcrumbs

¼ teaspoon chilli flakes

Wash the mussels in cold water. De-beard as necessary and tap any that aren't quite closed. If they don't close up straight away, discard them, along with any broken ones. Sit your mussels on a bowl of ice in the fridge until needed.

Peel and finely chop the shallot. Heat 1 tablespoon of the ghee or oil in a wide pan over a medium heat. Add the shallot and cook for 5 minutes or so until just softening. In the meantime, trim the lemongrass, remove its tough outer leaves and finely chop along with the peeled garlic. Add to the shallot, stir for a couple of minutes, then grate in the turmeric root and galangal – there's no need to peel them. Finely chop just the stalks of the coriander and add those too. (Be sure to keep back the leaves.) Stir everything for another minute or until nicely softening, then pour in the coconut milk, add some salt, and let it simmer gently for a few minutes.

Increase the heat and add the mussels. Put the lid on the pan and let them cook, undisturbed, for 4 minutes. While that is happening, heat the remaining tablespoon of ghee or oil in a small frying pan over a medium heat, add the panko breadcrumbs with the chilli flakes and toss around until nicely golden. Tip into a bowl.

Take the lid off the pan of mussels and you should see them excitingly opening. If some are still closed, replace the lid and cook for another 2 minutes, then remove from the heat and discard any that have remained closed. Chop the coriander leaves. Scatter half over the mussels and broth and stir the rest through the crisped chilli breadcrumbs. Finish by scattering the breadcrumbs over the top of the mussels and broth, and serve straight away.

Scallop and bacon bap

Don't let the simplicity of this fool you – cooking scallops in bacon juices before nestling them together into a fluffy white bap is a pretty much unbeatable way to enjoy them.

Its success lies in choosing top-quality produce: good bacon that will release fat and flavour into the pan, not lots of water; and scallops that have been dived for, not dredged. If you ever get the chance to hear Darren Brown of Shellseekers Fish & Game talk about the damage scallop dredging does to the seabed, you'll know just how important their sustainable sourcing is. A burger bun like the demi-brioche ones at Bread Ahead Bakery could be very happily substituted for the bap.

The only embellishment worth considering is a (good) tomato, sliced and cooked in the same pan.

Serves 1, but easy to scale up for feeding a hungry crowd

3 smoked or unsmoked back
   bacon rashers

3–4 scallops, depending on their size

1 bap

Heat a small frying pan over a medium heat and, when it is hot, add the bacon. There's no need to add any oil, as the bacon will start to render its own fat into the pan. Let the bacon rashers cook for a couple of minutes on each side so the fat can start to crisp. Add the scallops to the pan, sitting them around the bacon. They'll need about 3 minutes cooking on each side. The scallops are ready when golden brown on the outside and the flesh has become opaque. They should have a nice bounce to them when gently pressed.

If the bacon is ready first, take it out and sit it on the halved bap. Top with the scallops, pour over any pan juices, close the bap and eat straight away.

41

Fishmonger's pie with fish crackling

So called because the best fish pies don't start with a rigid set of ingredients, but with a conversation with the fishmonger about what is good and fresh and available. Aim for a mix of three or four fish. Not less than a third should be something smoked – ideally undyed smoked haddock. Then some chunky white fish – perhaps cod, pollack, coley or hake. And consider adding prawns and / or salmon too, so long as, like everything else, they are sustainably sourced.

Buy your fish fillets with the skin on and you'll be able to enjoy the recipe at the end for crisped fish crackling: a fabulous cook's perk, pre-meal bite, or to have with the pie.

Best served with peas, or wilted and buttered greens.

Serves 4 as a main

1kg fish fillets and shellfish (a mix
    of smoked haddock, salmon, hake,
    prawn etc – whatever you prefer)

500ml fish stock (bought, or see
    page 52)

100ml dry vermouth or white wine

Handful of flat-leaf parsley
    and tarragon

100ml whole milk

1–1.5kg floury potatoes, depending
    on the surface area of your
    baking dish

130g butter

30g plain flour

Large pinch of saffron threads

Nutmeg, for grating

½ teaspoon English mustard

200ml double cream

You will need a baking dish of approx.
1.8-litre capacity

Skin the fish fillets if necessary (see tip overleaf) and be sure to keep the skin for crisping.

Pour the stock and vermouth or wine into a large saucepan. Bring to a vigorous simmer over a medium heat and slide in half of the fish fillets. Poach for 3 minutes, then lift the barely cooked fillets out with a slotted spoon and transfer to the baking dish. Repeat with the rest of the fish. Gently mix the fish together, breaking it up into chunks and watching for bones. Chop the herbs, scatter over, and season with pepper. Set aside while you make the rest of the pie.

Add the milk to the poaching liquor and set aside.

Peel the potatoes, cut them into chunks, and simmer in a large saucepan of salted water for 15–20 minutes until tender. You can make the sauce while the potatoes cook, but keep an eye on them.

For the sauce: melt 30g of the butter in a medium saucepan over a low heat, add the flour and stir with a wooden spoon for a few minutes until it turns light brown, but take care it doesn't burn. Gradually pour in the reserved poaching liquid and keep on stirring to get it all worked into the flour. Add the saffron, a few good gratings of nutmeg and the mustard. Stir over a low heat for about 10 minutes until the sauce thickens, then add 150ml of the cream and stir again for a further 5 minutes or so until the mixture has a good sauce consistency. Remove from the heat and check the seasoning.

By now the potatoes should be nearly cooked. Once they are, drain them and mash well with the remaining 100g butter and 50ml cream. Salt generously.

Leave the fish, sauce and mash separate for at least 30 minutes and up to 2 hours until you are ready to get the pie in the oven.

Cont. overleaf

When you're ready to cook the pie, preheat the oven to 190C fan/210C/410F/gas mark 6.

Spread the sauce over the fish and then top with the mash, making sure the potato is tight at the dish sides to help stop the sauce bubbling over. Fork the mash into little peaks. Sit the pie on a large baking tray that can catch any bubbling sauce and bake for about 30 minutes (40–50 minutes if the fish and sauce are being baked from cold). Your pie is ready when the potato is crisp and browned. If it is being slow to crisp, put under the grill for a minute or two, but keep close watch to make sure it doesn't scorch.

To make the crisped fish crackling

Simmer the skins in boiling water for 3 minutes, then lift out and leave to thoroughly dry on kitchen paper or a clean tea towel. Use a spoon to gently remove any small bits of fish flesh on the skin. Heat a little olive oil in a frying pan over a high heat, lay the skins in the pan and let them bubble up and crisp. Turn them over and, when fully crisped, lift out and scatter over lots of salt.

HOW TO... skin a fish fillet

'You need a filleting knife for its flexible blade. Sit the fish on a chopping board, skin-side down. Hold it down firmly with one hand and use the other to insert the point of the knife between flesh and skin, at a slight downward angle. Work the knife in between the flesh and skin and move it along the length of the fillet, keeping the blade close to the skin to cut it away and pulling at the skin at the same time. It takes practice – be quick and be confident!'

Max Tucker, Furness Fish Markets

Bream fillets with buttered cobnuts and mixed beans

This meal feels disproportionately special for barely 15 minutes from start to finish – that is, so long as your fish fillets are at room temperature before you start cooking. It's hard to get gorgeously crisped skin otherwise.

Rather than buy fillets, you could use the skills guide on page 26 and fillet a whole round fish yourself. (That way you'd have the skeletons for stock, see page 52.) Other round fish such as sea bass, trout or mackerel, could be substituted in this recipe.

A mix of yellow, purple and green beans are a happy sight on a market stall and a plate, but at different times of year I'd switch those for purple sprouting broccoli cooked in the same way.

Serves 2 as a main

200g runner or French beans, ideally of different colours

30g cobnuts

2 sea bream fillets, at room temperature

75g butter

1 teaspoon rapeseed oil

1 teaspoon black mustard seeds

Preheat the oven to 100C fan/120C/250F/gas mark ½.

Bring a pan of salted water to the boil. Trim the beans, boil in the water for 3 minutes, drain, rinse under cold running water and set aside. Chop the cobnuts and set aside.

Season the skin side of the fish. Melt 25g of the butter in a large frying pan over a medium heat and add the oil. When the butter is frothing, sit the bream fillets in the pan skin-side down. Press them down to flatten them so the skin gets even heat. Season the flesh side of the fish but otherwise leave them alone and after a few minutes you'll see the flesh turning opaque. When the flesh is almost but not quite opaque all the way across the fillets, flip the fillets over and give them another 30 seconds. Lift the fish onto a heatproof plate and put into the low oven to keep warm.

Put the blanched beans into the pan the fish just cooked in, adding the black mustard seeds. Stir for a couple of minutes over a medium heat, then divide between two plates. Still using the same frying pan, add the rest of the butter along with the chopped cobnuts. Stir for a couple of minutes as the butter browns and the nuts toast. Take off the heat when the butter is just becoming nicely dark and nutty.

Sit the bream fillets on top of the beans and spoon the buttery nuts over the top.

Slow-cooked cuttlefish and white beans

Cuttlefish – like squid, which could be used in this recipe instead – are best when cooked either very fast or very slowly. We're going for the latter here, alongside fennel, aromatics and beans for something that becomes a cross between a stew and a broth.

Preparing the cuttlefish is a bit fiddly, so it is best done by the fishmonger. Ask to keep the ink sacs and freeze for later use with pastas, risotto, spelt or added into pizza or flatbread doughs.

Serve with bread to soak up the juices – perhaps following the advice of Olivier Favrel at Olivier's Bakery and go for a white sourdough.

Serves 4 as a main

650–750g cuttlefish body, wings and tentacles, prepared by the fishmonger

3 tablespoons olive oil

2 onions

1 fennel bulb

2 garlic cloves

2 bay leaves

2 sprigs of thyme

1 tsp smoked paprika

150ml fino or manzanilla sherry

1 orange

1 x 400g tin chopped tomatoes

300ml fish stock, bought or see page 52 (optional)

500g drained weight white beans (butter beans, cannellini beans… I used a large jar of Brindisa judion butter beans)

Small handful of flat-leaf parsley

Nutmeg, for grating

Slice the cuttlefish body and wings into strips approximately 1cm wide, and the tentacles into three sections. Set aside.

Heat the oil in a wide pan or a shallow casserole dish that can go on the hob. Peel the onion, slice into thin half-moons and cook in the hot oil for 10 minutes until softening. Trim and slice the fennel and add to the pan, leaving to cook for another 5 minutes. Peel and chop the garlic and add as well. Then the bay leaves, thyme sprigs and paprika go in – stir briefly for the paprika to release its colour and smell.

Mix in all the cuttlefish, followed by the sherry. Let it bubble for a minute before grating in the zest of the orange and adding the tin of tomatoes. Pour in the fish stock, if using – otherwise rinse out the tomato tin with water and add that. Stir, season, bring to a high simmer, then put a lid on, turn the heat as low as it will go and leave it to cook gently for 1 hour. Check occasionally that it isn't bubbling too fast, or in case you need to add more water to keep the cuttlefish just about submerged.

The drained beans go in for the last 10 minutes of the cooking time. Chop the parsley leaves, add to the pan and finish with a good grating of the nutmeg.

One-tin herb-stuffed fish on roasted vegetables

This way of roasting fish on a bed of vegetables, anchovies and herbs is intended more as a guide than a formal recipe. Please be led by the seasons for your choices of vegetables and fish. The red mullet here could be swapped for bream, bass, trout... Talk to your fishmonger about what's especially good and in season.

When the seasons turn, the summery courgettes and aubergines could be swapped for perhaps peppers, small peeled beetroots or cauliflower; and the light summer herbs for woodier thyme, rosemary or bay. When the new potatoes are done, maincrop potatoes will work just as well, and so would chunks of pumpkin.

This recipe is for one fish per person, but it's a good dish to scale up or down – you could make it for 1 person or 8 just as easily.

Serves 4 as a main

2 handfuls of a mix of tarragon, mint or chervil

2 tablespoons capers

½ lemon

4 red mullet (or other whole fish), about 600g per fish, scaled and gutted (with heads and tails on or off as you prefer)

750g new potatoes

100ml olive oil, plus 2 tablespoons

1 fennel bulb

2 green courgettes

1 large aubergine

8 garlic cloves

8 anchovy fillets in oil

3 bay leaves

1 orange

20 pitted black olives

Preheat the oven to 190C fan/210C/410F/gas mark 6.

Strip the leaves from the herbs and chop them. Rinse and drain the capers, chop those too, and mix with the herbs and a good squeeze of lemon juice. Stuff this mixture into the cavity of each fish. Set the fish aside.

Cut the potatoes into halves or thirds, depending on their size. Put them in a large roasting tray or baking dish, pour over 50ml of the olive oil, season well with salt and roast in the oven for 15 minutes to give them a head start on the other vegetables. Less time is needed if your potatoes are small.

Meanwhile, trim the top and bottom of the fennel bulb, remove the outside layer if it looks damaged, and then slice into rounds approximately 5mm thick. Chop the courgettes and aubergine into chunks, and put all these prepared vegetables into a large bowl with the unpeeled garlic cloves, the anchovies lifted out of their oil, another 50ml of olive oil and the bay leaves. Quarter the orange and add. Season well and mix. Add the potatoes to the bowl, mix again, then return the tray to the oven for a further 15 minutes or until the potatoes are nearly tender and browned.

Slash the skin of the fish three times on both sides, rub with the remaining olive oil, then sit them on top of the vegetables. Scatter the fish generously with salt flakes and roast for 20–25 minutes until the fish is starting to flake. Scatter the olives among the fish and vegetables and return the tray to the oven for a final 5 minutes.

Serve with an orange quarter on each plate so that their roasted juices can be squeezed over for a burst of sweet freshness.

Roasted cod's head with clams and seaweed

My respect for the fishmongers at Borough Market went up an extra notch when not a single eyelid was batted at my request for a whole cod's head. Quite right too. Cod's cheeks tend to get all the culinary glory, but there is plenty of meat to be had on the rest of the head too. They are too often considered waste, just when we need to be more aware of using every bit we can of the fish we have. (Page 28 has more on unusual cuts of fish ready to be discovered by savvy shoppers and cooks.)

Ask the fishmonger to prepare the head with the collar and a little of the shoulder attached. Roasted and served with seaweed, clams and wine-suffused juices, this cheap cut becomes a feast.

Serves 2 as a main

4 garlic cloves

4 bay leaves

4 sprigs of thyme

1 cod's head (approx. 800g–1kg)

3 tablespoons olive oil

40g dried seaweed

400g small clams (see page 25)

40g butter

25ml brandy

200ml white wine

2 sprigs of tarragon

Preheat the oven to 200C fan/220C/425F/gas mark 7.

Peel and slice the garlic cloves. Put them in the middle of a baking tray or dish along with the bay leaves and thyme sprigs to make an aromatic bed for the cod's head. Slash some holes in the skin of the head, sit it on the herbs and garlic, pour over the olive oil and scatter with salt flakes. Roast for 25 minutes, basting the head occasionally in the oil. Check after 20 minutes and if the skin isn't crisping up, increase the oven temperature to finish it off.

Meanwhile, soak the dried seaweed in cold water for 5 minutes, then drain and set aside. Wash the clams in cold water, discarding any with damaged shells, or any open ones that don't snap shut when tapped.

When the cod is nearly ready, melt the butter in a large saucepan over a medium heat. Once it's frothing, pour in the brandy and wine and bring to the boil. Straight away add the clams and drained seaweed. Turn the heat down a little and put a lid on. In 2–3 minutes the clams will be opening up. Don't eat any that stay shut.

To serve, divide the clams and seaweed broth between shallow bowls, with the cod's head as a centrepiece on the table to help yourselves to. Chop the tarragon and sprinkle over the cod and the clams. You might want some bread alongside for the broth.

Fish stocks

The single best benefit of filleting your own fish – aside from the satisfaction in your own skills – is knowing you'll have the fish 'frame' (its skeleton) to use for making stock. If the fishmonger is doing the filleting for you, don't be shy to ask for the frame. They'll very likely be willing to give you other frames too from a previous customer who didn't realise just how easy, and delicious, making their own fish stock would be.

Light fish stock

What fish to use:
Go for white-fleshed fish such as sea bass, halibut, haddock, pollack or sea bream. Oily fish such as mackerel, salmon or herring don't make for good stocks. Include the heads only if you've removed the eyes (they make it viscous) and the gills (they make it bitter).

To make:
Put the fish frames into a large pot. Roughly chop an onion, two carrots and a celery stick and put them into the pot too along with the flavour enhancers (see below) of your choosing. Cover with water and simmer gently for 30 minutes. Strain and your stock is ready to use that day or freeze. Reduce the strained stock further if you want a more concentrated end result.

Dark fish stock

Caramelising the frames before turning them into stock gives a richer, deeper flavour. Choose your fish as for Light fish stock, except:

- For this stock keeping the eyes in the head is good for flavour and texture – but still remove the gills.

- For better flavour and colour, let the frames dry out a little overnight in the fridge before using for stock.

To make:
Heat a little oil in a wide-based pan over a medium heat and, once it is hot, sit the frames in it in a single layer. Chop the frames into pieces if easier. Let them brown for about 5 minutes, turning them after 2½ minutes. Lift the frames out and set aside.

Roughly chop an onion, two carrots and a celery stick and put into the same pot. Let them soften, then add your chosen flavour enhancers (see right) and return the frames to the pan. Cover with water and simmer gently for 30 minutes.

Strain and your stock is ready to use that day or freeze. Reduce the strained stock further if you want a more concentrated end result.

Prawn / langoustine stock

The heads and shells of prawns and langoustines are too full of flavour to throw away if you are removing them to cook the shellfish (perhaps for the Hot and sour green papaya curry with prawns on page 184). Use them to make a rich stock.

To make:
Roughly chop an onion, two carrots and a celery stick. Heat a little oil in a wide-based pan over a medium heat and, once it is hot, add the vegetables and saute until softening. Add a tablespoon of tomato puree, then your raw heads and shells. Cook until they turn pink, add a tablespoon of brandy and your chosen flavour enhancers (see below). Cover with water and simmer for 30 minutes. Strain, really pressing at the heads and shells to get their flavour out. Add a squeeze of lemon juice and your stock is ready to use that day or freeze. Reduce the strained stock further if you want a more concentrated end result.

See page 34 for making stocks from crabs.

FLAVOUR ENHANCERS

Use your common sense on quantities, depending on how much fish you have for stock-making.

Essential: onion, carrot, celery.
Plus your choice(s) of: leek, garlic, bay leaf, fennel trimmings, parsley stalks and other fresh herbs, peppercorns, star anise, fennel seeds, coriander seeds, saffron threads, citrus zest, white wine.

Drinks

Coastal wines

Matching food with wines can seem like a complicated business. Expert traders will always be keen to help out, but for the non-experts it can be enormously reassuring to arm ourselves with a couple of key, easy-to-remember wine-pairing tenets. This one has stuck firmly in my mind since reading it in Jane Parkinson's column in *Market Life* magazine: match fish dishes and seafood with coastal wines.

Give it half a second's thought and it makes complete sense that when vines grow near the sea, the wines they produce speak of the saltiness in the air and the soil, and make perfect partners for the sea's bounty.

Greece, fairly obviously, has a lot of coast and so also an exciting breadth of coastal grapes and wine styles. Many of them herald from the Greek islands and remain true to the traditions of their wine heritage. Among the bottles sold by Marianna Kolokotroni at Oliveology are those from the island of Santorini. She calls it unique terroir and rightly so given the vineyards benefit not just from the saltiness of the sea but the flinty, high minerality of the island's volcano.

Assyrtiko is its most famous grape, producing some wines that are fresh and zesty, and others with a fuller body. The fish and seafood dishes they partner best with can run across that spectrum too.

THE
BUTCHERS

A farm and butchery specialising in rare and traditional breeds of cattle and sheep, Northfield Farm has been a stalwart of Borough Market for more than 20 years. Then it was Jan McCourt who travelled to London from the windy wilds of Rutland; today his son Dominic manages the shop and butchery in the Market, while his other son, Leo, takes care of life on the farm.

The quality of meat

Dominic McCourt, Northfield Farm

People presume there's such a thing as the 'best' lamb chop or steak. There isn't. I get a lot of customers who worry if they can't get the exact weight, cut or breed prescribed by a recipe – but your steak dinner isn't going to turn into a banoffee pie if you don't have precisely 350g of White Park rib-eye. What we have on the stall each day depends on what is ready and available. If you care about animal welfare and eating properly, it is part of your responsibility to accept that there will be this range, dependent on the seasons. Things are always going to be different at Borough Market, and that's the beauty of it.

That said, there are some ground rules to follow if you want to ensure the meat you buy is of the highest quality you can afford. Breed does matter. The advantage of the native breeds we rear is their good ratio of fat to lean meat. These characteristics can vary slightly between breeds, but not to the extent that you could really discern them. On our farm we currently have White Park and Aberdeen Angus cattle, and we do a bit of cross-breeding between the heritage breeds. All of them are native to the UK, which means the animals are well suited to the land and the climate. The same is true of our sheep: Border Leicester and Lleyn x Charollais. The same certainly isn't true of animals bred to live in feedlots in Argentina or the United States, where they spend their lives confined to tight pens.

Of course, the duration and quality of the animal's life also matters massively. It's almost cringeworthy saying it now, because it's a tagline that's misused by so many big food companies, but we raise our animals as nature intended – and that means enabling them to reach maturity. The older the animal is, the more time it has to roam, graze on pasture, build muscle and lay down fat, and the more flavour it has.

We want our cattle to live a little, and we sell mutton and hogget instead of lamb. At around the 12-month mark you have a good middle ground between the tenderness of a younger animal and the flavour that comes with age. If you're buying the meat of an animal killed at three to six months, it's going to be super-tender – but we have teeth for a reason. Let's use them to eat something that has a bit more going on.

Quality of life matters right to the end, with the delivery of the animal to the abattoir and its treatment while it's there. Relaxation is so important: if the animal is stressed, its cortisol levels will increase and that will cause lactic acid to build up, affecting the meat's flavour and texture. Taking care of our animals, making sure

The Butchers

Quality of life matters. The more time an animal has to graze on pasture, build muscle and lay down fat, the more flavour it has.

they're not stressed by transportation – these are ethical considerations, of course, but they influence quality too.

One of the most important – and useful – things to consider when buying meat is that there is a spectrum of cuts, based on the animal's physiology. In short, the harder the muscle works, the less tender and more flavourful it will be. Fillet steak comes from the muscle a cow uses to rotate at the hips, and you don't see cows rotating their hips much, do you? Shin, by contrast, comes from the muscle that supports the animal's entire weight. So, fillet is incredibly tender but has very little flavour, whereas beef shin has the most amazing flavour but needs to be cooked for hours to tenderise it.

When someone asks me which cut of meat is best, I say: 'That's like asking which golf club is best.' I don't know why I use a golf analogy, because I don't play golf – but I know enough to know that there isn't a 'best golf club'; there are different clubs for different shots, just as each cut of meat is good in its own particular way.

The good news is that the most flavourful end of the spectrum is also where the cheaper cuts of meat are found. Many of our best recipes have come from peasant food: pig cheeks in carbonara, beef shin in a ragu, lamb scrag (the neck) in a pie or stew. These cuts need low and slow cooking. By contrast, you're not going to get any more flavour out of a fillet steak by cooking it for a long time, you'll just lose that appealing tenderness.

The only things that suit a fillet steak are eating it raw – a carpaccio or tartare – or flash-frying it.

That same spectrum applies to ageing, too, at least as far as beef is concerned. Pork and lamb aren't aged really, but with beef, the harder the muscle works, the longer we will age it. A rump steak we'd age for about six weeks to get the right degree of tenderness, a sirloin or ribeye only needs four, and fillet doesn't need ageing at all. We age our beef in special fridges which control the temperature, air flow and humidity to draw out moisture and concentrate the flavour. Ageing also allows for enzymes to begin breaking down the fibres between the muscles, making the meat more tender.

Borough Market - The Knowledge

HOW TO... store meat

'I always tell my customers to take their joint of meat out of its wrapping, put it on a plate, and store it in such a way as to let the air circulate around it. If it's beef or chicken, put a piece of foil loosely on the top – don't cover it completely, because if it sweats, it will go off more quickly. If it's pork, leave it completely uncovered; that dries the skin out and makes for great crackling. Raw meat should always be stored at the bottom of the fridge – if you have it on a higher shelf, it can drip onto the food below. I recommend taking it out of the fridge two hours before cooking, for it to come up to room temperature; some people say 40 minutes, but I think two hours is better, especially if it's a big joint. Fresh meat can keep safely in the fridge for two to three days, maximum. In the freezer, you have around two to three months, but it varies from freezer to freezer, so you're best checking the manual.'

George Donnelly, The Ginger Pig

Wild duck

Season 1st September to 31st January.

Availability The mallard is the largest and most widely available bird from the duck family, which also includes wigeon and teal.

Uses One mallard feeds two generously, a tiny teal is only big enough for one, and a widgeon is somewhere in between. Roast them whole and serve them pink; like many game birds, the meat becomes tough when overcooked.

Partridge

Season 1st September to 1st February.

Availability French red-leg partridges are the most commonly available, with English grey-leg birds now a rarity.

Uses The mild and tender pale flesh of the partridge makes it perfectly suited to those trying game for the first time, while its diminutive size makes it the perfect roast for one.

Partridges in sloe gin with creamed Jerusalem artichokes, page 116.

Five game birds

Pheasant

Season 1st October to 1st February.

Availability The wild population in the UK is boosted each year by large numbers of pheasants reared for sport and released in July.

Uses Hen pheasants have more delicate flesh than the larger, more striking cocks. Early-season birds are ideal for roasting, but older pheasants are best employed for braises and pot roasts.

Game terrine with fennel, apple and radish remoulade, page 67.

Red grouse

Season 12th August to 10th December.

Availability Kicking off on the Glorious Twelfth, the grouse season heralds the start of the official game shooting calendar.

Uses The rich gamey flavour pairs well with early autumn ingredients, such as blackberries, girolles and rowans. Cover the breast with strips of fatty bacon or a liberal basting of butter, then roast.

Wood pigeon

No closed season.

Availability Pigeons breed all year round but are particularly plump and plentiful from May to October, when they gorge on famers' crops.

Uses Dark and full flavoured, pigeon breast lends itself to a variety of dishes. The whole bird makes for an economical and speedy roast for one.

Game terrine with fennel, apple and radish remoulade, page 67.

For decades, the Crouch family have been working directly with small-scale producers to import Italian meats and cheeses. The country's most famous cured meat is integral to the name of their Borough Market stand, but there's much more to Italian salume than Parma ham.

Five Italian cured meats

Esther Crouch, The Parma Ham & Mozzarella Stand

Prosciutto Maiale Nero di Parma

The hams from this salumificio, Carlo Peveri, are so large that we're forced to cut each leg in half before it can fit on our slicers. They come from rare-breed Maiale Nero pigs, which live entirely free range, grazing on nuts, roots and wild grains, so the final product is organic. Carlo Peveri salts and cures the hams in his facility near Piacenza for around 24 months. The prosciutto almost dissolves in your mouth, it's so soft and smooth in texture. The flavour is delicate and nutty, with rich, buttery fat.

Prosciutto San Daniele

There are around 200 registered producers of prosciutto di Parma – Parma ham. The town of San Daniele del Friuli near Trieste has only 30 makers of its own similarly lauded ham. Of these, we feel Prosciuttificio Prolongo is the best. Its San Daniele hams are cured for a total of 18–20 months in open curing rooms through which natural air currents are allowed to flow. A key difference to Parma ham is in the salting process: a San Daniele ham is salted over the same number of days as its weight in kilos – usually 14–15 days – whereas Parma ham is salted for up to 25 days. Personally, I prefer the San Daniele. It's softer and sweeter, because the lower humidity of the region allows the hams to cure slightly faster.

Coppa

Coppa is made from the muscle that runs from the pig's neck down to its ribs, then is placed in a natural bladder and cured for a minimum of six months. The marbling of buttery intramuscular fat in this cut results in a product that is particularly rich and umami. Ours is made by the Magnani family, whose Bré del Gallo production facility is based in Roccabianca, in the Po river valley close to Parma. They are experts in salume production and animal welfare, working closely with farmers and individually selecting each pig they use.

Pancetta affumicata

Our smoked pancetta – pancetta affumicata – is produced by the D'Osvaldo family in the small town of Cormons in the Friuli-Venezia Giulia region, north of Trieste. Meat from sustainably reared pigs is salted and spiced by hand, then smoked over laurel wood and rosemary. Many producers today use artificial smoking agents, but the D'Osvaldos continue to smoke their meat naturally. When people ask whether they should get smoked or unsmoked pancetta, I tend to say it depends what dish they're making: the smoked version works best with dishes based on tomato, chilli and spices – it's like adding smoked paprika. It brings so much flavour.

Guanciale Toscano

This is the perfect salume for a carbonara. It comes from the cheek – the guancia – of a Suino Grigio pig, which the Falaschi family coat in black pepper and garlic and cure for four months. It is commonly used in cooking, diced and warmed slowly to allow the fat to render, but it has a robust and spicy flavour that's nicely complemented by fresh soft cheeses if you eat it uncooked.

Game terrine with fennel, apple and radish remoulade, page 67.

Rabbit ragu pappardelle, page 70.

Broth of white beans and winter greens, page 219.

HOW TO... carve Spanish jamón

'A lot of Spanish carvers I've worked with will insist you can only be a real carver if you're Spanish – but I don't agree. It's a craft. If you take instruction, if you practise (and practise and practise), you can learn. We run a jamón school, at which you can pick up the basic principles. Carving jamón is not a routinely useful skill, but it is a fun and pleasant one, if rather esoteric. I find the process quite meditative; you need to watch the knife and keep it steady, and because some parts of the leg are more cured than others you have to work with each muscle individually. You want the slices very thin, as the greater the surface area, the greater the flavour impact. As a guide, 100g will provide a starter for two people or a meal for one greedy person, with fried eggs and potatoes. Make sure to bring the jamón up to room temperature before serving – if it's too cold, the slices might shred as you separate them, and you won't get the best of the flavour.'

James Robinson, Brindisa

At Wyndham House Poultry you'll find all kinds of seasonal birds, the best eggs, their incredibly delicious chicken stock, and the chickens they are perhaps best known for. Ask Lin Mullett on the stand any question about the age or breeding of their chickens and prepare to acquire more chicken knowledge than you thought possible. From how they're slow-grown, to their diet without hormones, 'growth promoters' or animal proteins, and why that all matters for delivering meat of exceptional flavour.

On pages 80–1 you'll find ideas for using the different parts of a jointed chicken. Here, Lin shows how to joint a high-welfare 'English Label' (formerly 'Label Anglais') bird – with a few different ways to achieve different styles of cut.

Jointing a chicken

^ Untruss the chicken and – if they are there - remove the giblets from inside. (The chicken neck is wonderful for gravies and stocks; the liver for pates, the heart for simply frying or skewering and cooking over fire...)

^ Sit the chicken breast-side up. Cut through the skin where the leg joins the main body. Use your hand to open the leg up, wriggle it loose, and 'pop' to release the ball and socket joint of the thigh bone.

^ Cut round to release the leg, taking the chicken 'oyster' with it. The oysters are especially delicious, small pieces of dark meat each side of the chicken by the thigh. Repeat for the other leg.

^ Keep the wings on the bird to help stabilise it as you continue jointing. Use a filleting knife with its flexible blade to release the breasts. Feel for the backbone and cut down one side of it in one smooth movement. Pull apart as you cut to help release the breast. Use smooth cuts rather than a sawing action.

^ Take the wing off with the breast for, perhaps, a supreme or kyiv. (OR: take the breast without the wing and cut the wing off separately, trimming its tip.) Repeat for the other side of the body.

^ To separate thigh from drumstick: find the natural line of fat where they join and cut along it, through the joint.

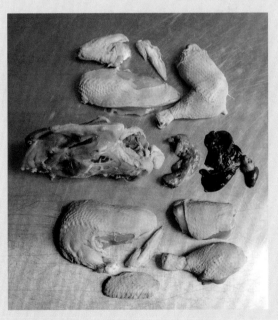

^ See page 82 for how to turn your chicken carcass into stock.

Five animal fats

Beef suet

This hard, raw fat from around the kidneys of a bullock is available vacuum packed at Wild Beef. 'It's pure fat, so you can render it down easily,' says Richard Vines of Wild Beef. Once melted, any leftover suet can be poured into a receptacle, where it will set for using at a later date. Suet is essential in steamed suet puddings (especially Christmas pudding) and is a traditional component of the mincemeat in mince pies. It makes wonderfully light, flavoursome pastry, too. or monkfish.

Oxtail with herbed suet dumplings and blackberry-braised shallots, page 88.

Dripping

'Dripping is the fat that comes from roasting a joint,' says Richard. His cattle tend to have a thick layer of fat, on account of their free-range lifestyle, forage-based diet and long lifespan. 'They get wodges of fat which the butcher normally cuts off, but some people ask for it to be left.' Dripping is perfect for spreading on toast, for general frying, for Yorkshire puddings, or for basting the potatoes and vegetables that accompany a roast.

Beef, leek and ale pie, page 90.

Goose fat

'Our tubs of goose fat are big, but goose fat freezes really well. We always say that you only want half a jar for a roast dinner,' says Lin Mullet of Wyndham House Poultry. Goose-fat roasties are the most obvious go-to: 'Melt the fat in the baking tray first, then tip the potatoes in before returning to the oven.'

Duck fat

Whereas geese are seasonal, available from September to the end of the year, duck fat is produced all year round, for use in roasts or for making confit vegetables and meats. 'Most people think that goose fat is better – but I defy anyone to tell me the difference,' says Lin.

Lard

Lard is rendered pork fat, traditionally used for frying, shortening and in shortcrust pastry, to which it adds a delectably flaky texture. Its relatively high smoke point and neutral flavour make it a particularly versatile fat to cook with. Good for deep-frying chips or using in cakes and puddings.

Deep celeriac, potato and gruyère pie, page 288.

Game terrine with fennel, apple and radish remoulade

This terrine – which in my house is always associated with Christmas – is a good way to become practiced at butchering birds. As you are cutting the meat up anyway to go into the tin, it doesn't have to be perfect or neat. Even if you are not too confident about it, it'll be fine. And if you are more experienced, you'll already know this is really a cinch.

The recipe says to use a whole pigeon but if you are unlikely to use the carcass for stock then just buy two pigeon breasts. The prosciutto I use here for its texture and flavour could be swapped for unsmoked streaky bacon or pancetta. In the past, I've made the terrine quite happily without breadcrumbs or egg.

Makes 1 terrine, about 8 slices

For the terrine

2 pheasants

1 pigeon or two pigeon breasts

450g wild boar sausage meat
(or other sausage meat)

2 sprigs of rosemary

2 sprigs of thyme

1 sprig of sage

1 tablespoon juniper berries

1 tablespoon black peppercorns

2 tablespoons fruit vinegar
(elderberry or blackberry would
be ideal)

40g breadcrumbs

1 egg

10 slices of prosciutto

You will need a loaf tin of approx.
19 x 9 x 6cm and 2 food tins as weights

Deal with your birds first. Sit a pheasant on a chopping board breast-side up and use a very sharp, small knife to cut along the breastbone so you can then cut out the breasts. Remove the skin and set the breasts aside. Now take off the legs, remove the skin and set them aside separately from the breasts. Really try to get as much meat off the bird as you can. Repeat for the other pheasant, then do the same for the pigeon, but remove the breasts only, as there's barely any meat on the legs. Save the carcasses for stock, following the guidance on page 82 for dark chicken stock.

Chop the pheasant leg meat as finely as you can, getting as much as you can off the bones, then mix in a large bowl with the sausage meat. Pick the herb leaves away from the stems of just one rosemary sprig, both thyme sprigs and the sage. Roughly chop and mix them in too. Crush the juniper berries and peppercorns using a pestle and mortar, then add them to the meat along with the vinegar and breadcrumbs. Beat the egg and mix in. Season with salt and use your hands to bring it all together.

Slice your pheasant and pigeon breast meat into strips about 1cm wide.

Line your loaf tin with a large piece of non-PVC cling film that overhangs the tin. Sit your remaining rosemary sprig in the base. Take a slice of prosciutto and – starting at one long edge of your tin – lay its short end halfway into the base, then up the sides and overhanging at the top. Repeat with a further three slices along that side, then use four slices to line the other side. The idea is that the two sides of prosciutto meet and overlap in the middle of the tin's base.

Spread half the sausage stuffing into the tin, top with half the pheasant breast meat, then the pigeon, and then the rest of the pheasant breast. Really press everything down well as you go, then finish with the rest of the sausage stuffing. It should all come nicely up to the top of the tin. Wrap the overhanging prosciutto over the top of the mixture and use your remaining two slices to fill any gaps. Fold the cling film over the mixture and wrap the tin tightly with foil.

Preheat the oven to 140C fan/160C/325F/gas mark 3.

Cont. overleaf

Sit the wrapped loaf tin in a large roasting tray and pour in enough water to come halfway up the sides. Transfer to the oven and cook for 1½–2 hours, until the internal temperature is 70C on a probe thermometer, or a skewer inserted into the middle comes out very hot.

Lift the loaf tin out of the roasting tray to cool, then – while it is still wrapped up – put it into the fridge on a plate and place another plate or board on top, weighted down with two food tins. Leave for at least 8 hours before turning it out, unwrapping and slicing. Make sure you take the terrine out of the fridge at least 30 minutes before eating. Well wrapped up, it will keep in the fridge for up to 5 days.

For the fennel, apple and radish remoulade

1 medium fennel bulb

150g mooli (daikon) radish (or other radishes)

200g apples

Juice of 1 lemon

2 tablespoons creme fraiche

1 tablespoon Dijon mustard

2 teaspoons capers

Make the remoulade shortly before serving the terrine. Trim the fennel, keeping back the perkiest of its fronds. Slice the bulb as thinly as possible and put it into a mixing bowl. Slice the radish very thinly too and toss it with the fennel. Quarter and core the apple(s), then slice them very thinly. Add them to the vegetables. (You could of course use a mandoline for all this fine slicing if you have one.) Squeeze the juice of the lemon into the bowl and toss. In a separate bowl, mix together the creme fraiche and the mustard with a little salt. Use to dress the vegetables and apple. Finish by draining, washing and then chopping the capers before adding those too, along with the reserved fennel fronds.

Serve slices of the terrine with the remoulade.

Rabbit ragu pappardelle

This is a meal for a cold, cold day. When a rabbit slowly braising will fill your home with the most delicious smells and build your anticipation for the hearty meal to come.

Choose wild rabbit, rather than farmed, for two important reasons: it will have had a much better life and will simply be more flavoursome. Ask the butcher to joint your rabbit into 6 or 8 pieces – and be sure to ask for the liver too and include it as you cook.

The ragu can be made a day or so in advance and kept in the fridge (or frozen).

Serves 4 as a main

1 leek

1 onion

1 carrot

1 celery stick

3 tablespoons olive oil

1 jointed rabbit (about 1.5kg)

60g diced guanciale (or pancetta)

4 garlic cloves

125ml dry vermouth

4 anchovy fillets in oil

2 tablespoons tomato puree

1 x 400g tin chopped tomatoes

2 bay leaves

1 sprig of rosemary

1 sprig of sage

4 sprigs of thyme

1 teaspoon Dijon mustard

400g dried pappardelle pasta

20g butter

100g parmesan

Finely chop the leek, peeled onion, carrot and celery. Set aside.

Heat 2 tablespoons of the oil in a large casserole dish over a medium heat. Brown the rabbit pieces all over and set aside. Do this in batches if necessary to avoid crowding the dish. Put the remaining tablespoon of oil into the casserole dish, followed by the prepared leek, onion, carrot and celery. Use just a splash of water to deglaze the base. Add the guanciale to the pan with some salt. Stir round and allow it all to cook for about 10 minutes, until the vegetables are softened and starting to colour, and the guanciale has rendered its fat and is crisping up. Towards the end, peel and crush or roughly chop the garlic, add to the dish and cook for another couple of minutes.

Pour in the vermouth and let it bubble for a minute, using a wooden spoon to rub at the bottom of the dish and deglaze. Chop the anchovies, then stir in. The tomato puree and the tin of chopped tomatoes go in next, then fill the empty tomato tin with water and add that too. Tuck in the rabbit pieces and herbs, bring to a simmer, then put the lid on and turn down the heat as low as it will go. Let it simmer very gently for 1½ hours, stirring halfway. through

Use a slotted spoon to lift out the very tender rabbit pieces. Let them cool a little, then pull off the meat with a fork, discarding any pieces of fat, gristle and bone. Remove the herb stalks and bay leaves from the rabbit and the casserole it was just cooked in. Shred the meat, set it aside, and bubble the rabbit cooking sauce over a high heat for 10–15 minutes until reduced by about a third. Reunite the rabbit meat with the sauce and stir in the mustard. Check the seasoning.

Borough Market - The Knowledge

When you're ready to serve, bring a large saucepan of salted water to the boil. Cook the pasta for 2 minutes less than the packet instructions. Meanwhile, reheat the ragu (if needed) and grate the parmesan. Drain the pasta, keeping a cupful of its cooking water. Add the pasta to the ragu, stirring to coat it well and adding the pasta water in stages to help bring it all together – you may not need it all. Stir in the butter and most but not all of the parmesan.

Serve with freshly ground black pepper and more parmesan added to taste.

Pork cochinita pibil tacos with black beans and x ni pek onions, by Nicholas Fitzgerald of Padre

Padre at Borough Market Kitchen is renowned for its tacos. It is run by Nicholas Fitzgerald whose passion for Mexican food was sparked by a stage at the renowned Mexico City restaurant Pujol. His Padre menu and the produce available at Shop Padre reflect the street food culture he found on his travels around the country.

This is a very special recipe from Nicholas. Cochinita pibil is a traditional Mexican dish from the Yucatán Peninsula. Marinated pork is slow-roasted in banana leaves for several hours, then served with the reduced marinade, black beans and the tangy, chilli-spiked quick pickle of the x ni pek onions that go hand in hand with the dish. Think of it as a project to immerse yourself in for several days, culminating in the most delicious sharing feast.

Start preparing the components at least a day before you want to serve, as the beans need overnight soaking; the x ni pek onions can be made up to a couple of weeks ahead.

Serves 8–10

1.5kg pork (a mix of belly, shoulder and hock is best, but if you can't use all three, opt for shoulder)

1 pack of fresh (or frozen and defrosted) banana leaves

For the x ni pek

500g red onions

1 fresh habanero chilli

150ml apple cider vinegar

100ml lime juice

100ml orange juice

For the beans

200g dried black beans

1 onion

4 garlic cloves

½ teaspoon dried oregano

At least a day before you want to serve, make the x ni pek. Peel and thinly slice the red onions. Destem and finely dice the habanero and combine with the onions in a large bowl. Mix the cider vinegar, lime juice and orange juice together, then add to the bowl of onions, stirring to coat. Cover and place in the fridge – the onions will keep for a couple of weeks at least.

Soak the dried black beans the day before you want to serve, make the adobo and for maximum flavour marinate the pork.

For the adobo (overleaf): tear off the veins and stems from the dried guajillo chillies, then make a small rip in the side of each chilli (this prevents it from behaving like a balloon when hydrating) and remove the seeds. Submerge them in a bowl of hot water for at least 20 minutes. You might want to weigh the chillies down with another bowl to ensure every chilli is submerged in the water. When they are soft and have turned from a deep brown to a bright red, they are ready.

Toast the peppercorns in a dry frying pan over a low heat for a couple of minutes until fragrant. Transfer to a bowl, then toast the oregano and ground allspice in the same pan for 1 minute. Peel and roughly chop the onions and garlic. Quarter the plum tomatoes. Then, while the chillies are still warm, put all the ingredients for the adobo in a food processor or blender and blend in batches, until smooth – it is best to add a little of everything, plus a splash of orange and lime juice (and some of the chilli soaking liquid if needed), every time you blend, in order to ensure everything blends smoothly, as the achiote is quite dense. Set aside.

Cont. overleaf

The Butchers

For the cochinita adobo

200g dried guajillo chillies

2 teaspoons black peppercorns

1 tablespoon dried oregano

1 teaspoon ground allspice

200g achiote (a dense spice paste also known as annatto, available from Spice Mountain)

200g white onions

100g garlic cloves (about 2 heads)

250g plum tomatoes

100g tomatillos (or green tomatoes)

25g salt

400g orange juice

200g lime juice

To serve

3 limes

Small bunch of coriander

30 corn tortillas

1 x 100g pack of chicharron (or pork scratchings)

Line a large casserole dish big enough to fit the pork with the banana leaves, overlapping them and leaving enough of an overhang to cover the pork. Spread a little of the adobo on the bottom of the lined roasting tin and add the pork, then cover the pork with the rest of the adobo and massage it in to ensure every part of the pork is coated. Fold the banana leaves over the pork to cover, put the lid on the casserole, and refrigerate for a minimum of 4 hours (24 hours is best).

The next day (or later that day), preheat the oven to 180C fan/200C/390F/gas mark 6.

Place the marinated pork in the oven for 30 minutes, then turn the oven down to 140C fan/160C/285F/gas mark 2 and cook for 4–5 hours, until the pork is meltingly tender. Once cooked, set aside until cool enough to handle.

While the pork is cooking, drain the soaked beans and add to a large saucepan with the peeled and halved onion, peeled garlic cloves, oregano and enough water to cover. Bring to the boil and simmer gently, uncovered, for 2–3 hours, or until soft. Top up with more water if the beans begin to look dry. Season with salt to taste and set aside while you finish the pork cochinita.

Remove the pork meat from the roasting tin and set aside on a chopping board. Discard the banana leaves and strain the leftover cooking juices through a sieve into a saucepan. Heat over a medium–high heat for about 30 minutes until the cooking juices reduce to a rich, thick sauce, occasionally skimming the surface and stirring to ensure it doesn't catch on the bottom. While reducing, chop the pork roughly into bite-sized chunks, discarding any bone or bits of cartilage, before returning it to the roasting tin. When the adobo sauce has reduced, add it to the roasting tin and mix through thoroughly until the pork meat is evenly coated.

Cut the limes into eighths and chop the coriander. Heat the tortillas in a hot, dry frying pan for about 20 seconds on each side until pliable, then wrap in a clean tea towel to keep warm. Serve the pork cochinita, black beans, x ni pek, tortillas, limes, coriander and chicharron on several platters around the table, allowing everyone to share and make their own tacos. Eat one yourself first to 'make sure' it is delicious.

Venison steak with samphire

This recipe calls for venison from the sika breed of deer, as its texture and flavour are well-suited to this kind of fast cooking – but really my best tip is to choose whatever breed is available and the butcher recommends for steaks that are fried just long enough to ensure the meat will be tenderly pink inside.

Marsh samphire, with its fresh flavour and vibrant colour, is most often partnered with fish yet it works very well with game meats or lamb too. I always like to get the different flavour elements of a dish working together, so here the samphire is cooked in the same pan the venison cooked in, before being deglazed with a fruity vinegar.

Crushed and buttered potatoes would be lovely on the side.

Serves 4 as a main

2 garlic cloves

1 teaspoon juniper berries

4 sprigs of thyme

2 tablespoons olive oil

4 sika venison steaks, about 120g each, at room temperature

30g butter

200g marsh samphire

½ tablespoon capers

1 unwaxed lemon

3 tablespoons raspberry or blackberry vinegar

Peel the garlic cloves and crush with the back of a heavy knife. Use a pestle and mortar to work into a paste with a good pinch of salt, the juniper berries and leaves picked from the thyme sprigs.

Heat the oil in a large frying pan over a low heat. Add the garlic mix and cook gently for just a couple of minutes until the flavours begin to be released. Sit the venison steaks in the pan on top of the garlic mix, increase the heat and fry them for 2 minutes on each side for meat that will be nicely pink.

Lift the steaks out and set aside to rest. Add the butter to the pan then, once it has melted, add the samphire. Drain, rinse and roughly chop the capers and add those too. Stir over the heat just long enough for the samphire to wilt. Grate over the zest of the lemon and divide the samphire between four plates. Pour the vinegar into the pan and let it bubble for 30 seconds or so, stirring and letting it reduce and deglaze the pan.

Slice the rested steaks on the diagonal, sit the meat on top of the samphire, and pour over the vinegar deglaze from the pan. Give a good grinding of pepper over the top and serve.

HOW TO... shop for venison

'Red, fallow, sika, roe, muntjack and Chinese water deer are the six species found in the UK. They're all rich, lean and delicious, but as each breed has a different habitat and diet, so the flavour and texture of the venison will differ too. Very lean roe deer meat, for example, is best cooked with plenty of fat. In general, haunches are good for steaks or roasting whole; cuts like the shoulder can be marinaded and slow roasted to retain moisture within the joint.'

Darren Brown, Shellseekers Fish & Game

Pork tomahawk

A tomahawk cut – a chop with some belly still attached and running down the bone 'handle' – can be from either a cow or a pig. I'm going for pork here. It's a spectacular chop to look at, to cook, and certainly to eat.

The principles here apply for cooking any pork chop, not just a tomahawk. As simple as a pork chop might seem, it – and the animal it came from – deserves you paying the respect of cooking it mindfully and well.

Brining the chop helps the meat to stay tender, with the bonus of serving as a reminder to bring the chop back to room temperature before cooking. You can buy the tomahawk pre-trimmed, or do it yourself with a very sharp knife, being sure to keep the trimmings for something else.

Serves 2 hungry people, or 3–4 less so

4 tablespoons sea salt

2 pork tomahawks, each about 700g untrimmed weight (about 400g when trimmed)

Make a brine by heating the salt with 1 litre of water in a large saucepan until the salt has dissolved. Set aside to cool.

If you're trimming your tomahawks, cut the meat off the long bone of each tomahawk. Then, trim the rinds off the fat – a line running about halfway through the fat is your guide for where to trim. Keep aside the rinds for crackling. Sit the tomahawks in a shallow dish and pour over the cooled brine to cover the meat end. Set aside for 1–2 hours.

Preheat the oven to 210C fan/230C/445F/gas mark 8 with a small roasting tray inside.

Use a very sharp knife to slash the skin of the rinds, then rub them with salt. Sit a frying pan over a medium heat and, when it is very hot, lay the rinds in it skin-side down. Give them a couple of minutes to start to brown, then turn over and repeat. Transfer the rinds to the hot roasting tray in the oven to crackle while you cook the chops.

Lower the heat under the empty frying pan as low as it will go. Sit the tomahawks in the pan fat edge down. The bone 'handles' will help you to keep the chops standing up. You want to slowly – very slowly – render the fat. It will take 12–15 minutes to turn translucent. A temperature probe inserted into the fat should read about 85C. Only then can you sit the tomahawks on their side to cook. They will need only 3 minutes or so on each side – you're looking for an internal temperature of 63C.

Lift the chops out to rest for 5 minutes. Serve the tomahawks whole for cutting into at the table, or slice the meat off the bone. You could still put the bones out for hungrier eaters to pick off any extra meat. Don't forget to serve alongside the crackling that's in the oven and which by now will be blistered and very likely in pleasing curls.

While the meat rests, use the fat that has rendered into the pan to cook whatever vegetables you fancy having.

Some ideas to serve alongside:

· Spelt and chard, page 85.

· Mixed root hasselbacks with miso butter, page 162.

· A big green salad with the sherry vinegar and mustard dressing option on page 162.

· Hot anchovy and garlic sauce for roasted purple sprouting broccoli and walnuts, page 109.

· Boil rice while the chops cook; then while they rest cook sliced calabrese broccoli in the pan the chops cooked in, adding chilli and soy sauce.

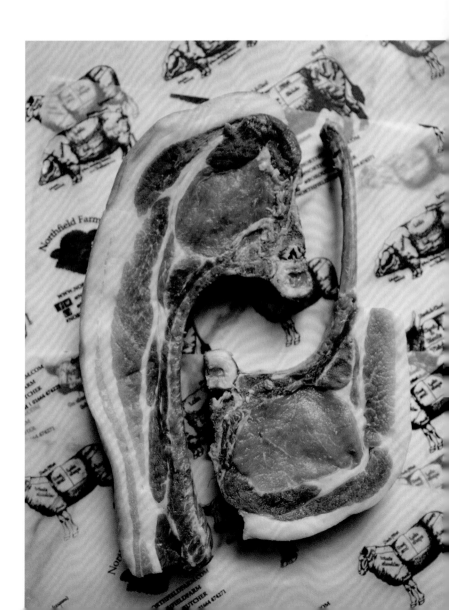

Borough Market – The Knowledge

Black pudding, cavolo nero, potato and egg breakfast pan

Maria Moruzzi had been a Market legend for nearly 20 years before deciding to hang up her apron once and for all. So this recipe comes in honour of Maria and is inspired by the bacon and bubble & squeak bap from Maria's Market Café that would be my go-to breakfast on many a Saturday morning, when I tend to get to the Market very early.

If you have some leftover cooked or roasted potato and leftover greens, you could use those instead of the cavolo nero and potato as the base for something that's even closer to its bubble & squeak inspiration.

My choice of black pudding is the wild boar from Shellseekers Fish & Game, though any good-quality black pudding, Spanish morcilla or French boudin noir will be great. Add eggs, then serve with hot sauce and some whipped herb labneh for a chill-busting way to start the day.

Serves 2 for breakfast, brunch or lunch

1 large potato

1 banana shallot

60g cavolo nero or kale

1 tablespoon olive oil

150g black pudding, morcilla or boudin noir

2 eggs

Hot sauce, to serve

For the herbed yoghurt

80g Greek yoghurt or labneh (see page 264)

Handful of chopped soft herbs, such as mint, chervil, dill or tarragon

½ lemon

Scrub but don't peel the potato, then halve it and put into a saucepan of salted water to simmer for 10–15 minutes until just about tender.

Meanwhile, peel and chop the shallot and strip the cavolo nero (or kale) leaves from their ribs. Cut away and discard the very woody end of each rib, then dice the ribs very finely. Heat the oil in a small frying pan over a medium heat, add the shallot and saute until just softening, then add the diced ribs. Cook for 5 minutes or so, until the ribs are softening too. If you get to this point and your potato isn't quite ready yet, just take the frying pan off the heat and wait before proceeding.

With the frying pan back over the heat, break up the black pudding and add it to the shallot mix. Drain the potato, cut it into small pieces and add it too. Tear the cavolo nero or kale leaves and put them into the pan along with 50ml water. Cover and leave to cook for 5 minutes, stirring halfway through and rubbing at the base of the pan with a wooden spoon to lift off any bits that are sticking. Make wells in the mixture to break the eggs into, crack an egg into each one, cover the pan and leave to cook for 5 minutes – you want the egg whites to be set but the yolks runny.

While the eggs are cooking, mix the yoghurt or labneh in a bowl with the chopped herbs and a good squeeze of lemon juice. Season.

To serve, grind black pepper over the cooked eggs, adding hot sauce to taste, and serve with the herbed yoghurt alongside.

A few ways with jointed chicken

Spend time at Borough Market and you can't help but begin to feel a greater connection with our food and where it comes from. That goes double for getting familiar with how to joint a chicken like the team at Wyndham House Poultry on page 64. When shopping for chicken only means picking up a pair of plastic-wrapped skinless fillets, it's perhaps understandable how easy it is to ignore thoughts about how the bird was reared, what breed it is, or its age. But buy a whole bird, joint it yourself, and those things will matter that bit more.

And, of course, you'll have some fantastic meat, the various cuts giving you so many cooking options. You could deep-fry the drumsticks, use the legs for a one-pot crammed with seasonal veg, turn the breasts into buttery kyivs... Here are just a few ideas to get things going.

Marinades

All the pieces of a jointed chicken are made even more delicious when given a tasty marinade for a couple of hours. You are aiming for a mixture that packs in flavour, with contrasts of sweet, sour and spicy. Perhaps:

- Soy sauce and honey with grated ginger, black mustard seeds and chilli.

- A spice blend such as Spice Mountain's baharat (cloves, mint and cumin) mixed with oil and lemon juice.

- Pomegranate molasses with mustard, dark brown sugar and poppy seeds.

- Paprika (sweet or smoked), rosemary and thyme with oil.

- Tahini with crushed garlic, cumin, lemon, sweet paprika and oil.

- Sriracha, honey and cider vinegar.

Roast, grill or griddle, as you prefer. The bonus of roasting in a tray means that when you lift the joints out to rest, there will be residual sticky marinade juices left behind, giving the opportunity to connect the flavours on your plate by using those juices to cook your vegetables in.

One-pot

Legs and thighs are especially good for a one-pot, but all the bird can be used. The meat cooks along with your vegetables, and perhaps you could add rice or potatoes in there too. Ideally use a shallow casserole dish that's large enough to take the chicken pieces in a snug single layer with the veg.

Two of my most-cooked chicken one-pots:

- Get some oil and butter good and hot in a large shallow casserole dish or roasting tray that can go on the hob. Add the chicken pieces skin-side down and let them brown. Lift out and set aside while you add to the same dish some chopped leeks, crushed garlic, sprigs of tarragon and rosemary, tinned anchovies, chunks of bright peppers, and potatoes cut into pieces. Return the chicken pieces to the pan, pour over fino sherry, wine or stock, season well, and cook uncovered in a 180C fan/200C/400F/gas mark 6 oven for about 40 minutes. Finish with a smattering of chopped herbs.

- Put orange quarters, sliced red onions, garlic cloves in their skins, whatever spices or herbs you are in the mood for, plenty of oil and some sherry vinegar into a large mixing bowl. Toss round, then toss in the chicken pieces too. Transfer the whole thing to a casserole dish or tray, making sure the chicken pieces are skin-side up. Season and bake in a hot 180C fan/200C/400F/gas mark 6 oven.

There are endless other options here.

Escalopes

To turn a breast into escalopes:

Put a large piece of non-PVC cling film on your worktop, sit the skinless chicken breast in the middle, and fold over the cling film so the breast is covered. Use a rolling pin (or meat mallet, if you have one) to bash at it and flatten it out. You are aiming for it to be about 5mm thick. If it's large, cut it in half to make two escalopes.

Then go old-school and fry in breadcrumbs until crisply golden:

Prepare one shallow bowl with egg beaten and a squeeze of lemon juice, and another shallow bowl with breadcrumbs. Dip the escalope first in the egg and then the breadcrumbs. Help things along by pressing the breadcrumbs in. Heat oil and butter in a frying pan over a medium heat and fry the breaded escalopes for 4 minutes on each side until cooked through.

Kyivs

Chicken kyivs don't require you to go as far as flattening the breast to an escalope. This is more about a little flattening and creating a pocket to fill with a delicious buttery filling.

For miso kyivs:

Make the miso butter as on page 162. Take a skinless breast, cut away the thin fillet tucked inside and keep it. Slit the breast down one side along its length, going in as far as you can without coming out the other side. You are trying to create a large pocket. Bash the breast with a rolling pin to flatten it a little, then fill its pocket with miso butter and seal the opening with the thin fillet you kept back earlier. Dip first in seasoned flour, then beaten egg, then breadcrumbs. Chill and repeat. Shallow-fry as for the escalopes, then transfer to a hot 180C fan/200C/400F/gas mark 6 oven to cook through for 10 minutes.

The kyiv butter filling is where you can get really creative. Switch out the miso butter for butter with anchovies, parsley, thyme or tarragon, cayenne...

Deep-fry

It's hard to better the satisfaction of eating (with your hands, obviously) a piece of freshly fried chicken, with its crisply spiced coating giving way to tender drumstick or thigh meat. Wings can be good too, although there's not really enough meat on them to be truly satisfying. This is not the time for chicken breasts – they simply take too long to cook in the fryer. Some tips:

- Sitting the chicken pieces overnight in buttermilk, yoghurt or kefir will help tenderise the meat. You could add some spicing to the marinade, but you'll need more for...

- ... the flour coating, which you need to season well with salt, pepper, and whatever spices (or spice blends – see page 212) appeal. Go a little heavier with the spicing than you otherwise might, as some will get lost in the frying oil.

- Take the pieces from the marinade to the flour to the fryer. For a thicker coating, go back to the marinade after the initial flour-dip, then back into the flour.

- Deep- or shallow-fry as you prefer. Just make sure the oil is 180C before you put the chicken in, and remember to keep an eye on both the oil temperature and the chicken's internal temperature. This might be a time for two thermometers.

- Drain and crunch.

Pie

Chicken pie always means thigh.

> Jointing won't leave you with much of a carcass, but what you have you can use for stock – see page 82.
>
> The wings make especially great stocks.
>
> A temperature probe is definitely your friend for cooking chicken. You are looking for 74C when you insert the probe into the middle of the chicken piece.

Meat stocks

Making stocks involves little more than simmering some bones with vegetables and aromatics, then straining those out. Really that's it. Okay, yes, sometimes you roast the bones first, but the point holds true: this is low-endeavour activity for high-achieving results. And, as I have said elsewhere, when an animal has given its life to feed us, the least we can do is respect every last morsel.

It is about minimising waste while capturing goodness and flavour. They'll resound through the rest of your cooking as you reach for the homemade stock in your fridge or freezer.

Broadly there are two kinds of meat stock:

- Light stocks, where the bones go directly into the pot. They give a lighter flavoured and coloured stock.

- Dark stocks, where the bones (and often the vegetables) are roasted first to caramelise and bring greater depth of flavour and colour. More suited to use in richer dishes.

The quality of your meat will determine the quality of your stock. High-welfare, heritage breeds of any animal are simply going to taste the best.

If you see a future for yourself as a stock-maker, your best investment will be a stockpot, far easier than fiddling around with saucepans that aren't quite big enough for the job in hand.

Chicken stock

Light chicken stock:
This is the stock to make with the stripped carcass of a roasted bird. If your chicken came with its giblets, you can add those to the pot too (but not the liver), and for extra oomph add some extra chicken wings – they make exceptionally good stock.

Put the chicken bones into a large pot, with the giblets and extra chicken wings (if using). Roughly chop an onion, two carrots and a celery stick and put them into the pot along with the flavour enhancers (see opposite) of your choosing.

Cover with water and simmer gently for 2 hours, skimming off every so often the froth that rises to the top.

Strain and reduce the strained stock further if you want a more concentrated end result, but note that for use in light dishes, a chicken stock can overwhelm other flavours if it is too concentrated. A lighter stock is often best. Let it cool, then spoon away most of the fat. Your stock is ready to use that day or can be frozen in batches.

Dark chicken stock:
A darker, richer chicken stock is made by asking your butcher for chicken wings and cooking those from raw specifically for stock.

Preheat the oven to 200C fan/220C/425F/gas mark 7. Spread 8 or so chicken wings in a single layer in a roasting tray and roast for 1 hour, turning occasionally. Transfer them to a large pot. Pour a little water or wine into the roasting tray to deglaze any chicken deliciousness stuck to the bottom and pour that into the pot.

Roughly chop an onion, two carrots and a celery stick and put them into the same tray. Roast for 15 minutes, then add to the pot along with the flavour enhancers (see opposite) of your choosing. Cover with water and simmer gently for 2 hours, skimming off every so often the froth that rises to the top.

Strain and reduce the strained stock further if you want an even more concentrated end result. Let it cool, then spoon away most of the fat. Your stock is ready to use that day or can be frozen in batches.

Poached chicken stock:

Poach a chicken in a pot with vegetables and aromatics and you will not only have fabulously tender chicken meat to feast upon, but ready-made stock too. Just strain it, cool, spoon away the fat, and reduce if you want to.

Pork stock

The recipe for gammon on page 113 leaves you with a pot of stock (and its poaching guide can be used for making stocks with other pork bones). Note that the resulting stock will be salty, and – as with lamb – pork stocks tend to taste clearly of themselves and so are best used only in pork dishes.

Beef stock

Beef bones make for flavoursome, rich stocks that are versatile to use. Marrow bones have so much goodness to give to stock, so aim for half your bone quota to be marrow bones, and the other half perhaps shin, shoulder or oxtail. As ever, talk to the butcher about what you are doing and see what they have that suits.

Preheat the oven to 200C fan/220C/ 425F/gas mark 7.

Spread the beef bones in a single layer in a roasting tray and roast for 1 hour, turning occasionally, until browned. Transfer them to a large pot. Pour a little water or wine into the roasting tray to deglaze and pour that into the pot.

Roughly chop an onion, two carrots and a celery stick and put into the same tray. Roast for 15 minutes,

then add to the pot along with the flavour enhancers (see right) of your choosing. Cover with water and simmer gently for 3 hours, skimming off every so often the froth that rises to the top.

Strain and reduce the strained stock further if you want a more concentrated end result. Let it cool, then spoon away most of the fat. Your stock is ready to use that day or can be frozen in batches.

Veal stock

Proceed as for beef stock, but don't roast the veg before adding to the stockpot.

Lamb stock

Proceed as for beef stock, but don't roast the veg before adding to the stockpot.

Note that lamb stocks have a distinctly lamby flavour and are best only used in lamb dishes.

FLAVOUR ENHANCERS

Use your common sense in terms of amounts, depending on the quantity of meat bones you have for stock-making.

Essential: onion (skin on – try red onion for a darker stock), carrot, celery.

Plus your choice(s) of: leek, fennel trimmings, celeriac trimmings, parsley stalks and other fresh herbs, peppercorns, star anise, fennel seeds, bay leaves, coriander seeds, citrus zests, red or white wine, fresh root ginger, mushroom peelings, halved garlic bulb with its skin left on.

Stuffed hogget leg with spelt and chard

Younger lamb can't match the depth of flavour of hogget (which is 1–2 years old) and mutton (2 years plus). For a roast joint like this, I think hogget is a great choice.

In this recipe, the joint is tunnel-boned for stuffing. The butcher should be happy to do that tunnel-boning for you. The cavity is then filled with flavours that pervade the meat as it cooks and gives every slice the benefit of its succulence and hit of paprika. Mix up what you serve this with as the seasons change – some thoughts on that appear opposite.

Serves 6 as a feast

65g cooked chestnuts

2 garlic cloves

3 anchovy fillets in oil

1 apple

2 sprigs of rosemary

2 sprigs of sage

Handful of dill and mint (about 20g)

2 teaspoons juniper berries

1 tablespoon sherry vinegar

2 teaspoons smoked paprika

30g breadcrumbs

About 2.5kg tunnel-boned hogget leg (roughly 3kg bone-in weight)

2 tablespoons olive oil

You will need butcher's twine

Chop the chestnuts, peeled garlic and anchovy fillets and put into a mixing bowl. Quarter and core the apple, then grate into the same bowl. Chop the leaves of the rosemary and sage, chop the dill and mint, and add all the herbs to the bowl too. Crush the juniper berries and mix those in along with the vinegar, smoked paprika and breadcrumbs. Season and set aside in the fridge for 30 minutes to firm up.

Preheat the oven to 210C fan/230C/445F/gas mark 8.

Sit your tunnel-boned joint in a roasting tray, skin-side down. At the shank end of the joint is a flap of meat. Tuck that in to block off one end of the tunnel, then pack in the stuffing, focusing on getting as much as you can in the middle. Use the twine to tie the centre first, and then do two more ties either side. Take care not to tie the joint too tightly or the stuffing will come out. But it has to be tight enough to hold it all together.

Turn the rolled leg skin-side up. Smear with the olive oil, scatter over some salt, then put into the oven for 25 minutes. At that point, turn the oven down to 140C fan/160C/325F/gas mark 3, cover the tray with foil and roast for another 2 hours. Halfway through, pour a small glass of water (or wine or cider if you have an open bottle around) into the tray to stop the joint drying out, but take care not to pour it over the meat itself. For the last 15 minutes of cooking time, uncover the meat and turn the oven back up to 210C fan/230C/445F/gas mark 8.

Take the joint out, cover again with foil and leave to rest for at least 30 minutes before carving. Keep the juices in the roasting tin for cooking your sides.

Gauging cooking times: for your weight of boned, stuffed lamb, allow 30 minutes per 500g, plus 30 minutes. The internal temperature should be 70C on a probe thermometer.

For the spelt and chard

400g spelt

400g chard

2 leeks

3 garlic cloves

Handful of mint

1 lemon

Make this while the lamb is resting. Cook the spelt for 20 minutes in boiling water. Trim off the very ends of the chard, then separate the leaves from the stalks. Set the leaves aside. Finely chop the chard stalks along with the leeks. Saute the chard stalks and leeks in the juices left in the roasting tray. Give them about 10 minutes, then peel, crush and add the garlic cloves. Go steady with salt as the lamb's juices will be packed with umami. Chop the chard leaves and add those along with some chopped mint and the juice of the lemon. Drain the spelt and stir through to serve.

More thoughts on sides:

- Creamed Jerusalem artichokes, page 116.

- Shaved kohlrabi, chickpeas and little gem salad, page 158.

- Warm borlotti bean and pea salad, page 160.

- Mixed root hasselbacks, page 162 (the version with sherry vinegar and mustard seed dressing).

And / or:

- Make some couscous and stir through chopped dried fruits and nuts.

- Slice potatoes and cook them in the same dish as the lamb, with some added stock for a boulangère.

Oxtail with herbed suet dumplings and blackberry-braised shallots

I don't think I'll forget the first time I saw at the Market a piece of oxtail unfurled from its neatly tied coil and looking like an actual tail. A reminder – along with the hearts, livers and kidneys from not just beef but other animals too – that when an animal has given its life to feed us, we owe it the respect of not wasting it.

The suet fat from around the bullock's kidneys makes for light dumplings that match perfectly with slow-cooked oxtail. Some steamed greens served alongside would bring a nice burst of colour, and a bitterness that complements the sweetly braised shallots.

Best made the day before serving so the flavours can develop.

Serves 6 as a main

2 tablespoons olive oil

50g butter

2kg oxtail, cut into its sections

1 onion

2 celery sticks

1 carrot

1 leek

1 tablespoon black mustard seeds

2 teaspoons freshly grated
  horseradish

4 anchovy fillets in oil

3 tablespoons plain flour

500ml red wine

2 teaspoons honey

1 star anise

1 cinnamon stick

2 bay leaves

1 red chilli

500ml beef stock (bought or
  see page 82)

Preheat the oven to 120C fan/140C/275F/gas mark 1.

Heat the oil and butter in a large casserole dish that can go on the hob and into the oven. Brown the oxtail pieces on all sides, working in batches so as to not crowd the pan. Lift out with a slotted spoon and set aside.

Peel the onion and slice into half moons; then cut the celery, carrot and leek into 2cm chunks. Put the vegetables into the casserole dish you just browned the oxtail in, and stir into the oil left behind from the beef. Give a good pinch of salt and cook for 10 minutes or so to soften the vegetables. Stir in the black mustard seeds and horseradish. Let those cook for a minute while you use a pestle and mortar to crush the anchovy fillets into a paste. Stir that through, then stir in the plain flour. Pour in a little of the wine and rub at the base of the dish with a wooden spoon to lift off any sticky bits.

Return the oxtail to the dish and mix with the vegetables. Stir in the honey. Pour over the rest of the wine and tuck in the star anise, cinnamon stick, bay leaves and whole chilli. Add beef stock until the meat is covered, topping up with water if you need to. Season and let it bubble for a couple of minutes, then cover and put into the oven for 3–3½ hours until the meat is so tender it wants to fall off the bones. Check occasionally that the meat is still submerged and add water if needed.

Remove from the oven and discard the whole chilli, bay leaves, cinnamon stick and star anise. Leave to cool, then chill overnight in the fridge for the flavours to develop.

When you want to eat it, preheat the oven to 170C fan/190C/375F/gas mark 5.

Spoon away the fat from the surface of the cold oxtail, then set the casserole dish over a medium heat to come to a simmer.

For the dumplings

100g shredded beef suet

225g self-raising flour

About 30g fresh herbs (any mix
of flat-leaf parsley, tarragon,
chervil or oregano)

1 egg

**For the blackberry-
braised shallots**

4 banana shallots

2 tablespoons olive oil

150g blackberries

2 tablespoons red wine vinegar
or sherry vinegar

To make the dumplings, mix together the suet and flour. Chop the herbs and add most but not all of them to the flour. Beat the egg and mix that in along with just enough cold water to bring it into a dough. Shape into 12 balls. Sit the balls on top of the gently bubbling oxtail, cover the dish and put it in the oven for 25 minutes so the oxtail warms through and the dumplings cook. Remove the lid halfway into the cooking time.

While the dumplings are cooking, peel and slice the shallots in half lengthways then into long thin strips. Heat the oil in a medium saucepan over a medium heat, add the shallots and saute until just crisping up. Stir through the blackberries, vinegar, and some salt and pepper, cover and cook for about 5 minutes.

Finish the dumplings with just a minute or two under a hot grill to brown them. Scatter over the herbs you kept back when making the dumplings, and serve with the blackberry-braised shallots alongside as a tartly jammy accompaniment.

Any leftover oxtail stew can be turned into a thick broth with the addition of a few more vegetables and some stock, or into a sauce for pasta.

Beef, leek and ale pie

This pie has a basic shortcrust pastry, but the key thing is that half the fat used to make it is beef dripping. That gives pastry which is simultaneously crisp, melting and very, very tasty. Dripping is also used for searing the beef, to harmonise and maximise flavours across the pie.

Ask for chuck steak at the butcher's. Cut from the shoulder, it is full of marbling and flavour but is also a little tough unless it gets low, slow cooking that can tenderise it (which is just what we're doing here). You'll also need to ask for the marrow bones to be cut just a little taller than your pie dish. They'll look glorious poking out of the top of the pie, their marrow having melted into the filling and the bone becoming a steam funnel. The filling can be made up to two days ahead of baking the pie and chilled until needed.

Serves 6–8 as a main

75g plain flour

1.5kg diced chuck steak

About 100g beef dripping

200g shallots

2 tablespoons rapeseed oil

3 leeks

500ml ale or beer

2 teaspoons mustard

500ml beef stock

2 sage leaves

2 sprigs of rosemary

3 sprigs of thyme

2 bay leaves

1 tablespoon soft dark brown sugar

2 marrow bones (see introduction above)

Greens of your choice, to serve

You will need a 27 x 20 x 6cm baking / pie dish

Preheat the oven to 120C fan/140C/275F/gas mark 1.

Season the plain flour and spread it out on a large plate or tray. Toss the chuck steak chunks in the flour. Heat 1 tablespoon of the dripping in a large casserole dish over a medium heat. Once it's hot, add a third of the beef and sear, getting it good and brown all over. Remove the beef with a slotted spoon to another large plate or tray and repeat for the rest of the meat, adding more dripping to the casserole dish as needed. Once all the meat is seared, there will be lots of its goodness stuck to the base of the dish. Deglaze this with a cup of water, rubbing at the base of the dish with a wooden spoon to lift off as much as you can. Pour into a bowl and set aside.

Peel and thinly slice the shallots. Heat the rapeseed oil in the casserole dish you used to sear the beef, add the shallots and cook over a medium heat. Slice the leeks into chunks about 2cm long and add to the dish just as the shallots are beginning to colour. Let the leeks cook to the point of collapsing but take care they don't burn. Pour in a little of the ale or beer to deglaze the dish again. Stir in the mustard with the rest of the ale, the beef, the stock, and the reserved deglaze from searing the beef. Finely chop the sage and rosemary leaves, pick the leaves from the thyme and add those along with the bay leaves and sugar. Season generously.

Bring to a low simmer, cover, and put into the oven for 2½ hours, removing the lid for the last hour. The meat should be very tender and the sauce still quite liquid. Use a slotted spoon to lift the meat and vegetables into the dish you'll be baking your pie in, discarding the bay leaves. Cover with foil so the filling cools in its own steam. Place the casserole with the sauce over a high heat to reduce it to a good gravy consistency. Test the seasoning. Once it has cooled, mix it into the meat and vegetables.

Continue to make the pie as described overleaf or store in the fridge and bring back to room temperature before baking the pie.

Cont. overleaf

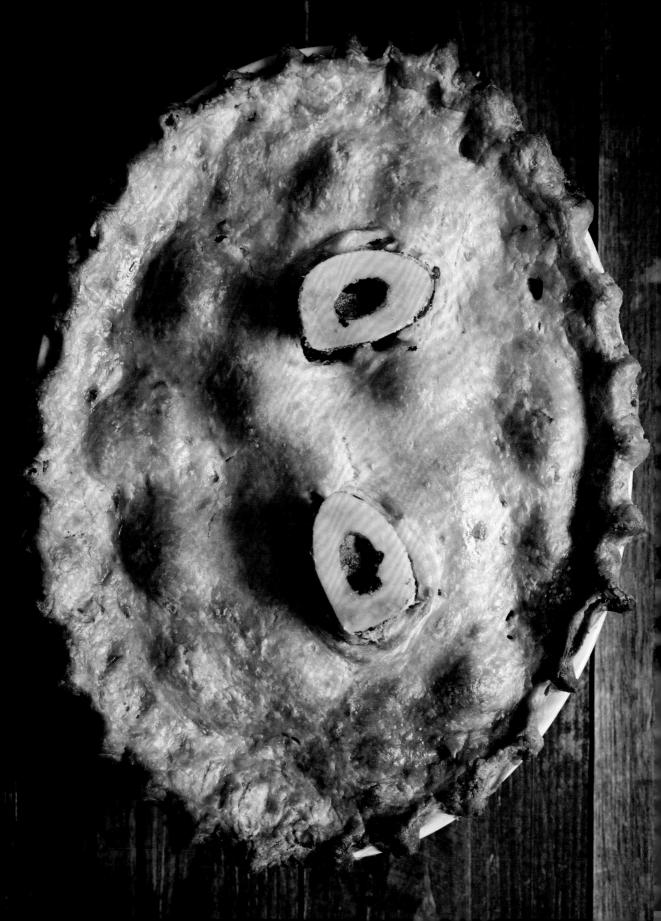

For the pastry

450g self-raising flour, plus extra
for dusting

½ teaspoon fine salt

100g cold beef dripping

100g cold butter

1 egg

To make the pastry, sift the flour and salt into a large mixing bowl. Cut the dripping and butter into dice, and use your fingers to rub them into the flour. Add a tablespoon of cold water and begin to work the mixture into a smooth dough. Add more water as needed, but as little as you can. Shape the dough into a disc, wrap and chill for 1 hour.

Preheat the oven to 170C fan/190C/375F/gas mark 5.

Stand the marrow bones in the pie mixture at even points in the middle. Dust the worktop with a little flour and roll the pastry out so that it will cover the pie dish. Make crosses where the marrow bones will be. Roll the pastry up onto a rolling pin, then unroll it over the pie dish, working it over and down the marrow bones so they are poking through. Crimp the pastry edges to seal the pastry to the dish. Beat the egg and mix with a tablespoon of water. Brush over the pastry.

Bake the pie for 40 minutes – the pastry should be golden and the filling hot.

Use that time to cook the greens of your choice quickly and over a high heat in a pan with butter, a little olive oil, salt and a small cup of water added towards the end.

To make this gluten free:
- *Use potato flour instead of plain flour to toss the beef in before searing.*
- *For the pastry: switch the plain flour for a gluten-free option adding 1 teaspoon xanthan gum when sifting it with the salt.*

Drinks

Syrah and shiraz

Two words for the same grape, and used by producers somewhat interchangeably. 'Syrah' is typically used in Europe, 'shiraz' in the Southern Hemisphere and Americas, although these lines can become a little blurry depending on the characteristics of the wine being produced.

The versatility of syrah / shiraz makes these wines a good choice for all kinds of meat dishes. But how do you choose which for what, and know what you are buying? Take advice from Mario Sposito, wine director / educator at Bedales of Borough:

'The softer and fruitier examples of syrah / shiraz are better paired with cuts and dishes like grilled sausages, duck or charcuterie. The complex and long-lived syrah from the Northern Rhône would instead be a top choice for refined and tender cuts of beef or venison or feathered game. The exceptionally concentrated and structured old-vine Barossa shiraz grapes are better suited for bolder recipes like a tajine.

The climate of the wine-producing region can be crucial in defining the primary fruit qualities of the wine. A moderate climate syrah / shiraz has fresh black fruit flavours, with herbal notes and black pepper aromas. A warm climate example would typically be full bodied with riper flavours of cooked black fruit and liquorice. Oak maturation is common with syrah / shiraz and is used to soften its tannins and to add flavours of smoke and spices.'

Bitter, porter and stout

Mike Hill, co-owner of Utobeer, has advice on beers to partner with meat dishes. These are listed in order of depth of flavour and weight (starting with the lighter beers), and are therefore suited to dishes that run that gamut too:

Best bitter: a beer that's making a bit of a comeback, according to Mike. Made in the pale ale style but more malty, they are best drunk with lighter meat dishes, with Mike steering this especially towards lamb which tends to be more aromatic than other meats.

Porter: a lusciously dark beer which typically has a balance of sweetness from the malt and hoppy bitterness playing through. Its place in the middle of these three makes it the most adaptable for serving with meats.

Stout: originally known as 'stout porter', which should give a clue to how closely related the two styles are. Their difference comes in the grain and how much is used. Stout tends to be sweeter, with more dark chocolatey profiles. In this chapter, Mike would put stout with the Oxtail with herbed suet dumplings and blackberry-braised shallots on page 88 – and, as he put it, would choose a robust stout at that. (His steer is to avoid 'pastry' – ie sweet – stouts with bourbon or coconut, which are more suited to desserts.)

Look for beer labels bearing the words 'bottle-conditioned' or 'can conditioned'. They have continued fermenting after bottling so will have sediment.

£2.25 FERMENTED FISH SAUCE £4.90

SAUCE £1.99   OYSTER SAUCE £3.45

SRIRACHA SAUCE £1.69 SRIRACHA SAUCE (THE ORIGINAL) £2.99

THE STORE CUPBOARD I

Though today home to a host of Greek speciality foods, Oliveology began, as the name suggests, with olive oil, grown and pressed by traditional, organic family farms on a part of the Peloponnese peninsula that has been cultivating olives for over 3,000 years.

Understanding olive oil

Marianna Kolokotroni, Oliveology

The best way to understand olive oil is to view it in the same way you would wine. Like wine, there are many different olive oils from numerous different regions – and, like wine, there are many factors that will affect the price and quality. The scale of production is one; if the plantation is large, and most of the harvesting and processing is done by machinery, the olive oil will be cheaper. One reason that olive oil from Greece is rarely cheap is because Greece is so mountainous; you inevitably have no choice but to harvest at least some of the olives by hand.

Another factor to consider is whether you're buying a single-variety olive oil or a blend. If the oil is produced from a single variety of olives from a single plantation, you can – again, like wine – really taste the terroir. Some producers blend two or three different types of olives, gathered from estates that don't grow enough olives to make their own oil. This can produce a good result, but blends are often used to hide faults in a particular harvest.

The more places the olives have come from, the less assured you can be of its quality. Kalamata olive oil will be a blend of olives from across the Kalamata region of Greece; Greek olive oil will be a blend from across Greece; European olive oil will be a blend from multiple countries. Our olive oil is a single variety, the Koroneiki variety, from a single estate in Sparta, Greece.

Of course, the main thing affecting the quality of the oil is the quality of the olives themselves. If you use pesticides and fertilisers on the crop, the quality will inevitably be affected, because these chemicals make their way into the harvest – you can't wash them away if they've been applied from the start. But growing organically is becoming a lot more challenging because changes in climate have resulted in more diseases, pests and extreme weather events.

Then there is harvesting. On commercial plantations, they let the olives fall to the ground. This makes them easier to collect but can result in some olives being bruised or rotting slightly. The longer the olives are left,

96   Borough Market - The Knowledge

"If an olive oil is produced from a single variety of olives from a single plantation, you can – like wine – really taste the terroir.

> "
> When you press at higher temperatures, the olives start to cook, the acidity of the oil increases, and the flavour deteriorates.

the worse this will be. Even for extra-virgin olive oil, you can allow up to 48 hours between harvesting and pressing. If those damaged olives go through the press, they will affect the result. Our producers pick the olives rather than allowing them to fall, then transport them to the press in less than two hours. Before pressing, they discard any that are defective; last year they had to discard 30–40 per cent. They would rather suffer that loss than damage their reputation.

Finally, there is the processing of the olives into olive oil. For an oil to be extra-virgin, the producer must cold-press the olives, meaning the temperature at which the oil is extracted is no more than 27C. At higher temperatures, the olives start to cook, the acidity of the oil increases, and the flavour and nutritional benefits deteriorate. Cold-pressing results in less yield, so you need to use more olives, but the lower the temperature, the higher the quality of oil. Each of our oils is labelled with a large number, which refers to the temperature of extraction. We're keen to teach people why this is relevant.

Any olive oil that is not labelled 'extra-virgin' will have been extracted at a higher temperature and made with poor-quality olives. 'Virgin' and other low-grade oils are simply a way of selling off bad olives. Sometimes people think they have a higher smoke point

so are better for cooking, but that's not true: extra-virgin olive oil has the highest smoke point of any type of olive oil. It's also a bad way of thinking about it, in my opinion. You're still eating it, you're still putting it in your body.

Another common impression is that greener olive oil is fresher and better – in fact, some manufacturers add green colouring because of this perception – but the colour of olive oil is not a guarantee of its quality. Olive oils that are unfiltered and cloudy are good to buy if you are going to use them quickly, but the sediment means they will deteriorate much faster. Our olive oil goes through a simple, natural filtration process – it is left in a metal tank until the sediment settles to the bottom.

I usually recommend that people go around Borough Market, try different olive oils from different stalls, and see which flavours they prefer. There are olive oils from Croatia, Spain, Italy – and Greece, of course. They are spicy, or bitter, or vibrant, or subtle. I don't believe there is a 'best' olive oil, in the same way that there isn't a 'best' wine. It is totally subjective.

HOW TO... marinade meat

'The style of marinade I use depends a lot on the meat. For cuts that are rich in flavour and carry a lot of their own fat, I'll base the marinade on a neutral oil – rapeseed or vegetable. In that case, I'm using the oil to help the spices adhere to the meat rather than impart flavour. If I were opting for a more herbaceous marinade with a cut of meat or poultry with a lower fat content, I would opt for olive oil as it will benefit from the flavour. When it comes to barbecue marinades, I sometimes use yoghurt or buttermilk rather than oil. They keep the meat really tender and help lock in those smoky flavours. If you have too much oil in the marinade it will flare up when the flames start kissing the meat, and the meat will end up tasting slightly acrid, like carbon.'

James Walters, Arabica

Five eggs

Century eggs (khai yiao ma)

Character Sold by Raya, these duck eggs are pickled in brine and buried in a mixture of clay and salt until the whites become dark and jelly-like, the surface is patterned, and the yolks have taken on a cheesy taste and texture and a deep, greenish hue.

Uses Traditionally served with pickled ginger root, or alongside a congee.

Salted duck eggs

Character Popular in China and Southeast Asia, these salted duck eggs from Raya have been steeped in brine. The process renders the egg whites almost rubbery when cooked – the recommended cooking time is 10–15 minutes – and the yolk somewhere between buttery and crumbly.

Uses Commonly enjoyed as a snack, on top of congee, or alongside everything from salad to stir-fries.

Goose eggs

Character About three times the size of a hen's egg and similarly flavourful. The pasture-reared geese that produce the eggs at Wyndham House Poultry enjoy a varied diet that results in richer, fattier eggs with yolks of a deep, sunset hue.

Uses Use in any recipe that calls for eggs, but take into account their large yolk-to-egg ratio. Goose eggs work particularly well in simple dishes that showcase their intense flavour and hue.

Duck eggs

Character Found at Ted's Veg, these are bigger than hen's eggs, with a wider range of colours, thicker shell, clearer white and significantly larger yolk, which gives them a particular richness when cooking.

Uses As versatile as any egg. Baking with duck eggs may require some recipe alteration, due to the size of the yolk.

Quail's eggs

Character The speckled shells of these diminutive eggs from Wild Beef conceal relatively large yolks and firm whites, which have a more intense flavour than many hen's eggs.

Uses The charming but insubstantial size of quail's eggs really demands they be cooked whole, either hard or soft boiled, or used to make miniature Scotch eggs.

The Store Cupboard I

From Field and Flower sources raw honey and honey-derived products from small-scale, independent beekeepers in Britain and further afield. Together with her husband Stefano, Samantha Wallace is committed to finding distinctive varieties that are deeply flavoursome and produced as sustainably as possible: two principles that invariably go hand in hand.

Samantha Wallace

From Field and Flower

You sell an extraordinary array of single-variety honeys – heather, acacia, lavender and so on. How is a single-variety honey created?

If necessary, bees can travel up to six miles for forage, but they try to be as economical with their effort as possible, pollinating the flowers nearest to them before moving further afield. By putting their hives in the middle of, for example, a crop of lavender, then closely monitoring the behaviour of the bees, a beekeeper can keep the varietals as pure as possible – the honey needs to be 85 per cent to be classed as a single varietal. Once that crop's season is over, the beekeepers extract the honey and move the hives elsewhere overnight – say to a chestnut woodland – to create a new varietal. Single varietals require lots of work, because you need a lot of hives and good weather to get long flowering seasons. That's why – with the exception of heather – you're more likely to find single varietals from Italy or eastern Europe than from the UK, where there aren't those big stretches of terrain with just chestnut trees or acacia.

Your honeys are unpasteurised. What's the difference between pasteurised and unpasteurised honey?

Mass-produced pasteurised honey is heated to above 60C for at least half an hour, before being bottled and rapidly cooled. This denatures the enzymes, kills any good bacteria and degrades the flavour. Pasteurisation means the honey is dead. It no longer has the properties that make it special. It's just sugar, without the layering and complexity of flavour – or the health benefits.

So why is most honey pasteurised?

Honey is a natural preservative: it's not going to go off. The main reason honey is pasteurised is to create a consistent product on an industrial scale. Industrial honeys are made from a huge number of sources, and each honey will vary wildly in colour and viscosity. So to make a uniformly consistent product, they blend them together and heat them to a high temperature. This also makes the honey very runny, meaning that thousands of jars and bottles can be filled rapidly. That's why it's so cheap. These honeys will usually carry the label 'EU and elsewhere', which means the honey could be from anywhere, and the ethics of how and where it is gathered and who gets paid for it are muddier. Beekeeping is a highly specialised craft requiring skill, patience and experience – but the way honey is sold leads people to think it should be cheap.

Do different honeys lend themselves to different uses?

Honeys vary greatly in flavour and texture, according to where and when they've been made. Generally, the rule of thumb is that the lighter the colour, the more delicate the flavour and the darker the colour, the deeper the flavour. Deeper doesn't necessarily mean sweeter, however: it's like going from a dry white wine to a more perfumed wine like a chablis, to a light red, to a dark red, to a brandy. If you're baking or cooking, a lighter honey will go well with summer fruits like raspberries and lychees, whereas darker honeys lend themselves to more intense, pruney flavours.

When it comes to bread, darker honeys are great with rye or very seeded breads, whereas lighter honeys are wonderful with white. Sourdough has a tang that will stand up to any honey, but I think it works best with an intensely floral, multi-perfumed honey with lots of butter. Butter's important. Some people think you don't need it, but if you really want a kick, I recommend a good amount of butter, honey and a sprinkle of sea salt.

What's the best honey for porridge?

Porridge is a mild base, but it also really absorbs flavour. If you use a light honey, you're going to have to use a lot to be able to taste it, so I'd recommend more of a medium honey, like cherry flower or late-season wildflower. Wildflower honeys are light and delicate at the beginning of the season, then as the season progresses you get more interesting floral flavours.
Three-cheese bourek with honey and nigella seeds, page 253.

Labneh with watermelon, honey and mint, page 264.

Chestnut honey and rosemary ice cream, page 120.

Ramón Peña sardines in olive oil

Contents Sardines caught off the coast of Galicia, canned by Ramón Peña, which has been preserving fish and seafood for more than 120 years, and brought to Borough Market by The Tinned Fish Market.

Character Plump sardines, carefully selected at the harbour and traditionally canned in high-quality olive oil.

Pepus mussels in escabeche

Contents Mussels grown and harvested in Galicia, hand-selected for size and preserved by another favourite supplier of The Tinned Fish Market, Pepus – a traditional business with a contemporary eye for can design.

Character Large mussels fried in olive oil and packed in an aromatic marinade of olive oil, vinegar and spices.

Five tinned

PEPUS

MEJILLONES EN ESCABECHE
MUSSELS IN MARINADE

GRANDES
LARGE

Ramón Peña

SARDINAS
En Aceite de Oliva picantes
SARDINILLAS

20/25 piezas

SARDINES IN SPICY OLIVE OIL

Nardín beech-smoked anchovies

Contents Nardín, a famed Basque conservas and supplier to Brindisa, only sources anchovies which have been sustainably caught in the Cantabrian Sea.

Character Soft, plump anchovies are brined and cold-smoked whole over beechwood, lending them a sweet, smoky flavour. After filleting, they're tinned in olive oil.

Ortiz yellowfin tuna belly

Contents Yellowfin tuna, line-caught off the coast of northern Spain and preserved by another Brindisa supplier, Conservas Ortiz, a family-owned company founded in the Basque Country in 1891.

Character The most prized part of the tuna is carefully cooked to preserve its long, tender flakes, melting texture and rich but gentle flavour.

Niçoise bundles, page 110.

Cântara stuffed squid

Contents Squid caught off the Atlantic coast, prepared by La Gondola cannery in northern Portugal, which was established in 1940 by Italian immigrants. Sold by The Tinned Fish Market.

Character Small squid stuffed with onion, rice and tomato, delicately cooked and preserved in sunflower oil.

fish

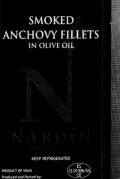

Five vinegars

Vinegar is created through two natural processes that play out in sequence. Yeasts feed on sugars and turn them into alcohol. Acetic acid bacteria then get to work, converting the alcohol into acetic acid: vinegar. The word 'vinegar' derives from the French for 'sour wine', but anything that can be turned into alcohol can be made into vinegar. Although the word 'vinegary' is often used to describe mouth-puckeringly sour flavours, the wealth of vinegars available at Borough Market belie this association, with varieties offering a far more complex flavour experience, ranging from floral and aromatic, to fruity and sweet.

Unió moscatel vinegar

This single varietal white wine vinegar – made in the Catalan province of Tarragona and imported by Brindisa – is produced using the 200-year-old Schützenbach method: a slow acetification process that ensures the floral aromas and honeyed stone fruit flavours of the moscatel grape remain distinct above the vinegar's gentle tang.

Emilia 12-year-old balsamic vinegar of Modena

Produced in line with the strict rules that govern balsamic vinegar of Modena, Bianca Mora's signature product starts with the must of organic grapes from a vineyard local to Modena. 'There is no sugar, no caramel: just fermented grape must and a bit of wine vinegar,' says Ewa Weremij of Bianca Mora. The vinegar is aged for 12 years, passing through a sequence of wooden barrels, becoming ever more concentrated as it matures and evaporates. The resulting liquid is intense and fruity with woody notes.

Valdespino sherry vinegar with PX

Valdespino is one of the oldest sherry producers in Jerez, southern Spain, with a storied, centuries-long history. This vinegar, available at Brindisa, is derived from the sherry wine of palomino grapes grown in Valdespino's own vineyard. It is aged for six years in American oak casks that once contained pedro ximénez sherries. The result is a vinegar of striking mahogany colour, with rich notes of oak.

Mastri acetai aceto di melograno

Among the most unusual vinegars at Borough Market is this sweet, tangy and intensely pink vinegar, which is made from the fermented juice of ripe Sicilian pomegranates and sold at Condiment Pantry, another of Ewa's ventures. 'It's made like a wine vinegar, but from fermented pomegranate juice,' says Ewa. 'I have it with plain yoghurt or drizzled on pancakes.'

Gustoso organic apple vinegar

This sweetly sour, distinctive yet versatile vinegar from The Olive Oil Co is made from pure organic apple juice. Produced in the northern Italian region of Emilia-Romagna, it is naturally fermented in wooden casks.

Pickled habanero and serrano chillies with lemongrass

It's not at all unusual for me to get overexcited at the grocer's stall by the sheer range and beauty of the fresh chillies on display. I buy a bagful, then get home and remember the dish I'm intending to cook calls for just one. That's when this pickle comes into its own. I think it's best made with a mix of (not too fiercely hot) chilli varieties.

A white wine vinegar – especially a slightly sweet moscatel – would work very well too instead of the cider vinegar. Either way, the pickling brine is useful for adding a chilli hit to salad dressings.

Fills 1 x 500ml jar

150ml cider vinegar

1½ tablespoons salt

1½ tablespoons caster sugar

1 lemongrass stalk

10–12 mixed chillies
(habanero, serrano, etc)

You will need a 500ml jar, sterilised

Put the vinegar, salt and sugar in a saucepan with 150ml water and heat just until the salt and sugar have dissolved. Remove from the heat and set aside.

Trim the lemongrass, remove its tough outer leaves, and slice in half. Bruise it with the back of a heavy knife. Prick each chilli a couple of times with a skewer.

Now pack the jar with the chillies, slipping in the lemongrass halves as you go. Pour over the pickling brine – the chillies should be just submerged; if they're not, add a little more vinegar.

Seal, label and date, then store in a cool place for at least 10 days before using. They'll keep in the fridge for up to 2 months.

The pickled chillies are great with charcuterie, or in salads, or thinly sliced for sandwiches. I often add them to the Mediterranean vegetable picnic loaf on page 292.

Hot anchovy and garlic sauce for roasted purple sprouting broccoli and walnuts

This version of garlic and anchovy bagna cauda sauce relies on making good choices about the anchovies you use in it. My anchovy essential – the beautiful box I am never without a fair few of in my store cupboard – is Ortiz from Brindisa. As wonderful as they'd certainly be in here, this recipe tempts me instead to head to De Calabria to find ones just as glorious, and somewhat closer to the sauce's Italian roots.

Anchovies are a wonderful partner for broccoli, and so especially delicious with the purple sprouting variety. Roasted walnuts bring texture and flavour to a dish that works as a side, as a starter, piled on toast for lunch, or even tossed through pasta.

Serves 4 as a small plate or side

250g purple sprouting broccoli

2 tablespoons olive oil

70g walnuts

For the anchovy and garlic sauce

6 garlic cloves

150ml milk

12 anchovy fillets in oil

120g unsalted butter

120ml olive oil

1 tablespoon creme fraiche

Preheat the oven to 190C fan/210C/410F/gas mark 6.

Trim off any very woody ends of the broccoli, then slice the stems horizontally into thinner lengths, being sure to keep the leaves. Toss in the olive oil and arrange in a single layer in a roasting tray. Season lightly. Roast in the oven for 12 minutes, until starting to char. Use that time to lightly crush the walnuts, then scatter them over the broccoli and return the tray to the oven for a further 3 minutes.

While the broccoli is roasting, prepare the sauce: peel and halve the garlic cloves, removing any green in their centres. Put the milk into a small saucepan, add the garlic cloves and cook gently over a low heat until tender – it will take about 15 minutes. That's almost exactly as long as the broccoli and nuts take to roast, but if they are ready first, just set the tray aside out of the oven while you finish the sauce.

Take the pan off the heat and mash the tender garlic cloves into the milk. Drain the anchovies of their oil and stir them into the milk until dissolved. Dice the butter into pieces then, over a low heat, whisk in with the olive oil and creme fraiche.

Serve the sauce with the broccoli and nuts while it is all still hot.

Niçoise bundles

The classic niçoise salad is served here as individual bundles that are perfect for a summer lunch or starter. I'm giving you two versions: one layers up blitzed olives and capers with egg and an anchovy; for the other, flaked tuna sits on an olive bed with tarragon mayo.

Their simplicity makes it important that each ingredient is chosen for maximum flavour. Perhaps especially the fish. I make these with (my favourite) Brindisa Ortiz anchovies and the same maker's yellowfin tuna belly 'ventresca', which in one bite of its long, tenderly rich flakes took me from thinking I didn't really like tinned tuna to stockpiling it. Head to page 104 for more fabulous tinned fish.

Serves 4 as a main or 8 as a small plate or starter

16 leaves of little gem lettuce and / or red chicory

For the tarragon mayonnaise

1 egg yolk, at room temperature

1½ teaspoons moscatel wine vinegar

¼ teaspoon English mustard powder

100ml sunflower oil

50ml mild olive oil

1 sprig of tarragon

For the olive and tuna mix

½ teaspoon raspberry vinegar

8 basil leaves

100g pitted black olives, drained weight

110g tinned yellowfin tuna

For the egg, olive and anchovy mix

2 hen's eggs or 4 quail's eggs

150g pitted black olives

2 teaspoons capers

1 garlic clove

75ml peppery olive oil, plus 1 tablespoon for drizzling

½ lemon

8 anchovy fillets

Wash and dry the lettuce or red chicory leaves.

For half of the little gem / chicory leaves:

Make the mayonnaise by gently hand-whisking the egg yolk with a pinch each of salt and ground pepper. Stir in the vinegar and the mustard powder, then hand-whisk in both the oils – drop by drop to start with, then in a steady, thin stream – until you have a lovely thick, shiny mayonnaise. Check the seasoning, chop the tarragon leaves and stir through.

Sprinkle a little raspberry vinegar, salt and pepper inside eight of the little gem / chicory leaves and line with a basil leaf. Chop the olives and sit them inside. Top with flaked tuna. Serve with the tarragon mayonnaise on top, or alongside to be spooned over.

For the other half of the leaves:

Hard-boil the 2 hen's eggs (or 4 quail's eggs) and set aside to cool.

Put the olives, drained capers, peeled garlic, 75ml of olive oil and a good squeeze of lemon juice in a blender and blitz to a paste.

Peel the hard-boiled eggs. Quarter them if hen's, halve if quail's. Spoon the olive relish inside the lettuce / chicory leaves, sit a piece of egg inside too and then lay over the top the whole anchovy fillet. Drizzle with the remaining olive oil.

Serve the bundles on platters for people to help themselves, or portion up two of each type per person.

You will almost certainly have some of the blitzed olive and caper mix left over, but it's so good for other things. Chop a couple of anchovies into it and use it as a relish, as a dip, for pasta, to have with fish or chicken, spread on a sandwich, or baked into a roll...

Truffled lentils with radicchio and carrots

It is the final ingredient on the list here that works the hardest and is the one that brings together all the other elements of this dish – truffle oil. But as Mario Prati of Tartufaia points out on page 139, you do have to be a little careful when shopping for truffle oil. I definitely suggest reading his piece before choosing your bottle.

Mario advocates partnering truffle oil with strong flavours, and that is certainly what we're doing here. There are carrots roasted into mellow sweetness, radicchio wilted down so its bitter edge just comes through, caraway for another layer of bitterness, then truffle oil to smooth it all out deliciously.

Serves 4 as a main or 6 as a side or small plate

350g carrots with tops

4 tablespoons olive oil

300g small green or brown lentils

3 sprigs of woody herbs of your choice, such as thyme, oregano or rosemary

1 large leek

3 garlic cloves

2 teaspoons caraway seeds

100ml dry vermouth, cider or vegetable stock (bought or see page 147)

250g chioggia radicchio

2 teaspoons truffle oil

Preheat the oven to 190C fan/210C/410F/gas mark 6.

Wash but don't peel the carrots. Trim the green carrot-top leaves to just a couple of centimetres and be sure to keep them for later in the recipe. Slice any thicker carrots lengthways before laying them all in a roasting tray, tossing them in 2 tablespoons of the olive oil and some salt and putting into the oven. They'll take about 20 minutes to tenderise and begin to crisp a little.

Meanwhile, rinse and drain the lentils. Bring a saucepan of water to the boil with whatever herbs you are using in there too, then simmer the lentils until just about tender – it'll take 10–15 minutes, depending on your lentils.

Use that time to heat the rest of the olive oil in a large frying pan or another saucepan. Trim the leek, keeping the offcuts for stock (see pages 52, 82 and 147). Slice the leek into half-moons about 1cm thick and cook in the oil until softening. Peel and chop the garlic cloves and add to the leeks, stirring for about 5 minutes. Add the caraway seeds, then the vermouth (or cider or stock) and let it bubble. If the lentils are ready, drain them and add them to the pan; or take the pan of leek mixture off the heat and wait for the lentils to tenderise. Toss the lentils in the leek mix and season well. Shred the radicchio and mix that in too, then cover the pan and let the radicchio wilt over a low heat for 5 minutes or so. Stir in the truffle oil and check the seasoning, then spoon it all into a serving dish.

Your carrots should hopefully be just about ready. When they are, lift them onto the lentil mix along with their cooking oil. Chop a handful of the carrot tops and scatter them over. Serve hot, and note that this reheats well, so you can make it ahead if you wish.

Baked gammon with Market preserve glaze

A bone-in, beautifully glazed gammon is one of the most impressive of sights on a table, as suited to a Christmas feast as a summer's garden picnic.

The glaze is where you can really use your culinary imagination with jams, marmalades, honeys, mustards and soy sauces. The key is for it to be a balance of sweet and tart, and exactly what I use will change each time I make this according to the Market preserves I've got excited about using. This time it's Taste Croatia's fig and orange preserve – two flavours that go brilliantly with all things pork.

Almost the hardest thing about this recipe is finding a stockpot big enough to take the joint. Note that the gammon can be cooked up to 3 days before you bake it with the glaze.

Serves 12

5kg bone-in unsmoked gammon

1 celery stick

1 onion

Handful of herbs of your choice, such as thyme, rosemary, sage or bay

1 tablespoon black peppercorns

330ml bottle of beer or cider

2 tablespoons black treacle

For the glaze

1 tablespoon whole cloves

5 tablespoons dried fig and orange preserve

1 tablespoon Dijon mustard

2 teaspoons soy sauce (optional)

The gammon stock will be full of flavour from the pork and the aromatics you've added. Strain it, store it and use for all kinds of vegetable, meat or cheese soups. Bear in mind it will be quite salty, though.

Take the gammon out of the fridge at least an hour before starting. Sit it in a large stockpot, adding the celery and peeled onion cut into chunks, the herbs, peppercorns, beer or cider, and treacle. Fill the pan up with water, hoping to cover the gammon. If the water doesn't cover it, you'll need to carefully turn the joint halfway through the cooking time.

Bring to the boil, then turn the heat down and simmer gently uncovered for around 2 hours. As it cooks, skim off any scum on the water's surface, and top up with more water as needed. The gammon is ready when the temperature inside the joint is at least 70C on a probe thermometer. Let the joint cool in the pot, then carefully lift it onto a baking tray.

Proceed straight to the glazing, or keep the gammon in the fridge for up to 3 days and then glaze.

Preheat the oven to 200C fan/220C/425F/gas mark 7.

Trim off and discard the skin that covers the fat. Score the exposed fat with crosses and stud the centre of each with a clove. Mix together the fruit preserve and mustard, adding the soy (if using). You're trying to achieve a sticky glaze that isn't too runny. Protect the exposed meat end of the joint with a piece of baking paper or foil held tight to the meat with more cloves or cocktail sticks. Smear about two-thirds of the glaze over the gammon, covering all the fat. Put it into the oven straight away. Bake for 15 minutes, then spoon over the rest of the glaze, taking care to cover any bald sections of fat. Bake for another 15 minutes. Remember you're not trying to cook the gammon, just colour the glaze. Go as dark as you dare.

Remove from the oven and let the joint rest for at least 30 minutes before carving. It will keep for up to a week in the fridge.

Partridges in sloe gin with creamed Jerusalem artichokes

Sloe gin is great to cook with. Gin's usual botanicals of juniper berries, coriander seeds, some citrus and perhaps some herbs are amped up with the plummy acidity of sloes – that's a lot of flavour to bring to all kinds of savoury (and sweet) cooking.

Here it cooks in with partridges and garlic, with then more sloe gin added for a sauce that brings together the roasted game with the Jerusalem artichoke mash. You could apply the core flavours of this recipe just as well to any of the other feathered game on pages 60–1. Removing the wishbone makes the partridges easier to carve – it's a good thing to know how to do for other game birds too.

Serves 4 as a main

4 partridges

½ lemon

1.2kg Jerusalem artichokes

400g floury potatoes

Handful of fresh oregano

2 whole garlic bulbs

4 tablespoons olive oil

125ml sloe gin

90g butter

1 tablespoon double cream
  or creme fraiche (optional)

Prepare the partridges by cutting out their wishbone: sit on a board breast-side up and use a small, very sharp knife to cut down either side of the wishbone. Find the wishbone's point where it connects and cut there to release it, then just pull the wishbone out. Repeat for each of the birds and set them aside.

Put plenty of water into a frying pan or casserole dish and squeeze in the juice of the half lemon. Peel the artichokes and cut them into chunks, then put them straight away into the acidulated water. Do the same for the potatoes, putting them into the same pan as the artichokes. To this point can be done an hour or so ahead of time.

Preheat the oven to 180C fan/200C/400F/gas mark 6.

Sit the partridges in a flameproof baking tray or dish and stuff them with the fresh oregano. Cut the garlic bulbs in half through their equator and sit them cut-side up with the partridges. Pour the olive oil over the birds and garlic, then approximately half of the sloe gin just over the birds, and finally scatter salt over it all.

Drain the water in the vegetable pan, cover the artichokes and potatoes with fresh water, add some salt, and put it on to simmer over a medium heat. Once the water is simmering, put the partridges into the oven and cook them for 25 minutes, basting them occasionally. That should be enough time for the vegetables to cook through.

Use a slotted spoon to lift the partridges and garlic onto a plate and set them aside somewhere warm to rest for 10 minutes. (If the garlic halves aren't yet tender, just lift out the partridges and give the garlic more time in the oven.)

Drain the tender vegetables, season and mash with half the butter. Sit the tray the partridges cooked in over a medium–high heat. Add to its juices the rest

of the gin and the remaining butter. Use a wooden spoon to deglaze any sticky bits on the base of the tray, and let it bubble for a minute or so to create a light sauce. Season. This is where you can add the cream or creme fraiche (if using). Return the partridges and garlic halves to the dish and serve with the creamed artichokes.

Store cupboard suppers

This chapter and The Store Cupboard II are full of thoughts on culinary staples – from oils and vinegars to salts, teas, spice blends and more. Yet just as important as these basics are the store cupboard amplifiers, those ingredients that can give meals an easy-win quick hit of flavour. They're invaluable for the kind of midweek cooking when we all need to rely on what we already have to hand. Here are four of the Market's most useful amplifiers, and some ideas for how they can lift your store cupboard suppers.

Tahini

Shop:

- White tahini is made by crushing hulled and roasted white sesame seeds into a paste. This is the best choice for adding to dips, dressing and marinades.

- Whole tahini retains some or all of the sesame seed hull, sometimes toasted, sometimes not. This darker tahini is a little more bitter than white tahini, and its richer flavour makes it more suited to using where the tahini is the star.

Use:

- For dips. Stretch beyond the tahini hummus classic with this suggestion from Oliveology, who do glorious organic tahinis: blitz white tahini with pre-cooked gigantes beans, walnut oil, lemon juice and salt, then finish with toasted sesame seeds sprinkled over to serve. Switch in any of the enhancers in column two.

- Mix with yoghurt for a salad dressing.

- Make tahini sauce: mix 150g white tahini with 150ml water, 2 tablespoons lemon juice, 1 crushed garlic clove, salt and any of the enhancers below. Kept in a jar in the fridge for up to a week, it will be ready to use as a marinade for chicken pieces, and to toss amongst vegetables before roasting them (or after they've been cooked in any way). Think cauliflower, carrots, tomatoes, brussels sprouts, peppers, beetroots, squashes...

- Because supper sometimes is a piece of toast and not much more: spread it with whole tahini, perhaps first mixing the tahini with honey or date molasses (this also works very well as a pancake filling).

- When supper finishes with a scoop or two of ice cream, give vanilla or chocolate a drizzle of white or whole tahini.

Flavour enhancers:

Tahini's creamy texture and slightly bitter, nutty flavour make it a perfect bed for layering on other flavours. Think about soy sauce or tamari, miso, honey, ginger, ground cumin, ground cinnamon, walnut oil, toasted sesame oil, lemon or orange, pomegranate seeds, or fresh herbs. Arabica restaurant uses tahini with the pickled mango condiment, amba – that's a good flavour lead on adding other fruity pickles and vinegars to tahini too.

Kimchi

Shop:

- The classic kimchi vegetables are Chinese leaf cabbage and mooli radish (daikon), but those aren't the only elements you might find lacto-fermented into kimchi's distinctive hit of hot and sour. Perhaps also carrot, spring onion and / or apple.

- For extra crunch, the Chinese leaf is sometimes swapped out for white cabbage, which is more usually seen in that other fermented cabbage condiment, sauerkraut.

- Consider what other companion flavours have been packed in there and how they'll achieve flavour balance: perhaps there's ginger, chilli, soy sauce or tamari.

Use:

- Keep front and centre kimchi's traditional use as a condiment, which for amping up simple suppers means you could: serve a spoonful alongside eggs, add it to a grilled cheese sandwich or into a burger, have it with grilled fish, or spoon it over steamed rice and vegetables.

- Stir through when cooking noodle dishes.

- Cook into soups or layer into vegetable gratins.

- Stir-fry kimchi with greens, soy sauce and some sliced spring onions.

Flavour enhancers:

Kimchi itself is the enhancer, although you could add more fire or flavour to your kimchi by augmenting it with ginger, chillies, soy sauce or tamari.

Preserved lemons

Shop:

- Seek out salted Egyptian baby lemons that have been prepared with punchily sharp, fragrant, nuanced flavour balance.

Use:

- Before you use them, take a moment to think what a preserved lemon is: a flavour bomb of bitter, sour, salty and sweet. The only basic taste profile it is missing is umami, so think about partnering with umami-heavy foods, such as mushrooms, tomatoes, seaweeds, or heavier meats like lamb or venison.

- Reduce the saltiness: soak them in water before using.

- Thinly sliced preserved lemons pep up simple salads of rice, quinoa, spelt, couscous or lentils.

- Stir-fry leftover rice with sliced preserved lemons and lots of chopped herbs.

- Slice into a basic salad dressing, remembering to reduce the amount of vinegar / lemon juice you'd normally use. Add your choice of the flavour enhancers (see right).

- Deglaze a pan you've cooked fish or meat in with a little wine, cider or water and make into a quick sauce with chopped preserved lemon, capers, parsley and perhaps creme fraiche or yoghurt.

- Chop preserved lemons into a salsa with olive oil, mint and a little lemon juice, perhaps adding some chopped tomato too. Great as a quick side for fish, meats or roasted vegetables.

- Puree the pulp into soups.

Flavour enhancers:

Think about: creamy goat's curd, labneh or yoghurt; mint, dill, basil and really all the bounty of soft herbs; pomegranate; orange; chilli; garlic; capers; olives; paprika.

Hot sauce

Shop:

- Having a bottle (or two, or more...) of hot sauce in your store cupboard is a sure fire way to add, well, a little fire but also flavour to a quick store cupboard supper. The hot sauces of different culinary cultures will each add something distinctive to your dish.

- At the Market keep an eye out for Habanero Guacachile at Mexican specialist, Shop Padre. It's a very, very spicy habanero hot sauce with garlic, onions, and habanero ash in there alongside the confit habaneros.

- De La Grenade take hot sauce in a different direction with their Pepper Sauce. Its scotch bonnet peppers deliver plenty of heat that is then married with spices, nutmeg and fruit.

Use:

- Add a couple of dashes to avocado or cheese on toast.

- Pep up simple omelettes or scrambled eggs.

- Give some heat to a burger or chicken wings.

- Turn a fairly basic stir-fry of meat, vegetables or tofu into something far more memorable.

- Mix with mayonnaise for a sandwich.

- Give a dash or two over a rice bowl.

- However you use your hot sauce, go steady at first. You can always add more, but there's no going back.

Chestnut honey and rosemary ice cream

At From Field and Flower you can do a wonderful tasting tour of honey styles that is a real honey education. You start with the mildest, the very lightest of honeys and work your way along maybe a dozen or so varieties to end up with the deeper, darker styles. And that is where chestnut honey sits in all its woody, smoky, even slightly salty magnificence.

Those attributes translate to this ice cream. It is a distinctly grown-up scoop. Choose a milder honey if you like, but it'll be sweeter than the chestnut, so you might need slightly less of it. (See pages 102–3 for more on honey varieties.)

Honey ice cream doesn't set firmly hard, making this almost soft-serve in style and one I'd partner with little more than some kind of plain but crunchy biscuit or wafer.

The rest of your chestnut honey will be glorious in a glaze for a roast; spread on toast, or drizzled over cheeses - especially the blues.

Makes about 500ml (enough for 4)

4 egg yolks

40g caster sugar

350ml whole milk

150ml double cream

1 sprig of rosemary

75ml chestnut honey

Use a hand whisk to beat the egg yolks and sugar together in a large mixing bowl until they become lighter in texture.

Pour the milk and cream into a large saucepan along with the rosemary and heat until almost boiling (about 80C). Transfer the rosemary to whatever container you intend to chill the custard in, then whisk the hot milk mix into the sugared egg yolks, adding it a little at a time so as not to scramble the yolks.

Pour it all back into a clean saucepan and stir continuously over a low-medium heat to make a custard that is thick enough to coat the back of a wooden spoon. Remove from the heat and pour it over the reserved rosemary in the container. Pour through a sieve if you are at all worried about lumps. Cover and wait until it is just about tepid, then stir in the honey. Chill in the fridge for at least 8 hours.

Remove the rosemary, then churn the custard in an ice cream machine according to the manufacturer's instructions. Freeze until needed.

Remember when it comes to serving that this ice cream won't have set very hard, so don't get it out of the freezer too early. It'll need just a minute out of the freezer to be scoopable.

Honeys can crystallise over time. It's a natural process, and that's what 'set' honeys are: just honeys that have been allowed to granulate. To revive a crystallised honey the best thing to do is put the jar in a warm water bath and let it stand for 15 minutes to loosen it – then give it a stir and repeat the process until you're satisfied.

Salted nut butter millionaires

This version of millionaire's shortbread layers in a couple of things that make all the difference to the classic's rich indulgence.

First, the nut butter – which isn't instead of any of the usual ingredients, it's plus. And what a plus. Elevating the caramel layer from being 'just' sweet to having scrumptious nutty depth. I use ButterNut of London's ABC for its mix of buttery Spanish almonds, toasted Bolivian brazil nuts and creamy Goan cashews; but then something like their Coconut Cardamom Cashew butter would take it all in a subtly different and very tasty direction. Your call.

The nut butter also helps to (very simply) achieve beautiful decoration, and then there's salt scattered over to finish. Because chocolate + caramel + salt is always a yes.

Makes 12–16 pieces, depending how large you cut them

For the shortbread

120g caster sugar

240g unsalted butter, at room
    temperature, plus extra
    for greasing

120g fine cornmeal or semolina

240g plain flour

¼ teaspoon fine salt

For the nut butter caramel

200g unsalted butter

150g soft light brown sugar

50g soft dark brown sugar

400g condensed milk

50g smooth nut butter

2 teaspoons salt

For the topping

200g dark chocolate

1 tablespoon smooth nut butter

Salt flakes, for sprinkling

You will need a 20cm square baking tin

Preheat the oven to 160C fan/180C/350F/gas mark 4 and grease the baking tin with butter.

First, make the shortbread. Beat the sugar and butter together in a mixing bowl with a wooden spoon until smooth. Add the cornmeal or semolina, the flour and salt. Work into a dough, but don't overwork. As soon as it holds together, it's done.

Use your hands to press the dough into the greased tin, getting it as flat and even as you can. Prick it all over with a fork and bake for 25–30 minutes until becoming golden and firm to the touch. Remove from the oven and set aside to cool in the tin.

Once the shortbread base is cool, make the nut butter caramel. Put the butter, sugars, condensed milk, nut butter and salt into a medium saucepan and heat until the butter has melted and smoothly come together. Simmer very gently for 10–15 minutes, stirring often, until thickened. Pour the mixture over the cooled shortbread, smooth the top and set aside to cool. Chill for 3 hours to really firm up.

Once the caramel base is set, break the dark chocolate into a heatproof bowl and sit it over a pan of simmering water to melt (making sure the bowl doesn't touch the water), then pour it over the caramel.

Working quickly, spoon the nut butter into another heatproof bowl and put that over the same pan of hot water until it becomes runny. Drizzle it over the still-soft chocolate topping, using a cocktail stick or skewer to swirl it into as pretty a pattern as you fancy. Finish by scattering over salt flakes, then leave to thoroughly cool and set (you can do this in the fridge if you want to be certain / fast).

Ease the shortbread out of the tin and cut into the shapes and size of your choice. It will keep in an airtight tin in the fridge for up to 5 days.

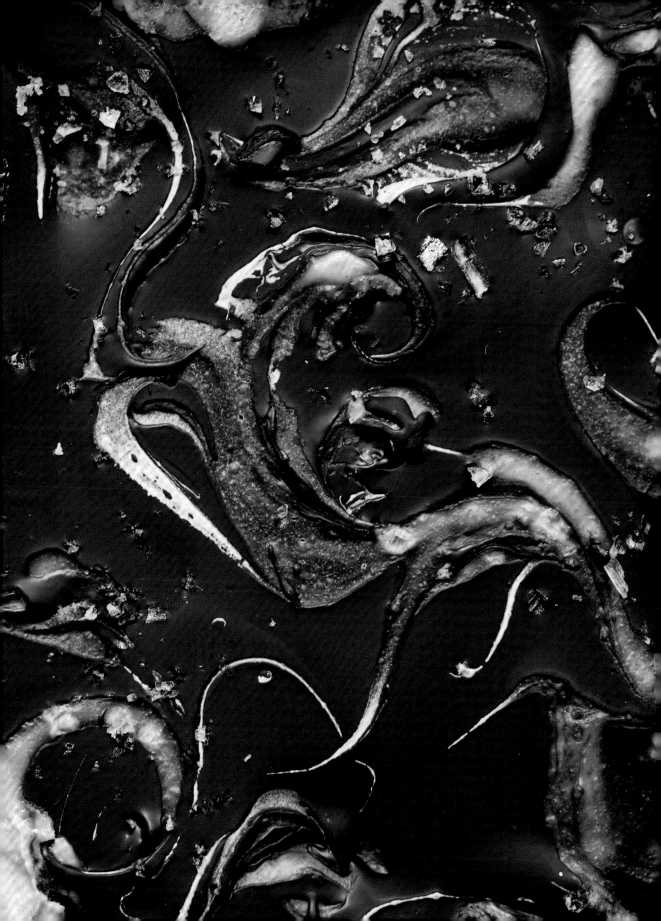

Chocolate olive oil cake with figs and hazelnuts

This is a pleasingly elegant cake to serve as a dessert. It's not overly rich, and has a lovely tangy bite from the yoghurt topping, with hazelnuts giving that topping crunch as well as flavour.

This is the place for using a good, but not necessarily the absolute best, olive oil. Marianna Kolokotroni of Oliveology explains more about that on page 96. You want something with a mild flavour that isn't going to overwhelm the other elements.

Serves 10

150ml mild olive oil

60g carob flour or cocoa powder

2 teaspoons hazelnut liqueur

200g golden caster sugar

3 large eggs

125g self-raising flour

A pinch of fine salt

200g thick Greek yoghurt

2 ripe figs

100g skinned hazelnuts, toasted

You will need a 23cm springform cake tin

Preheat the oven to 170C fan/190C/375F/gas mark 5. Grease the sides of the cake tin with a little of the oil, and line its base with baking paper.

Sift the carob flour or cocoa powder into a bowl, then whisk in 125ml boiling water and the hazelnut liqueur. Set aside.

Put the sugar, the rest of the olive oil and the eggs into a large mixing bowl. Use an electric whisk to beat them together until thickened: you are trying to get lots of air into the mix. Beat in the carob flour / cocoa powder mixture, then sift in the flour and salt. Gently but thoroughly fold the flour in – you don't want to lose all the air you've just beaten in – then pour the mixture into your prepared cake tin.

Bake for 35–40 minutes until just about set. Remove from the oven, cool on a wire rack for 10 minutes, then remove from the tin and leave to cool some more.

Once the cake is cool, spoon the thick yoghurt on top. Slice the figs and arrange those on top too. Chop the hazelnuts, scatter over and slice.

You can bake the cake ahead of time and store it without the topping in an airtight tin. It will keep well unadorned like that for up to 3 days. Once topped with the yoghurt, figs and nuts it is best eaten that day.

The carob tree produces a pod with a sweet pulp that can be dried, roasted, then ground, to carob flour. It can be used in place of cocoa powder or plain flour. De Calabria suggest trying it in smoothies, bread dough or pancake batter, or just sprinkled over yoghurt or ice cream.

Pomelo cocktail bitters

The pomelo is a very large fruit and so comes with a lot of rind. Rather than just discarding that en route to the fruit's flesh, this is a way of making the most of the rind's own flavours by turning it into cocktail bitters.

A high-proof base alcohol is needed to extract maximum flavour from the zest and the other botanicals. My hunt for that led me to discovering East London Liquor Co.'s Louder Gin which is 47 per cent ABV and so perfect for this.

Most cocktail bitters include gentian root for its bittersweet, spicy, floral notes. Here I am going instead for Spice Mountain's cinnamon berries to bring similar flavour profiles, along with gentle cinnamon and pepper notes too.

Just one pomelo makes a lot of bitters, but you'll be the best friend of any cocktail lover if you gift them a vial of this.

Makes 500ml

1 pomelo

1 teaspoon coriander seeds

1 teaspoon juniper berries

½ teaspoon cinnamon berries

1 mace blade piece

500ml high-proof gin

1 tablespoon mild honey

You will need a 750ml jar, sterilised

Preheat the oven to 90C fan/110C/230F/gas mark ½ and line a baking tray with baking paper.

Use a vegetable peeler to pare the peel of the pomelo. Set half aside and arrange the other half in a single layer on the lined baking tray. Put it into the oven to dry out for 30 minutes. You'll soon be able to smell the wonderful citrus pomelo aroma.

Meanwhile, cut the remaining pomelo peel into pieces about 5cm long and put them into your sterilised jar. Add the spices.

When the peel has had its time in the oven, let it cool a little before adding it to the jar. Mix well, then add enough alcohol to just about cover the peel. Seal the jar and set aside out of direct sunlight for 2 weeks, shaking it daily.

Strain through clean muslin (cheesecloth) and squeeze at it to get all the liquid out. Discard the solids and strain twice more. Stir in the honey, return the pomelo bitters to the jar and seal. Let the jar sit untouched for 3 days – again, out of direct sunlight – then strain once more through muslin to catch any remaining sediment or debris.

Decant into smaller bottles, label and date, and the bitters are ready to use in your cocktail making. They'll keep for up to a year – to be used in a gin and tonic, whenever a cocktail recipe calls for grapefruit bitters (the two fruits are related), or for experimenting with. Try them in the Dark rum egg nog on page 274.

Drinks

Cocktail cabinet

The well-stocked cocktail cabinet is to the curious drinker what a well-stocked larder is to the clever cook. Meaning: that with the core stock of basics, and a smattering of interesting flavour flashes, you will never be thirsty or hungry. Or bored.

Not that it needs to be an actual cocktail cabinet. What your bottles are housed in matters far less than thinking what you might want to get hold of if curating a 'cabinet' from scratch. There's no-one better to steer your way through that than Siggi Sigurdsson, general manager of East London Liquor Co., whose stand at the Market is a cocktail lover's haven. The shelves bear a range of their own gins, whiskies and vodka all distilled in beautiful copper stills at their distillery in Bow, in east London. Amongst them are rums imported from Jamaica and Guyana, and an eclectic, exciting range of locally produced alcohols.

These are Siggi's tips for three classic cocktail styles (and the basic kit to make them), which together can form the foundations of creative and delicious home cocktail-making.

Martini

Shop:

Gin (or vodka), dry vermouth, lemon (or other citrus), olives.

- Dry, citrusy gins that aren't too heavy, such as East London Liquor Co.'s Brighter gin, are suited to martinis garnished with a citrus twist. Note that while lemon is the classic, orange gives a little sweetness, lime is more perfumed, and grapefruit is a terrific mix of all those attributes.

- For a Dirty martini (with an olive and little olive brine), your gin choice can be heavier to match up. Perhaps something more herbaceous. In the East London Liquor Co. collection that would be the Louder gin.

- Your vermouth choice needs to be bitter and dry. What it doesn't need to be is especially expensive. Remember that vermouth is fortified wine, and to keep it in the fridge once opened.

Mix:

- Siggi's mix: 60ml gin to 10ml vermouth. Use more or less vermouth to make a wetter or drier martini.

- Stir the gin and vermouth over lots of ice and strain into a chilled Nick & Nora glass or coupe.

- Garnish with citrus peel or an olive. Or even go for both.

Options:

- Add a few dashes of orange cocktail bitters. (Or the pomelo bitters on page 126.)

- Add a pickled baby pearl onion and a little of its pickling brine for a Gibson martini.

- For a Martinez martini use Old Tom gin and sweet vermouth.

Sidecar

Shop:

Cognac, orange liqueur, lemon or lime, sugar.

- The Sidecar is one of the daisy style of cocktails, which mixes a spirit with a liqueur plus lemon or lime and sugar. Some daisies use an optional egg white too. Have in stock a bottle of orange liqueur, such as triple sec or Cointreau, and you are set for making all kinds of daisy cocktails.

Mix:

- The citrus element means daisies need to be shaken for the ingredients to combine. Egg white, if using, helps that too.

- Siggi's Sidecar: shake 40ml cognac, 20ml orange liqueur and 20ml lemon juice over ice. Strain into a chilled coupe that is rimmed with sugar.

Options:

- The Sidecar proportions are the same for all daisies – swap the cognac for gin in a White Lady; and for tequila in a margarita (giving the margarita glass a salt, not sugar, rim).

Old-fashioned

Shop:

Bourbon, sugar, Angostura bitters

- Choose a bourbon with more corn for extra sweetness.

- Siggi calls Angostura bitters 'the bitters of all bitters'. Hugely versatile for adding depth to lots of cocktails.

Mix:

- In a cocktail stirring glass – or the rocks glass you're serving it in – crush a sugar cube (or use a little sugar syrup). Mix with 60ml bourbon and 3 dashes of Angostura bitters. Serve over ice.

Options:

- Having bourbon in your cocktail cabinet means that with the addition of sweet vermouth you are well on your way to Manhattans.

EQUIPMENT AND GLASSWARE

- *Ice* – the single most important element of all in cocktail-making
- *Measuring jigger*
- *Strainer*
- *Cocktail shaker / stirring glass* (although a measuring jug or glass jar can work just as well)
- *Stirring spoon* – the professional spoons have a long twisted handle for extra grip

- *Always try to chill your glasses first:* give them a few minutes in the fridge or freezer, or put some ice cubes in them while you prepare the drinks

These three classic glasses will cover the cocktail bases:

- *'Nick & Nora'* (preferred by Siggi, with its more rounded sides, to the more conventional 'Y' cocktail glass)
- *Coupe*
- *Rocks*

THE GREENGROCERS

The Dawson family have been farming fruit and vegetables on the flat, fertile fields of Lincolnshire for over four generations, selling first to the supermarkets and then independently to farmers' markets around the country. About 25 years ago, they decided to stop using chemicals and rely instead on natural solutions to manage disease, insects and soil health.

Farming the old way

Kath Dawson, Ted's Veg

If you could see my fields right now, you would see weeds. You'd also see bugs – hundreds of them. The insect population has increased tenfold since we stopped spraying with chemicals. When we have weeds, we use the tractor to scuffle them, or a hoe to clear the fields. Sometimes we get the chance to do that, sometimes we don't, and that's okay. If we have aphids, we have to hope we have ladybirds. I hang teabags in the greenhouse to discourage spiders. The other day Ted found a caterpillar in his purple sprouting broccoli at dinner. I can't do anything about that, and nor would I want to. That's what comes with organic farming. People seem to want organic produce, but they don't want the bugs that come with it. The thing is, you can't have one without the other.

We do farm organically here – we don't use any pesticides, herbicides or any other chemicals – but we don't have organic certification because I think it's too expensive and too easy to manipulate. There aren't random inspections, which I believe there should be, and spraying with natural chemicals is still allowed. 50 years ago, everyone farmed 'organically'; now it has become a buzzword, and I don't

think that's helpful. Here, everything is done as it always was, and as it should be. We don't spray anything. That's what organic means to me.

We use crop rotation – we'll plant a crop like peas or beans between years to help replenish the soil with nitrates – or we'll leave the field fallow for a year and sow it with clover and grass. That helps with the weeds, it helps restore nutrients to the ground, and we will hopefully find a local farmer who wants to graze their sheep on it. That gives the land a chance to get back on its feet. It isn't easy or cheap: growing organically takes a lot more manpower, and you can lose an entire crop because it comes too early or is infested with blackfly. But, for the first time in 20 years, we have thrushes in the garden because they have bugs to feed on. We have more birds and more bees. Everything is making a comeback.

We sell or give away everything we grow. We don't just select the best-looking vegetables and leave the rest. Some things can look weird or ugly and still taste fantastic – and fortunately our customers aren't picky: they buy for taste, every time. The other day I had a cucumber that looked

"People seem to want organic produce, but they don't want the bugs that come with it. The thing is, you can't have one without the other.

> "
> We don't just select the best-looking vegetables and leave the rest. Some things can look weird or ugly and still taste fantastic – and fortunately our customers aren't picky: they buy for taste, every time.

like a bangle because it got caught up in a leaf and just grew around itself. I loved it. Just because something looks perfect doesn't mean it's got flavour.

In fact, one of the advantages of produce that's been farmed without chemicals is that the flavour is often better because the root systems are more established. Another advantage is that there's no obligation to peel anything or remove the outer leaves because there are no trace chemicals. You just need to wash them to remove any soil and insects. Just because you've been brought up throwing away the lush, green outer leaves of a cabbage or cauliflower doesn't mean that's the only way to do it.

Personally, I don't peel anything unless I absolutely have to because I'm lazy, and because the skin is where the fibre and a lot of the flavour lives. Besides, if you peel carrots and beetroot, they bleed; you just need to scrub them well. I don't peel parsnips and potatoes either. Admittedly, my kids don't like it when I serve mash or roast potatoes with lots of skin, but personally I think they're better with their jackets on.

Turnips are renowned at the Market for their beautiful mushroom displays, with so many different sizes, colours, shapes across the varieties.

Some of them take a little preparation, as Tomas Lidakevicius shows here. Each mushroom is treated in his hands like a gem that he is taking the time to clean and trim into the best possible version of itself.

The principles are the same across the ceps and girolles pictured here.

Preparing a mushroom

> Use a damp cloth to gently clean the top of the mushroom cap. Only wash it if very gritty.

> Take a small knife and peel the stem and trim the base.

> Clean under the mushroom cap with the damp cloth, or a mushroom brush. (A pastry brush will do the job.)

Five radicchio varieties

Chioggia

Character The best known and most widely grown radicchio variety, with tight crimson leaves. It combines classic bitterness with a piquant edge and a satisfying crunch.

Uses Excellent roasted, grilled or raw in a mixed salad.

Truffled lentils with radicchio and carrots, page 112.

Castelfranco

Character Often called the 'tulip of winter' on account of its seasonality and shape. Rarer than the chioggia and milder in taste, its absurdly pretty leaves retain a slight crunch when raw.

Uses A mildly bitter and beautiful addition to a mixed salad. Also good in risottos, on pizza or with pasta.

Tardivo

Character A mild, crunchy radicchio, with protected geographical indicator (PGI) status. Tardivo means 'late' in Italian: it is harvested in late autumn, then left in tanks of running water until new sprouts germinate.

Uses Most recipes call for it to be grilled or roasted, but the crunchy leaves also lend themselves to being served raw with extra-virgin olive oil and salt.

Treviso

Character Oval in shape and with closely compacted leaves, treviso leans toward the more bitter end of the radicchio spectrum.

Uses While roasting or grilling softens their sharp bitterness, the raw leaves' triangular, almost spoon-like shape renders them the perfect vehicle for cheese or spreads.

Rosa de Veneto

Character One of the more modern varieties of radicchio, developed through cross-breeding to accentuate its ethereal pastel-pink shade and comparatively sweet flavour.

Uses The delicate colouring disappears during the cooking process, so it is best served raw.

A former chef, Mario Prati has been sourcing the finest truffles from his Italian homeland and, more recently, from selected suppliers in Spain and Australia since 2006, selling them either in their natural state or in an array of homemade products, including truffle butter, honey and mayonnaise.

Mario Prati

Tartufaia

*Is there any material difference
between wild and farmed truffles?*

There are only two species of truffle
that can be farmed, and only one
that is farmed actively around the
world: the black winter truffle. No
one has yet managed to find a way to
farm the white truffle, which grows
only in Italy.

When wild truffles are good, they
are way better than farmed truffles,
but they are inconsistent. The
beauty of farmed truffles is the
degree of control. There are so many
different elements that influence
the development of truffles:
temperature, altitude, rainfall, how
deep in the soil they are, how many
stones are in the soil. The problem
with stones is that the truffle grows
around them, which distorts their
roundness, and the rounder the
truffle is, the better it will be. Truffle
farmers can choose flat land and
remove as many stones as they
can. That said, there is still a high
percentage of failure with farmed
truffles, and you don't know if you've
been successful until your first crop,
seven to 10 years after starting the
process. It's not a great business
model, which is why there's not
much difference in price between
farmed and wild truffles.

How do I select the right truffle?

Look at the seasons: truffles vary in
quality, flavour and price according
to the time of year. For black winter
truffles, the best season is January;
for white winter truffles, you're

better buying in November – in
December, they will double or triple
in price. The white spring truffles
and black summer truffles are
cheaper than the winter truffles, but
less flavourful and pungent, with
less of that distinctive truffle aroma.
Our truffles start at 20g, and we
recommend anything between 3g
and 10g per serving, depending on
the dish. If it's just a simple omelette,
3g will be enough; if there are more
flavours going on, you're likely to
need more.

*How do I get the most out of
my truffle?*

A whole truffle will keep for seven
to 10 days in an airtight container.
Cutting into it will halve that time,
because of evaporation, which is
why we only sell fresh truffles whole.
You should use the truffle as soon
as you can, but if you have some left
over, we recommend that you grate
it into a bowl of room-temperature
butter: about 10g of truffle for 100g
of butter. Mixed together, wrapped in
paper and kept in the fridge, truffle
butter will last a fortnight; to extend
its life even further, it can also be
frozen. You can throw it into your
dishes at the last minute whenever
you want to add a bit of flavour.

What is truffle oil?

Truffle oil is the only product we sell
that is made with truffle essence,
not actual truffle. The flavour and
smell of truffle only clings to animal
fat; it doesn't stick to plant fats
at all. When you see bits of black

truffle in a bottle of truffle oil, it's
just there for show. We make our
truffle oil ourselves, using a high-
quality essence we get from Italy
– and we don't add black truffle
because it's wasteful. It's also quite
misleading: the essence in truffle
oil is designed to mimic the flavour
of white truffle, not black. The
mistake chefs sometimes make is
to add truffle oil to dishes that also
contain black truffle in order boost
the flavour, but that just masks the
delicate taste of the fresh truffle.
There's nothing wrong with truffle
oil, but it needs to be used sparingly
and in combination with other
strong flavours, otherwise it can just
overwhelm a dish.

*Truffled lentils with radicchio and
carrots, page 112.*

*Asparagus with quail's eggs and shaved
truffle, page 147.*

Five flavour roots

Ginger

Ginger, one of the key building blocks of Indian cuisine and an important ingredient across much of the continent, is probably the most familiar of all Asian roots. 'In Thailand we use ginger a lot for its warm fragrance, but we don't use it in curry pastes,' says Worawan Kamann, owner of Raya and Khanom Krok, who hails from Bangkok. 'We normally use it in a stir-fry of beef or chicken, or to flavour rice or a dipping sauce. Another popular dish is a Thai sausage, fermented and served with fresh ginger alongside as a complement.'

Moong dal dosa with tomato chutney, page 215.

Liquorice root

Liquorice root is often added to hot liquid to make an infusion, syrup or sauce. 'I like to stir it in green or black tea instead of using sugar – it's naturally sweet,' says Massimo Maggioni of Maggio's Confectionery. 'I've also heard of people using it to give up smoking – apparently cigarettes taste horrible after chewing it.' The powdered form works well as a rub for slow-cooked meat, particularly lamb.

Fig and liquorice sorbet, page 189.

Turmeric

Turmeric root is small in size but strong in flavour. 'If you use too much, it overpowers all the other fragrances, so we use it sparingly and mostly for its colour,' says Worawan. 'We pound it with chilli and use it in curries. Whereas here in the UK most people use dried turmeric, we use the fresh roots because they're in our backyard, and they grow all year round.'

Hot and sour green papaya curry with prawns, page 184.

Horseradish

Horseradish, part of the brassica family, is a root that packs a punch. 'Here in the UK, it's grated and mixed with a vinegar or mustard base to make horseradish sauce,' says Gary Voight at Elsey & Bent. Sometimes it's mixed with a mayonnaise base – it depends on how hot you want it.'

Deep-fried oysters with horseradish sauce, quick-pickled ginger and spring onion, page 36.

Galangal

Galangal looks a little like ginger, to which it is closely related, but has smoother skin and a sharper flavour. 'We use galangal in tom yum and in curry pastes after breaking it down in a pestle and mortar,' says Worawan. 'We also bruise it and cut it into chunks for soup.' Older roots are fibrous, but younger roots are softer and can be sliced thinly as a garnish.

Mussels in lemongrass, galangal and turmeric broth, page 39.

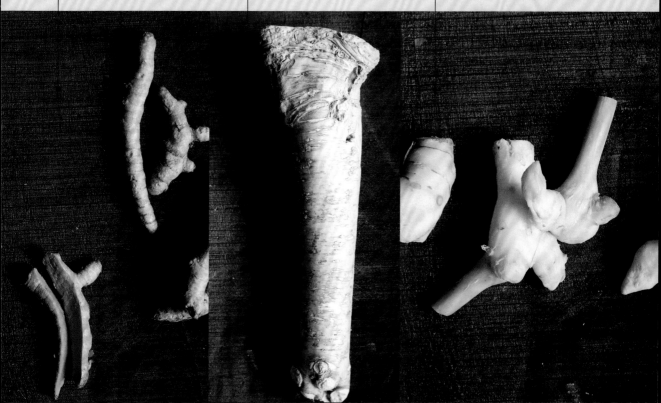

Tomatoes fermented with celery and lime leaves

A ripe tomato in peak season needs little more than salt and olive oil to be amongst the best things you'll eat all summer. But, as that season threatens to end, you might want to find ways to prolong this pleasure and preserve them. This is one of the best things you can do – fermenting them into sour, punchy nuggets of flavour.

Choose ripe (but not over-ripe) tomatoes that are unblemished and firm, and use distilled or filtered water if you can. The high water content of tomatoes means this is a slightly saltier brine than keen fermenters might be used to.

Fills a 1.5-litre jar

1 litre distilled or filtered water

40g sea salt

700g tomatoes

Small handful of celery leaves

8 dried makrut lime leaves

You will need a 1.5-litre jar, sterilised

Make a brine by gently heating the water with the salt in a saucepan, just until the salt dissolves. Set aside to cool to room temperature.

Wash your tomatoes, celery leaves and lime leaves. Pack the jar with the tomatoes, interspersing the celery leaves and lime leaves, but keeping back a couple of the larger celery leaves. Pour the cooled brine into the jar to cover the tomatoes, then sit the reserved celery leaves on top to help the tomatoes stay submerged.

Close the lid and keep the jar at room temperature away from direct sunlight. Open the lid every day to release gases and stir with a scrupulously clean long spoon. Tomatoes' sweetness makes them prone to developing yeast in the jar, and stirring helps limit its chance of forming. White yeast is no problem if it does appear, just scrape it off. Mould – which is more a mixture of colours and textures – is a problem. If you see that then you will sadly have to scrap the project and start again. It is worth taking the time to limit that potential and make sure everything is super-clean before you start.

Test the tomatoes after 4 days – they should be starting to get fizzy and sour. Carry on fermenting them until they reach the intensity that suits you (for me that's at about 10 days), then store in the fridge to stop them fermenting any further.

Use in salads or with cheeses.

Celery leaves are always too delicious to just throw away – use them in salads, soups, stocks or stir-fries.

Watercress soup with lemon and thyme breadcrumbs

This beautiful flecked-green soup is a bowlful of spring flavours. And like many a spring day, it can be warm or chilled. It's a great way to use watercress that is a little past its perky best.

I've provided a swap for the amontillado sherry in case you don't want to use it. It really does give the soup extra depth, though. (For more on sherry styles, see page 309.)

Serve with slices of a strong, hard cheese on oatcakes to make this light soup into something heartier.

Serves 4

1 onion

1 celery stick

40g butter

300g potatoes

300ml whole milk

50ml semi-dry amontillado sherry (or 2 tablespoons sherry vinegar)

300ml chicken or vegetable stock (bought or see pages 82 and 147)

400g watercress

50ml double cream (optional)

For the lemon and thyme breadcrumbs

1 tablespoon olive oil

50g breadcrumbs

Leaves from 2 sprigs of thyme

½ unwaxed lemon

Nutmeg, for grating

Peel and finely chop the onion, then chop the celery. Melt the butter in a large saucepan over a low heat. Add the onion and celery and cook until they soften but are not turning brown. While that is happening, peel and dice the potatoes. Stir the potatoes into the softened onion and celery, then stir in the milk, sherry (or vinegar) and the stock. Season, increase the heat to bring to the boil, then reduce the heat, put the lid on and simmer gently for 25 minutes or until the potatoes are very tender.

Add the watercress, keeping back a few sprigs for garnish. The watercress will need only a minute to cook. Take off the heat.

Use a blender to liquidise the soup until it is as smooth as you like it, adding the cream if you think it needs thickening. Check the seasoning.

To fry the breadcrumbs, heat the olive oil in a small frying pan over a medium heat, then add the breadcrumbs and thyme leaves. Stir continuously for about 3 minutes until they have browned and crisped. Remove from the heat. Grate the zest of the lemon half and stir through.

Serve the soup warm or cool; garnished with the reserved watercress sprigs, the crisped breadcrumbs and a grating of fresh nutmeg.

This soup freezes well, but fry the breadcrumbs just before serving.

Asparagus with quail's eggs and shaved truffle

It seems odd to begin this recipe by declaring myself a truffle sceptic, but there you go. Or rather, I am a former truffle sceptic. Tartufaia gave me a truffle taste epiphany and now I pester them at the stall asking advice on what truffle to use with what and when. Not that they ever seem to mind – read Mario Prati's truffle insights on page 139 and you'll understand that he is a trader passionate about his wares.

This recipe could be made with shavings of fresh spring truffle, and that's what I would do if scaling it up for more people. But for such a small amount for one person have on standby a small jar of sliced summer truffle, which Tartufaia preserve in sunflower oil.

Serves 1 as a breakfast, lunch or light supper

1 bundle of asparagus spears, about 250g

1 tablespoon olive oil

2 quail's eggs

1 teaspoon shaved summer truffle in oil

Preheat the oven to 190C fan/210C/410F/gas mark 6.

Snap the tough ends off the asparagus spears (keep them for stock – see box). Sit the spears in a roasting tray, drizzle with the oil, toss to coat and scatter over some salt. Roast for 6–10 minutes, depending on how thick the spears are. They are ready when tender to the point of a knife and charring.

While the asparagus spears are roasting, bring a small saucepan of water to the boil. About halfway through the asparagus cooking time, lower the eggs into the water and simmer for 1½ minutes, then drain and run under cold water to stop them cooking further.

Lift the cooked asparagus spears onto a plate. Drizzle over the oil left behind in the roasting tray. Scatter over the truffle shavings, then peel the shells from the eggs and nestle them around the asparagus so that when you cut into them their soft yolks envelop the spears. Finish with lots of freshly ground black pepper and serve immediately.

MAKE YOUR OWN VEGETABLE STOCKS

All manner of vegetable trimmings and peelings can be kept for making vegetable stocks. Store them (washed) in a resealable bag in the freezer. As the bag gets a bit full, make your stock:

· Empty your bag of trimmings etc into a stockpot with an equal volume of water. Add some salt and herbs if you have any to hand. Simmer for about 1 hour, then strain. The stock is now ready to use or store in the freezer for up to 3 months.

· Use: asparagus ends, the green parts of leeks, onion skins, carrot peel, stringy bits of pumpkin, celery ends, fennel trimmings...

· And / or: add fresh vegetables into the stockpot.

· Avoid: potato peelings, cabbage leaves and trimmings.

Globe courgettes with wild mushrooms and nuts

Summer's courgettes are one of the many stunning visual highlights of the Market year. You'll see on the stalls all shapes and sizes, but it is the round (globe) ones – green or yellow – which are especially good for stuffing. Here their filling is a satisfying mix of wild summer mushrooms that are just coming into season at the same time, with nuts, raisins and herbs.

My nut choice will always be the almond nibs from Food & Forest. If you haven't yet, now is a good time to head to page 209 and read Charles Tebbutt of Food & Forest explaining why not all nuts are equal. The flavour and textural difference of high-quality, sustainably sourced nuts has been a revelation to me.

These are great served with a sauce of seasoned yoghurt stirred through with lemon juice, mint and dill.

Serves 4 as a light main or side

1 tablespoon dried mushrooms

2 tablespoons raisins

4 globe courgettes

6 tablespoons olive oil

2 garlic cloves

2 tablespoons rapeseed oil

150g wild seasonal mushrooms, such as St George, morels, chicken of the woods, or fairy ring (mousseron)

1 sprig of rosemary

4 tablespoons almond nibs, flaked almonds or pine nuts

2 tablespoons cherry vinegar

60g breadcrumbs

12 basil leaves

4 teaspoons balsamic vinegar

Preheat the oven to 190C fan/210C/410F/gas mark 6.

Put the dried mushrooms and raisins in a small heatproof bowl, cover with 100ml hot water and set aside.

Cut the tops off the courgettes, about 1cm down from the stem. Set aside the tops to use as lids later on. Scoop out (and keep) the courgette flesh inside, leaving a thickness of about 5mm. Rub the shells all over with 2 tablespoons of the olive oil, sprinkle with salt, sit on a roasting tray and roast for 10 minutes.

Peel the garlic cloves and crush with the back of a heavy knife. Heat the rapeseed oil and 2 tablespoons of the olive oil in a large frying pan over a medium heat and cook the garlic in that for a minute or so. Add the wild mushrooms and rosemary sprig. Cook, stirring, for a couple of minutes, then add the rehydrated mushrooms and raisins along with their soaking juice. Stir in the almond nibs (or whatever option you have gone for – if you are using flaked almonds, give them a gentle crush first). Season well and stir in the cherry vinegar. Roughly chop the saved courgette flesh, add to the pan and cook over a gentle heat for 5 minutes. Discard the rosemary and stir in the breadcrumbs.

Pack the baked courgette shells evenly with the stuffing mix. Drizzle over the remaining 2 tablespoons of olive oil and return to the oven for 10 minutes, then chop the basil and scatter it over the courgettes. Top with the reserved courgette lids, drizzle the balsamic vinegar all over the courgettes and return to the oven for 5 minutes. Serve hot or at room temperature.

Parsnip gnocchi and smoked garlic butter with crisped sage leaves

Parsnips bring such sweetness and nuttiness to these gnocchi. They are silky, somehow luxurious for all the humility of their ingredients, and just so incredibly tasty.

Using smoked garlic makes all the difference. You absolutely could use unsmoked, but it will lack the depth that the smoking brings. I usually shop for extra of these burnished bulbs to make more garlic butter, which can then be wrapped to store in the fridge or freezer, and used on toast, over vegetables or meats.

Serves 2 as a main or 6 as a starter

300g parsnips

250g floury potatoes, such as King Edwards

80–100g 'oo' pasta flour, plus extra for dusting

1 egg yolk

½ smoked garlic bulb

75g butter, at room temperature

16 sage leaves

Peel and chop the parsnips and potatoes into chunks and put in a saucepan of salted cold water. Simmer for about 20 minutes until tender. Drain, tip them back into the pan to dry for a minute, then push through a potato ricer into a large mixing bowl (the parsnip cores might be reluctant).

Add 50g of the flour, the egg yolk and some seasoning to the riced vegetables and mix it together. Keep adding more of the flour until you achieve a smooth, non-sticky dough – you might not need all the flour. Knead briefly, then pull into four equal pieces. Dust a large chopping board with flour, then roll each piece of dough into a long sausage about 2cm thick. Cut each sausage into 3cm-pieces and press the tines of a fork into each piece to leave indentations. You can prepare the gnocchi an hour or so ahead of time, covering them with a clean tea towel until you want to cook them.

To make the smoked garlic butter: peel and chop the garlic cloves, then use a pestle and mortar to work them into a paste with a good pinch of salt. Work in the butter too, then wrap in baking paper and set aside.

Preheat the oven to 100C fan/120C/250F/gas mark ½.

Bring a large saucepan of salted water to the boil. Just as the water is starting to get hot, put a small frying pan over a medium heat. Melt a third of the smoked garlic butter in the frying pan, then sit the sage leaves in, turning them after a minute or so to crisp. Lift out and sit the leaves on kitchen paper to dry. Add the rest of the garlic butter to the frying pan but turn off the heat – you want it just to melt in the residual warmth.

By now the water should be boiling. Place half the gnocchi into the water and – after a minute or so – you will see them start to rise to the surface. As each one reaches the surface, use a slotted spoon to lift it out and onto a tray, then keep them warm in the low oven. Repeat for the rest of the gnocchi.

Divide the gnocchi between serving bowls. Spoon over the melted smoked garlic butter, top with the crisped sage leaves and finish with plenty of ground pepper. Eat immediately.

(Gnocchi traditionalists will note I make my gnocchi mixture in a bowl rather than on a worktop. That's just a greater level of mess than I am comfortable with. Make on a worktop if you prefer.)

Grilled sweetcorn cobs with toasted coconut, lime and Urfa chilli

These whole cobs have more than a bit of 'wow' factor, with their husks gorgeously charred, and leaves pulled back to reveal bright, tender kernels that have cooked in an equally bright mix of coconut, coriander, lime and chilli. There are even more of those flavours spooned over the top for extra wow.

Urfa chilli brings a lovely smokiness, which you can enhance by cooking these over fire on a barbecue. But the cobs are just as good made in the kitchen on a griddle pan or under the grill.

Serves 4 as a light main

4 sweetcorn cobs with husks

80g fresh coconut (see tip below on opening a fresh coconut and extracting the meat)

6 tablespoons coconut oil

Handful of coriander (about 30g)

1 lime

½ teaspoon Urfa chilli flakes

The team at Raya set me straight on how to choose a good coconut: give it a shake to ensure there's plenty of water inside – a sign of freshness.

To open it, find the three 'eyes' near the top, pierce with a skewer, then shake out the water. Use the handle of a hammer to firmly hit around the coconut's equator line – it will separate into two halves. Wrap each half in foil and bake for 1 hour at 190C fan/210C/410F/gas mark 6. After cooling, the meat should come away easily. Use a vegetable peeler to remove any brown skin from the meat, then wash and dry. You can freeze what you don't use.

Peel back the husk leaves of each cob, taking care not to pull them off at the base. Remove and discard the silky threads.

Grate 20g of the fresh coconut and mix it in a bowl with 4 tablespoons of the coconut oil. Finely chop the coriander stems and add those too, along with the juice of half the lime, the chilli flakes and a pinch of salt. Mix into a paste. Divide the paste evenly between the cobs, pressing it onto the corn. Bring the husk leaves back up to enclose the corn and twist the ends together to seal.

Grill, griddle or barbecue the cobs for 20 minutes, turning them every few minutes. You want the husks to char and the kernels inside to cook. Transfer the cooked cobs onto a serving dish or plates, cover and set aside for a few minutes.

Use that time to finely chop the rest of the fresh coconut. Heat a small frying pan over a medium heat, add the coconut and toast for a few minutes, keeping it moving so it doesn't burn. Tip the toasted coconut into a bowl. Chop the coriander leaves and add those, along with the juice from the remaining half lime. Melt the remaining 2 tablespoons of coconut oil in the empty frying pan, add it to the coconut and coriander mix and season.

To serve, peel back the sweetcorn husks to reveal the tender yellow kernels and spoon over the toasted coconut and coriander mix. Eat while still hot.

Black rice and feta-stuffed chard with spiced yoghurt

Rainbow chard is right up there among the most aesthetically pleasing vegetables at the Market. It's almost two vegetables in one, really, as its leaves and stems should be respected for how they cook at different paces.

Here they're cooked separately, then reunited in bundles filled with spices, feta and black rice. You'll find black rice at specialist stockists like Spice Mountain, and it's well worth seeking out for its exceptional flavour and colour, which isn't so much black as a divine deep purple.

Kath Dawson at Ted's Veg is absolutely right that choosing vegetables shouldn't be about perfection (see page 132), but for this you do need leaves that are as perfect as possible. The filling would otherwise fall through any holes.

Serves 3–4 as a main or 8 as a side or small plate

250g black rice

12 rainbow chard stems with large undamaged leaves (or Swiss chard, or a mixture)

1 leek

4 tablespoons olive oil

5 garlic cloves

1½ teaspoons fennel seeds

1½ teaspoons ground cumin

250ml white wine or vegetable stock (bought or see page 147)

200g feta (drained weight)

Handful of mint and dill

For the spiced yoghurt

200g natural yoghurt

2 teaspoons dukkah

Rinse and drain the rice. Bring a large saucepan of salted water to the boil, add the rice and simmer for about 30 minutes until tender (check the packet instructions first, as varieties can vary in cooking time). Drain and set aside.

While the rice is cooking, prepare the chard leaves and stuffing. Trim off and discard the very woody ends of the chard stalks. Separate off the leaves and at their very base cut out a 'V' pointing up the leaf (this makes them easier to roll). Bring another large pan of salted water to the boil and wilt the chard leaves in it for just 2 minutes, then drain, rinse in cold water and drain again. Set the leaves aside.

Dice the chard stalks along with the leek. Heat 3 tablespoons of the olive oil in a large frying pan over a medium heat. Saute the diced chard stems and leek until softening but not colouring. Peel and crush the garlic cloves with the back of a knife, then chop and add along with the fennel seeds and ground cumin. Cook for another 10 minutes, then pour over 150ml of the wine (or stock) and let that bubble for a minute or so to reduce. Take off the heat and, when the rice is tender and drained, stir the vegetable mixture through. Crumble in the feta, chop the herbs and add those too. Taste for seasoning.

Preheat the oven to 180C fan/200C/400F/gas mark 6.

Unfurl the chard leaves and lay them out flat, with their ribs uppermost. Spoon the feta and rice stuffing into the middle of each leaf. Roll the point of the leaf over the filling, tucking the sides in and working tightly down to where you cut away the stem. Sit each roll in a baking dish, seam-side down. Pour the remaining 100ml of white wine (or stock) into the baking dish and brush the tops of the chard rolls with the remaining tablespoon of olive oil.

Bake for 20 minutes. Use that time to make the spiced yoghurt by simply mixing the yoghurt with the dukkah. Season well and serve alongside the baked, stuffed chard.

Charred hispi cabbage with bottarga cream sauce

The cabbage family runs the gamut of shapes, sizes and seasons. From the round wrinkly Savoy and January King's vibrant purple and green leaves; to smaller, crisp pak choi with its peppery notes, and many more. (Without even considering that vegetables such as cauliflower and broccoli are technically part of the cabbage family too.)

This recipe calls for elegant hispi cabbage – aka sweetheart or pointed cabbage – because it holds its shape once cooked. It's very much the star of this dish, gorgeously accentuated by the umami-laden bottarga. I'd read about this salted and cured roe of tuna or mullet but never tried it before stumbling across some at Gastronomica. Now I grate it onto many vegetables for a savoury hit.

Serves 4 as a main or 8 as a small plate

1 hispi cabbage (about 400g)

2 tablespoons olive oil

For the bottarga cream sauce

50g bottarga

2 tablespoons olive oil

2 garlic cloves

1 mild fresh red chilli

1 lemon

150ml white wine, dry vermouth,
    dry cider or vegetable or fish stock

100ml double cream or creme fraiche

Preheat the oven to 180C fan/200C/400F/gas mark 6 with a baking tray inside to get hot.

Cut the cabbage into quarters through its core. Heat the 2 tablespoons of olive oil in a large frying pan over a medium heat, then sit the hispi quarters in the pan, with the outer-leaf-side down. Leave to char for 2 minutes before turning onto one cut edge for 2 minutes, then onto the other cut edge for another 2 minutes. Using tongs will make this easier.

Transfer the hispi quarters to the hot baking tray, sitting them on their outer leaves so the 'point' is upwards. Season lightly with salt and bake for 5–8 minutes until tender.

Use that time to make the sauce: finely grate the bottarga and set aside. Put the same frying pan you have just used for the cabbage over a low heat with the remaining 2 tablespoons of olive oil. Peel and halve the garlic cloves and add to the pan along with the whole chilli and cook for 2 minutes to release their flavours into the oil. Take care the garlic doesn't burn. Lift out the garlic and chilli, keeping the chilli – you'll need it in a minute. Stir half the grated bottarga into the pan, followed by the juice from the lemon and whatever alcohol or stock you are using. Let it bubble to reduce a little, then cut half the chilli into thin diagonal slices and return those to the pan along with the cream or creme fraiche. It will come together into a fabulous sauce.

By now the hispi should be tender. If not, just take the sauce off the heat until it is. Either sit the hispi back in the pan, nestled on the sauce, or spoon the sauce between shallow bowls and sit the charred hispi on top. Finish by scattering over the rest of the grated bottarga and serve immediately.

Shaved kohlrabi, chickpeas and little gem salad

Serving this as a large sharing platter for people to help themselves to really helps show off the elegance of its blending shades of white, cream and pale greens. With just a few flecks of chilli hidden in there to pep things up.

The kohlrabi is sliced so thinly, it doesn't need cooking to be tender – the gentle heat of the charred little gem and warmed-through chickpeas is enough to relax it. (The recipe here calls for a weight of the specific Brindisa chickpeas that I love, but any standard 400g tin is fine. Other pre-cooked beans would do too – use what you like or have to hand.)

Serves 4 as a main or 8 as a side or small plate

2 limes

4 tablespoons peppery or fruity olive oil

½ teaspoon dried chilli flakes

2 kohlrabi (about 700g in total)

2 little gem lettuce

1 x 325g jar of chickpeas (see introduction above)

2 spring onions

1 tablespoon pumpkin oil

Grate and set aside the zest of the limes, then mix together in a bowl the limes' juice with half the olive oil and the chilli flakes. Set aside.

Peel and trim the kohlrabi, then slice into thin slivers, using a knife, a mandoline or even a vegetable peeler, as you prefer. Arrange on a serving plate and salt generously.

Quarter the lettuces through their core. Heat the remaining olive oil in a large frying pan over a medium–high heat, then sit the little gem pieces in the pan to char for a couple of minutes on each side. Tongs will help you turn them. When they're done, add to the kohlrabi slices.

Drain the chickpeas. Heat them through in the pan the lettuce just charred in and then add them to the kohlrabi plate too. Arrange everything as prettily as you like. Pour over the lime dressing you made at the beginning. Finish it all off by thinly slicing the spring onions and scattering them over along with the reserved lime zest, the pumpkin oil, and plenty of freshly ground black pepper.

Switch the jarred or tinned beans for soaking and cooking your own – see page 221 – adding them straight from the cooking pot to the platter of kohlrabi without warming them through in the frying pan.

The Greengrocers

Warm borlotti bean and pea salad

Almost the best thing about this recipe is the sheer relaxing pleasure of time spent podding the peas and borlotti beans. Their freshly cooked heat then releases the flavours of the lettuce and tomatoes that are bang in season at the same time – because this is a meal for high summer. Try not to be too sad that the purple-speckled borlottis will lose their colouring as they cook. You have the memory of seeing their beauty first on the grocer's stall and then as you pod them.

This salad is delicious just as it is, though non-vegetarians could add a shaving or two of parmesan and / or a few anchovies, or serve it with a piece of fish or some fried prawns.

Serves 4–6, depending on what, if anything, you are serving it with

500g peas in their pods
   (about 250g podded weight)

500g borlotti beans in their pods
   (about 150g podded weight)

10 sprigs of thyme

1 little gem lettuce

2 medium, very ripe tomatoes

125ml mild olive oil

2 tablespoons red wine vinegar
   or sherry vinegar

2 spring onions

6 sprigs of mint

6 sprigs of basil

Bring a medium saucepan of salted water to the boil. While it is getting hot, pod the peas and borlotti beans into separate bowls. Tip the peas into the bubbling water and cook for about 3 minutes until tender, then use a slotted spoon to lift them out of the water and into a mixing bowl. Set aside.

Put the podded borlotti beans and thyme sprigs into the water that the peas cooked in and simmer for 15–20 minutes until tender.

While the borlotti beans are cooking, slice the little gem lettuce in half through its root and cut out the core. Slice the lettuce leaves and add to the peas in the bowl. Quarter the tomatoes, cut out and discard the core and seeds, then chop the flesh and add to the peas and lettuce. Toss to combine.

Drain the borlotti beans when they are tender, discard the thyme sprigs, and toss the beans into the bowl of peas along with the oil, red wine vinegar or sherry vinegar, and plenty of salt. Trim and thinly slice the spring onions, then add those too along with the mint and basil, tearing the leaves as you go. Finish with a grinding of black pepper and serve the salad while it is (ideally) still slightly warm.

HOW TO... store and preserve herbs

'Compared with other countries, British people tend to underuse herbs, or not use enough of them when they do. If I'm making pasta with fresh basil, I use a whole bunch of basil. If you use fistfuls of coriander and parsley, not just a sprig, you'll have far more flavour and far less wastage. Use the stalks of soft herbs as well as the leaves – they're full of flavour, and you can introduce them early on in the cooking process so you get more of a background note. If you take care of herbs, they will last about a week – longer for hardy herbs like thyme and rosemary. The best way to store them is in the fridge, in an airtight container. I know some people like to store them in a glass of water, but I find it's not worth the hassle; they still wilt a bit. If you do have some left over, either make a pesto, or turn them into a paste and freeze in ice-cube trays, ready for cooking. You can also use herbs in pickles; the classic example is cucumbers with loads of dill. I love marinading mushrooms, and submerging them in olive oil with chopped thyme. They're perfect for pasta or omelettes.'

Matt Tarantini, Elliot's

Mixed root hasselbacks with miso butter

All kinds of root vegetables can be hasselbacked into crisply delicious glory. Potatoes, carrots, parsnips, beetroots, small turnips, salsify, parsley root... Just give them a scrub and get going. Serve the hasselbacks with chicken, meats, fish, lentils, or on their own with just a few leaves. A vegan alternative to the miso butter is given below.

Serves 4 as a main or 8 as a small plate or side

1kg mixed root vegetables

3 tablespoons olive oil

120g unsalted butter, at room temperature

60g red miso paste

2 tablespoons white sesame seeds

Preheat the oven to 200C fan/220C/425F/gas mark 7.

Wash and dry the vegetables. Trim them, leaving a few centimetres of roots and tops intact. There's no need to peel them. Working one at a time, sit each vegetable on a chopping board between two wooden spoons and use a very sharp knife to slice two-thirds of the way through at 5mm or so intervals. The spoon handles are there to stop the knife going all the way down. Put the hasselbacked vegetables into a roasting tray that can fit them in one layer, then toss them in the olive oil, making sure they remain cut side up. Sprinkle over a little salt.

The roasting time will depend on what roots you have chosen – beetroots and turnips will take about 50 minutes, for instance, but carrots and parsnips only about 25 minutes.. Baste the roots occasionally with the oil as they roast. They are done when tender and crisped. If some are ready ahead of others, just take them out, set aside, and put them back into the tin towards the end to warm through.

Meanwhile, make the miso butter. Put the butter and the miso paste into a bowl and use the back of a spoon to mix them together. Don't mix them too thoroughly – a bit of a ripple effect works well. Use baking paper to wrap the butter into a log shape, twist the ends and put into the fridge until needed.

When the vegetables are ready, toast the white sesame seeds in a small dry frying pan over a low heat, then scatter the seeds over the hasselbacks. Grind over plenty of black pepper and serve with miso butter slices on top and more at the table for people to help themselves.

Sherry vinegar & mustard seed dressing:

Instead of the miso butter: mix together 75ml olive oil, 50ml sherry vinegar, 1 tablespoon maple syrup and plenty of salt. Just before serving, toast 1 tablespoon black mustard seeds (you could use the same pan as for the sesame seeds) and add those to the dressing before serving with the roots. There will be plenty for also dressing the leaves or lentils you might serve with the hasselbacks.

The miso butter here can be made ahead as it keeps in the fridge for up to a week, and freezes well. It's usually a good idea to make more than you need – once you've tried it, I imagine you'll be finding lots of things to spread miso butter onto.

A few ways with pumpkin and squash

Every autumn and winter brings the sheer joy of seeing all the pumpkins and other squashes displayed across the Market stalls – so many different shapes, colours and sizes – and seemingly endless ways they can be used in all kinds of cooking.

Shop

The ripest pumpkins and squash will give a hollow sound when tapped. Stored in a cool, dark place, they can keep for months, should you want to. Different varieties come with different flavours and textures, and the following are particularly wonderful to cook with:

Acorn squash: Unsurprisingly, shaped like an acorn, with dark green ridges that, when sliced into, give a scalloped-edge appearance. Its flesh is a beautiful yellow with a mild, nutty flavour, but a little watery, so not the best for grating. Instead, it's ideal for soups or sauteing.

Crown prince: These absolute beauties have a pale blue-green skin that's so thick it can be hard to cut into, so take care. Once in, prepare to be stunned by the vivid beauty of its deep orange flesh that holds its shape well on cooking. Great for roasting. They store well too.

Harlequin squash: This one looks a bit like an acorn squash, but this time with speckled creamy green skin. Its watery flesh means it can disintegrate on roasting or grating. Best for soups or sauteing.

Onion squash: A small, teardrop-shaped squash that's bright orange inside and out. It has a nutty flavour, is a little less sweet than others, and may not keep well for quite so long. Great for roasting.

Turban squash: Looks like a small stripy squash on top of a larger one. Its pale yellow flesh is, again, a little watery, and is better for soups than grating or mashing.

Cook

Roast:

Roasting hollowed-out, sliced or chopped pumpkin or squash – particularly a crown prince – is very probably the very best thing you can do with it. It protects and develops the inherent flavour, opening up a world of culinary opportunity for what you can do with it once cooked.

Slice open and remove the stringy insides and the seeds. Don't throw away the seeds – see page 165.

Remove the skin if you want to for the final dish, but keeping it on helps with flavour and it's easier to remove the skin after cooking.

Slice or chop, add to a roasting tin, then toss in oil or ghee along with spices and aromatics of your choosing – rosemary, sage, oregano, za'atar, cumin, paprika, cinnamon, caraway, etc – and a splash of balsamic or sherry vinegar.

Roast in a hot oven at 200-210C fan/220-230C/425-445F/ gas mark 7/8 for 20–40 minutes, depending on the variety and the sizes you are roasting.

(If you do remove the skin before cooking, keep it to make pumpkin-peel crisps: just toss the peels in oil and salt and roast in a very hot oven until crisped.)

Then perhaps:

- Serve as a winter salad with other roasted vegetables (maybe cauliflower or beetroots), feta, quinoa or spelt.

- Roast a mix of varieties and tear some kale or puntarelle into the roasting tray for the squashes' last 10 minutes to take on flavours and crisp up. Add halloumi pieces if you like.

- Mash the tender flesh to use for kofte, gnocchi, as part of the filling for a tart or pie, as a bed for seared scallops / langoustines / fish / meat, stir into a risotto finished with crisped sage leaves, parmesan and lots of black pepper, or simply have it mashed, with lots of butter and grated parmesan.

- Blitz into soups.

- For roasted stuffed squash: Halve your squash, scoop out its strings and seeds, slash the flesh, rub with oil and salt, and roast cut side down for 30 minutes. (Use that time to make your stuffing by cooking whatever mix of grains, greens, herbs, spices, beans or meat you fancy.) Then turn it the other way up, stuff and bake some more to finish.

Simmer:

- Bring pieces of pumpkin to tenderness by cooking them directly in all kinds of tagines, stews, dals and curries. It's best to peel the skin away first.
- The simplest lunchtime soup is made by simmering peeled chunks of pumpkin in stock and then blitzing. Other flavour layers are optional.
- Cook peeled and diced pumpkin with onion, spices and coconut milk to use as the filling for a dosa.

Grate:

- To include in the filling for dumplings, ravioli or tortellini.
- For baking into cakes, muffins and breads.
- Add to the batter of a chickpea-flour pancake, or to flatbreads as on page 294.
- For fritters.
- Simmer grated squash with apple or pear and spices as a porridge or granola topping.

Raw

- Use a mandoline or vegetable peeler to make ribbons you can toss in olive oil, sherry vinegar and salt.
- Very thin slices of raw pumpkin are great deep-fried in a light batter as tempura.
- Make a pumpkin pickle.

Seeds

Wash the seeds to remove the bits of string (they can be used for stocks). Spread the seeds out on a baking sheet and roast just as they are – no oil or salt yet – at 180C fan/200C/400F/gas mark 6 for about 10 minutes or until turning golden and dried out. Use them as follows:

- Toss with olive oil, some grated citrus zest and soy sauce, then roast in the hot oven for snacking on.
- Toast in a dry pan with honey (or maple syrup) and salt, then let them cool on a plate until you can break them like praline for a sweet snack.
- Add when making granola.
- Use in flapjacks.

> **FLAVOUR ENHANCERS**
>
> *Think about:* strong cheeses (such as feta, cheddar, parmesan, and the blues like gorgonzola); anchovies; chilli; fennel or fennel seeds; sage; bitter leaves like kale, puntarelle and spinach; celery; lemongrass; coconut; mushrooms; nutmeg; soy sauce; lime; spices; tahini; miso; balsamic vinegar.

Borough Market – The Knowledge

Drinks

Chardonnay

Chardonnay wines can vary hugely in style, from appley and crisp to smoky and buttery – good news for the versatility of pairing chardonnay with a breadth of vegetable (and other) dishes, but it does mean you need to give proper consideration to the style of chardonnay you choose. Two of the main considerations that Natacha Jaune of Borough Wines urges the prospective chardonnay-drinker to think about are where the wine is from, and its ageing.

Location first. The inherent sunshine of New World countries is going to make chardonnays that bit sweeter, with tropical fruit notes coming through. Whereas cool climate, Old World chardonnays (like a chablis or meursault) will be drier, more lemony and with more minerality.

Young unoaked or lightly oaked wines are at the lighter end of the chardonnay spectrum. Others are given time in oak barrels to bolster their waxy, buttery credentials. Full-bodied or oak-aged chardonnays are what you want to reach for with creamier and richer vegetables like squash, pumpkin, mushrooms and sweetcorn. And then there are the more mature barrel-aged or fermented chardonnays, which are superb with vegetables that have powerful accompaniments, such as toasted nuts or truffle.

The Borough Wines team advise keeping an eye out too for lower-intervention 'pet nat' sparkling chardonnays (*pétillant naturel*, meaning 'natural sparkling'), or chardonnay natural wines. As Natacha says, 'Every bottle can have its own magic. Experiment!'

Lager, pale ale and IPA

Mike Hill of Utobeer has lots of great advice when it comes to choosing beers to serve with food, but perhaps none better than this: think about what you like. To Mike, that is far more important a consideration than what might be considered a classic match. Beyond that most sensible point, it's about deciding whether you want the flavour profiles of the beer to complement or offer contrast to the flavours of the food. Either can work.

Here are three styles of beers especially suited to dishes with vegetables at their heart:

Lagers can be gorgeously light and summery and are best-suited to similar styles of food.

Pale ales vary quite a bit in their lead flavours, meaning that if you intend to match your pale ale with food it is definitely worth taking the time to find out about its profiles. And then go back to Mike's thoughts about flavours complementing or contrasting.

IPAs (India pale ales) are more hop-forward than pale ales – with a higher ABV, too – so come to the food-pairing fore when the intensity or depth of food flavours start to go up a notch. IPAs can handle spice, or anything in the salty and / or fried line of things. Their more hoppy characteristics mean there's more going on with the aroma too. Serve an IPA in a wider glass (rather than a straight-sided pint glass) to give space for the aromas to play. Similarly, give an IPA time out of the fridge before serving: as the temperature warms the beer, it opens up its flavours.

THE FRUITERERS

ESTABLISHED
1756

BOROUGH
MARKET

You don't need a calendar to know what month it is at Borough Market. You just need to walk past the Turnips stall, run by the Foster family, where the kaleidoscopic bounty of quality seasonal fruit and vegetables – sourced from a network of independent farms around Britain and far beyond – serves as a vivid guide to the time of year.

Why seasonality matters

Charles Foster, Turnips

For every single piece of produce, there is a place in the world where it grows best. We firmly believe that. It's not just about the country – every region, every plot of land, every corner of that plot is different. Flavour is in the soil. And with fruit in particular, it's in the climate. One area will be wonderful for strawberries, another for apples, another for blackcurrants. We source our fruit accordingly. We start here in London, and slowly work our way outwards until we find what we consider to be world-class produce.

If we could find the perfect mango in Sussex, we'd stop there – but of course, we can't. So for the short time they're in season – about six weeks of the Indian summer – we ship over kesar and alphonso mangoes from India. It's a good example of a product that grows far away, but which is so good we want to celebrate it. If you look at the percentage of our stock that we import over such long distances, it is tiny. We only really steer towards exotic fruits in the winter, when northern Europe can't offer those sweet flavours. To get them, you have no choice but to go further afield.

Those exotic fruits have seasons too, though. When their season's over, we don't stock them. The only way to extend the natural season of a fruit is to grow it off the ground in a greenhouse – but that makes for an inferior product, because so much of the flavour comes from the soil. There are mega-farms in this country and elsewhere that buy up all the land around them, fill it with greenhouses and polytunnels and produce as much as they can, as quickly as possible, with as little labour as possible. Economically it makes sense, and it meets the consumer desire to have all things at all times, but it kills the seasonality completely and it undercuts the small-scale producers who are growing produce naturally. Mass production makes for a cheaper product, but it's too cheap. It means people don't want to pay the real price for the land and labour that go into a seasonal product grown naturally.

For example, there aren't many small-scale producers of strawberries in England any more. The real English strawberry season is a similar length to that of asparagus – it's four to five weeks in the summer. This means that most of the English strawberries you find through the

"

Buying local isn't always best. Sometimes it's better to have a product that has travelled some distance but has been produced in a sustainable way.

> I'm often asked what we sell that people can't find at their local supermarket – and my answer is everything. Every single product.

year are grown in greenhouses or polytunnels. That's why we sell a French strawberry variety, the gariguette, early in the season, and the fraise de bois – the wild strawberry – later in the year. We do sell British strawberries for the short time they're in season, but it's hard to find producers that align with our ethos of quality over quantity.

People tend to think they're always doing the right thing by buying local, but sometimes they're not. Sometimes it's more sustainable to have a product that has travelled some distance but has been produced in a sustainable way. The producer we buy most of our apples from is French. The branches of the trees are trimmed to concentrate the minerals going into the fruit, making them bigger and more flavoursome. The time of year matters, the geography matters, but so does the producer. Are they trying to get the biggest yield or the most flavour? That's why we tend towards France for apples and strawberries – because their general culture and attitude toward produce is focused more on the latter.

You'll end up paying more for seasonal produce, but you'll also have better flavour. When something is more flavourful, you need to use less. The average supermarket passion fruit is half the price of our Vietnamese passion fruit, but the Vietnamese one is twice as big, and so much more flavourful. You would have to buy two vines of tomatoes to get the same flavour as one of our large Italian ones. Our Sicilian pomegranates are smaller than the standard Turkish

ones, but they're much sweeter and tangier and packed full of seeds.

If you want to shop for the best of the seasons, avoid the supermarket, where the range is dictated by the volume they can sell: strawberries, blueberries, bananas and so on. In the UK, you're more likely to find gooseberries and mulberries in a hedgerow than a supermarket, where produce is flown in from all over to meet customer demand all year round.

It is so, so much better to wait. For example, you can get fairly average satsumas all year round, but from late November to February the very best citrus in the world grows naturally in Italy and the south of France. Buy more, preserve some while it's in season, then leave it alone until it's good again. One thing I get asked a lot is what we sell that people can't find at their local supermarket – and my answer is everything. Every single product. Because each one is a specific variety, from a specific producer who grows it in a more sustainable way in a certain part of the world.

HOW TO... reduce fruit waste

'When it comes to reducing fruit waste, the headlines are: a) use your senses to judge if something is off, not just a date on a packet; b) love your freezer, particularly when it comes to delicate summer fruits (before bagging them, separate them out on baking trays so they don't clump together); and c) cooking is often the answer. If your fruit is starting to look a bit old or soft, you can still cook with it – in fact, you'll often get even more flavour. The same goes with steeping fruit in alcohol. Make sure to remove any mouldy specimens: old is fine but mould is not.

If you're juicing fruit, the leftover pulp can be used in cakes or pancake batter. Fruit peel can also add an oomph of flavour: bake it low and slow until dry, then pulverise into a fruit powder which you can bake with or use as a decorative sugar. Usually, I've zested my citrus already before eating it, but un-zested citrus peels can be candied for baking. Come Christmas time, it's really satisfying to make mince pies and stollen with your own peel.'

Chloë Stewart, nibs etc.

Candied citrus, page 195.
Greengages in bay, cardamom and calvados, page 197.

Five stone fruits

Greengage

Known in France as a reine claude, this small, olive-green dessert plum boasts luminous green-gold flesh, the jammy sweetness of which lends itself as happily to desserts, jam (of course) and pastries as it does to being devoured whole. In season through August and September.

Greengages in bay, cardamom and calvados, page 197.

Damson

The dark, dusky purple skin of the damson gives way to golden flesh and a sizeable stone. Although tarter and trickier to cook with than larger, fleshier plums, damsons are well worth the effort, particularly for using in crumbles, cakes and to make the classic damson gin. You'll find them in the late summer months and into the autumn.

Damson-ripple sourdough ice cream, page 302.

Mirabelle

Famously associated with the Lorraine region of France, these golden, orb-like plums resemble sunshine in both taste and appearance. Available in the high summer months, they are endlessly versatile. The small stone detaches easily and the golden flesh can be made into jam, poached, baked into a traditional galette, or transformed into a gleaming liqueur.

Kesar mango

Kesar translates as 'saffron' – a nod to this mango's gorgeous colour. You could almost warm your hands on its deep orange-yellow flesh, so reminiscent is it of late afternoon sunshine. The texture of the flesh is smooth, and the flavour floral and intensely sweet, lovely in a lassi, or simply diced in a bowl. Find this type of mango from April to July.

Rainier cherries

So delicious and difficult to cultivate is this cherry variety, it has its own national celebration day in the United States, its country of origin. With its superior taste and delicate yellow, red-blushed skin, it is better suited to special occasion desserts and salads – or just savouring on its own – than for cooking into crumbles and jams.

The Fruiterers

Five citrus fruits

Citron (cedro)

Character One of the four original species of citrus that went on to parent all modern varieties. A giant, wrinkled lemon-like fruit, prized more for its aromatic zest and fleshy, delicate pith than its juice.

Uses In Italy, its skin is used to make candied peel – a compulsory component of panettone – and cedro liqueur. The mild pith, with its marshmallowy texture, can be eaten raw in a salad of black pepper and olive oil, atop a bruschetta, or in a risotto with parmesan and sage.

Pomelo

Character Similar to the grapefruit in appearance, although the pomelo is sweeter, and more tangy than bitter. It has a thick rind and yields relatively little fruit.

Uses In Southeast Asia, pomelo is generally eaten in savoury salads or for dessert. Combine with mint, chilli, lime and peanuts, and serve with shellfish and noodles. The rind can be candied or even slowly braised in a sauce in place of tofu or meat.

Pomelo cocktail bitters, page 126.

Finger lime

Character The flesh consists of tiny, glassy beads, known as lime caviar, which pop in your mouth as you eat them, releasing a burst of sweet-sour juice. A simple slice down the middle and a gentle squeeze yields a flurry of zesty pearls.

Uses For millennia the finger lime has been used as both medicine and food by the indigenous people of Australia. Makes a pretty and citrusy garnish for desserts and salads, and elevates seafood dishes and cocktails.

Yuzu

Character Intensely aromatic, with a sweetly sharp flavour reminiscent of both mandarin and grapefruit. Less valued for its flesh than its juice and zest, which are used in Japan and Korea to add zip and brightness to an array of dishes.

Uses Lovely in cakes, cocktails, salads and sorbets, or to bring a touch of bright acidity.

Bergamot

Character One of the most highly perfumed and acidic of all citrus fruits, with a bitter yet intensely flavourful rind. Although edible, the bergamot is most sought after for its distinctive, fragrant oil – a key component of perfumes, cosmetics and Earl Grey tea.

Uses The juice is a good match for stronger meats and seafood, particularly when partnered with woody herbs and spices like nutmeg and cinnamon. The zest is versatile but intense, so best used with care.

With over 50 years of collective experience of selling fresh produce at Borough Market, father and son team, Jock and Richard Stark, are better placed than most to advise on picking out the highest-quality fruit.

Richard Stark

Stark's Fruiterers

How can you be assured of the quality of the produce you sell?

For the most part, it's experience – experience and seasonality. Seasonal produce will always, always have more flavour than produce that's out of season. It's about knowing your suppliers too. For example, I have a really good Italian importer. He drives to Italy twice a week and buys the best produce available in that season. I don't even need to try his produce because we've worked together for years, and I know it's always good. I just meet him here or in Covent Garden every Thursday evening. That Friday and Saturday, I know I'll have great produce

How ripe do you want the produce to be?

I always try to buy fruit that's fairly ripe because that's most people's preference. They want to eat it there and then; they don't want to take something home and have it take forever to ripen – or worse, not really ripen at all. If there's lots of ripe fruit available, that's often because it's in season at the time and there's an abundance of it. And when fruit is in season, it tastes better and it's usually cheaper.

BOROUGH MARKET

What are you looking out for when sourcing fruit?

Appearance, feel and flavour – and smell to some extent. You know how ripe or fresh something is by the feel of it. With stone fruit, for example, the skin should be tight, and the fruit should be firm but not overly firm. If the skin is wrinkly, you know it's dead old. Flavour is, of course, the most important thing. Other than the Italian produce, I sample everything before I buy it. Some things can look good and have no flavour. Part of the problem with wholesale produce is refrigeration. Big wholesalers put berries in a cold fridge to stop them deteriorating. When they bring them out, they look good, but they turn to mush within hours. That's why you're always better buying berries in season, as fresh as possible.

You often have class one and class two produce at your stall. What's the difference?

Class ones are superb – a superior product – but their main advantage is that they're more perfect in shape and size. They're what restaurants and high-end retailers look to buy. Class two is more of a jumble. They can be misshapen in shape or size, but they're often just as delicious and grown with the same ethos.

How to do advise your customers to store fruit?

Some fruits just shouldn't go in the fridge, ever: avocados go black in the fridge, and so do bananas. Bananas shouldn't go in a fruit bowl either, because the gas they release will ripen other fruit. Tomatoes don't like the fridge – the cold affects their texture and flavour. Most fruits should be fine stored in there, provided it's not too chilly: six degrees and above is okay.

Blood orange, watermelon radish and purple kale salad

Late winter and early spring are when you'll find blood oranges and watermelon radishes together on the Market stalls. Their shared vibrancy of colour and flavour is a sign of brighter days to come and is enormously welcome. They are married here with purple kale to make a pretty salad that's a wake-up call for the palate.

In the balance of sweet, sour, sharp and nutty elements working together, the sweetness here is courtesy of De La Grenade's nutmeg syrup, which I always have to hand (not least because it is my favourite topping for the crumpets on page 263). Swap in honey or maple syrup if you prefer.

Serves 2–3 as a main or 4–6 as a side or small plate

2 blood oranges

2 watermelon radishes, or other radishes (about 200g in total)

1 teaspoon fine sea salt

250g purple kale (or green kale or cavolo nero)

3 tablespoons fruity olive oil

2 teaspoons nutmeg syrup

¼ teaspoon ground cinnamon

½ teaspoon nigella seeds

Cut the top and bottom off each blood orange, then use a very sharp knife to cut down the fruits and remove the skin and pith. Follow the curve of the fruit and take off as little of the flesh as you can. Cut along the membranes to release the segments, put them into a bowl and pour over the juices left on your chopping board. Squeeze the skins over to get out every bit of blood orange juice and flavour.

Peel the watermelon radishes and trim to reveal their vibrant flesh. Slice them as thinly as you possibly can, using a mandoline, vegetable peeler or sharp knife – whatever works best for you. Add to the blood oranges and toss them together with the fine sea salt.

Pull the kale leaves away from their ribs. Shred the leaves and put into a serving bowl or a plate. Give them a pinch of salt, then use your hands to massage the kale for a minute. You'll feel it wilt and soften.

Lift the radishes and blood orange segments out of their juices and arrange over the kale as artfully (or not) as you please. Whisk the olive oil, nutmeg syrup and ground cinnamon into the left-behind juices. Taste and add more syrup or cinnamon as needed – how much you need will depend on the juiciness of your oranges. You want the dressing to be sweetly punchy. Pour it over the salad.

Toast the nigella seeds in a dry frying pan for barely a minute, scatter them over the salad and serve.

Charred pineapple and soused mackerel with cucumber and mint

Using fruits in savoury dishes is always a balancing act of judging how their inherent sweetness can temper or accentuate other flavours. Pineapples, being especially sweet, are useful as a counterpoint to acidity and sourness, so they do a super job partnered here with mackerel fillets soused in vinegar. Diced cucumber makes a great accompaniment to the mackerel that is part salad, part salsa. This dish has a really lively bounce of flavours.

As the mackerel are soused rather than cooked in heat, you really do need the freshest fish you can get. In The Fishmongers chapter you'll find tips for choosing fresh fish and filleting your own round fish like mackerel (see page 26).

Serves 4 as a light main

4 mackerel fillets

1 tablespoon fruity olive oil

2 sprigs of dill

1 small red onion

250ml white wine vinegar
   or vermouth vinegar

1 bay leaf

1 teaspoon coriander seeds

½ teaspoon black peppercorns

For the salad

½ pineapple (about 500g)

1 ridge cucumber

2 sprigs of mint

3 tablespoons fruity olive oil

½ teaspoon finely chopped red chilli

First, souse the mackerel. Place the mackerel fillets skin side down in a shallow dish. Rub the oil into the flesh and sit the dill sprigs on top. Peel and thinly slice the onion into half-moons and put into a saucepan with the vinegar, bay, coriander seeds, peppercorns and a pinch of salt. Bring to a low simmer then pour over the fish, making sure the fish is immersed. Set aside to cool, then cover with non-PVC cling film and leave in the fridge for at least 6 hours or overnight. Remove from the fridge an hour before serving.

To make the salad, slice the pineapple into rings about 1cm thick. Run a knife around the inside edge of each slice to remove the skin and 'eyes'. Cut out the core of each slice and cut each ring in half. Place a large frying pan or griddle pan over a medium heat and let it get hot – don't add any oil – then char the pineapple pieces in batches for about 2 minutes on each side until nicely browned. Set aside.

Cut the cucumber in half lengthways and scoop out the seeds. Dice the cucumber and put into a mixing bowl. Lift the onion slices out of the sousing juice and add those to the cucumber. Dice the charred pineapple, roughly chop the mint leaves and add to the bowl along with the olive oil, chilli, and 4 tablespoons of the sousing juice from the mackerel. Season liberally with salt and mix.

To serve, lift the mackerel fillets out of the sousing juice and arrange on plates. Grind over some pepper and serve with the pineapple and cucumber alongside.

Hot and sour green papaya curry with prawns, by Worawan Kamann of Khanom Krok

The small khanom krok coconut pancakes that are a Thai street-food delight gave their name to the street-food stall that Worawan Kamann runs with her husband, Michael. There you might find Worawan working with the distinctive dimpled pans they are made in, or serving up their curries, laabs and noodle dishes.

If Worawan isn't there, she's most likely found over at Raya selling the most exciting breadth of Southeast Asian store cupboard essentials and fresh ingredients, and doling out advice to anyone needing tips on how to use them.

Krachai, listed here, is a slightly unusual ingredient, perhaps, but one that Worawan urges you to seek out if making this dish. Also known as fingerroot, it is part of the ginger family. Note that you will have more chilli paste than you need for this recipe, but it keeps in the fridge for 7–10 days and also freezes well. Try it with white fish, or vegetables such as green beans or cauliflower.

Serves 2 as a main

For the gaeng som chilli paste

50g dried long Thai red chillies

10g salt

1g turmeric root

70g krachai (see introduction)

100g red shallots

20g shrimp paste

For the curry

150g green (unripe) papaya

100g raw shell-on king prawns (4–5 per person)

400ml fish stock or water

100g white fish fillet, eg. sea bream or bass

40g gaeng som chilli paste

30ml tamarind sauce

30g palm sugar

2 teaspoons fish sauce

½ teaspoon salt

First, make the gaeng som chilli paste. Cut the chillies in half lengthways and remove the seeds. Pound the chilli and salt in a mortar with a pestle until well mixed. Peel and chop the turmeric root, krachai and red shallots. Gradually add to the chilli, pounding to combine, and finally add the shrimp paste. Keep pounding until all the ingredients form a fragrant paste.

Now to prepare the curry. Wash the papaya thoroughly, remove the stem and peel the away the skin. Cut the unripe fruit in half lengthways and scoop out the seeds with a spoon. Cut the flesh into thin slices.

Rinse, peel and devein the prawns, then remove their heads and set aside.

Place the fish stock (or water) in a saucepan over a medium heat and bring to the boil. Add 30g of the fish fillet and poach gently for a couple of minutes until it is cooked, then turn off the heat and remove the fish with a slotted spoon. Pound the fish in a pestle and mortar until smooth. Cut the remaining fish fillet into large dice.

Bring the stock back to the boil, then add the chilli paste and the pounded fish. Once it comes to the boil again, add the sliced papaya, cover the pan with a lid and simmer for about 10 minutes until the papaya softens – the pulp becomes clearer when it is ready. Season with the tamarind sauce, palm sugar, fish sauce and salt. Finally, add the raw prawns and diced fish and simmer over a low heat for a couple of minutes until just cooked, then serve with jasmine rice.

Perfect jasmine rice for two

150g jasmine rice

175ml water

Rinse the jasmine rice twice, then put into a saucepan with the water. Bring it quickly to the boil, then cover with a lid, reduce to a low heat and cook for 12 minutes. When cooked (all of the water will have been absorbed), remove from the heat and allow to rest with the lid on for a further 10 minutes, then gently fluff up the rice so as not to break the grains.

Roast duck legs with spiced quince and charred sprout tops

Quince are often described as being a bit like apples, and a bit like pears, which seems to me to be selling quince a bit short – they are a glorious fruit in their own right and to be prized. Their hard, bitter flesh has to be cooked to reveal its flavour. Here they are mulled in wine and spices that exaggerate the quince's own tendency to turn a little pink upon cooking.

This is a dish where the various elements meld and contrast and complement before they even hit the plate. The greens cook in the fat the duck legs release into the pan, the finishing sauce is made with the liquor the quinces poached in – it all comes together.

Serves 4 as a main

4 large duck legs

1 fennel bulb

1 red onion

200g sprout tops (if they have any tiny sprouts attached to them, use those too)

For the poached quince

400g quince (1 or 2 fruit, size depending)

½ orange

1 tablespoon black peppercorns

2 bay leaves

1 sprig of rosemary

1 star anise

1 cinnamon stick

1 teaspoon juniper berries

2 tablespoons honey

250ml red wine

First, poach the quince. Scrub the quince under cold running water. Peel them, cut into quarters or sixths (depending on the size of the fruit) and remove the core, then put each piece into a bowl of cold water to stop them turning brown. Use a vegetable peeler to remove the peel from the orange in strips, taking as little of the white pith as possible. Put the pared peel and the juice of the half orange into a medium saucepan along with the peppercorns, bay leaves, rosemary, star anise, cinnamon, juniper berries, honey and red wine. Bring to a simmer over a medium heat, then add the drained quince pieces. Add 150ml water or however much is needed to submerge the fruit. Sit a piece of greaseproof paper on top of the fruit, put a lid on the pan, and simmer for 10–15 minutes or until the quince pieces are tender.

Remove the quince with a slotted spoon and set aside. Strain out and discard the orange peel, herbs and spices, but keep the poaching liquor. You'll need 150ml of it for this recipe, but the rest can be reduced and kept in the fridge for pouring over ice cream, desserts or topped up with soda water for a drink.

Preheat the oven to 170C fan/190C/375F/gas mark 5.

Pat dry the skin of the duck legs and season the tops of the legs with salt. Put a flameproof casserole dish or large frying pan over a medium heat to get hot. There's no need to add any oil. Sit the duck legs in skin-side-down. Season the side facing you and leave for 10 minutes for the fat to begin to run and the skin to brown. Turn them over and transfer to the oven, uncovered, for 35–40 minutes. Trim the fennel, peel the onion, thickly slice them both and then, halfway through the duck roasting time– remembering the pan handle(s) will be HOT – add them to the duck pan, tossing them in the released duck fat.

The duck legs are ready when their internal temperature tested with a probe thermometer is 74C and the juices run clear (pierce them in the thickest part of a leg with a sharp knife to test). Lift them out of the pan onto warmed plates, cover and set aside to rest while you prepare the sprout tops. The fennel and onion can either travel with the duck legs, or stay in the pan to continue cooking with the sprout tops.

Roughly chop the sprout tops. Put the pan the duck cooked in over a medium heat on the hob. Saute the sprout tops in a couple of tablespoons of the duck fat (spoon out any excess), until tender and lightly charred. Slice the poached quince into lengths about 1cm thick and, when the sprout tops are nearly done, slip the quince slices into the pan to heat through. Divide everything in the pan between the warmed plates with the duck.

Pour 150ml of the reserved quince poaching liquor into the pan the sprouts just cooked in and bubble over a high heat to deglaze the pan and reduce to a sauce. Pour over and serve straight away.

Sprout tops are the rosettes of leaves you find at the top of a sprout stalk and are definitely not to be discarded. Other vegetables you could use include cavolo nero, chard leaves, savoy cabbage or collard greens.

The Fruiterers

Borough Market – The Knowledge

Fig and liquorice sorbet

Plumply sweet black figs are very much the star here, so naturally sweet that relatively little extra sugar is added. Liquorice is just the undertone, enhancing the flavour of the figs and giving depth. (If you are a liquorice lover and that is at all disappointing to read, simply add a little more of Spice Mountain's liquorice powder.)

The optional egg white gives the sorbet a slightly smoother texture. But if you don't want to use it, any lack of egg white air is more than compensated for by churning the sorbet in an ice-cream machine.

Makes about 700ml

3 liquorice roots

80g caster sugar

550g black figs

1 teaspoon liquorice powder

1 egg white (optional)

Peel the liquorice roots with a vegetable peeler. Put them into a saucepan along with the sugar and 250ml water, heat until the sugar has dissolved, then cover and turn off the heat. Leave for 30 minutes for the roots to infuse the sugar syrup with flavour.

Use that time to prepare the figs. Peel them by lifting up a little of the skin near the stem and pulling it down the fig. Repeat all the way round and don't worry if you don't quite get all the skin off. Cut off the stem. Repeat for all the figs, then roughly chop them and put into a large mixing bowl.

When the 30 minutes infusing time is up, discard the liquorice roots and stir the liquorice powder into the syrup along with a pinch of salt. Use a hand-held blender to start pureeing the figs, adding the syrup as you go along. (Or you could do all this in a stand blender, of course.)

Chill the fig and liquorice puree for at least 1 hour. If you are using the egg white, whip it to soft peaks in a bowl shortly before you want to churn the sorbet.

Churn the sorbet in an ice cream machine according to the manufacturer's instructions, adding the whipped egg white towards the end if you are using it. Spoon into a container and freeze.

The sorbet will serve best if you let it sit in the fridge for about 10 minutes before scooping out.

Apple snow with fennel and rosewater biscuits

This elegant dessert is well named – from the first spoonful it really is as light as snow. The trick is to choose apples whose flesh will collapse and fluff-up on cooking. That's as much why some apples are considered cooking apples (rather than eaters) as any difference in sweetness. Bramley apples have become rather ubiquitous as far as British cooking apples go, but as the autumn harvest arrives at the Market stalls, so will many other varieties. As ever, ask what will be good.

Serves 6

For the apple snow

1 unwaxed lemon

3 large cooking apples, such as Cox's
    orange pippin, Discovery
    or Bramley

80g caster sugar

2 egg whites

100ml double cream

1–2 tablespoons demerara sugar,
    to serve

**For the fennel and
rosewater biscuits**

1½ teaspoons fennel seeds

90g butter, at room temperature

45g caster sugar, plus extra
    for dusting

180g plain flour, plus extra for dusting

1½ teaspoons rosewater

1 tablespoon dried rose petals

*You will need 6 individual
serving glasses*

Grate the lemon zest into a saucepan, then halve the lemon and squeeze in its juice. Peel and core the apples and chop into chunks. As you go along, put them into the pan with the lemon and stir around so that the acidic juice stops the apple turning brown. Add the sugar, cover the pan, and cook over a medium heat for 10 minutes until the apples are soft and starting to collapse. Remove from the heat, blend until smooth and set aside to cool.

Put the egg whites in a spotlessly clean bowl and whisk until they form meringue-like stiff, glossy peaks. In a separate bowl, whip the cream until stiff. Use a metal spoon to gently fold the smooth apples, egg white and cream together, being sure to keep as much air in it all as possible. Spoon the snow into whatever glasses you will be serving it in and chill for at least a couple of hours (but not more than about 4 hours or the snow will start to split). This gives you ample time to make the biscuits.

Heat a small dry frying pan over a medium heat, add the fennel seeds and stir them around for barely 20 seconds to toast and release their flavours. Take care they don't burn. Tip the toasted seeds out of the pan and set aside.

In a large mixing bowl, beat together the butter and caster sugar until light. Sift in the flour, add the toasted fennel seeds and rosewater and mix together until it forms a smooth dough. Shape into a flat circle, wrap in non-PVC cling film and chill for at least 30 minutes.

Preheat the oven to 160C fan/180C/350F/gas mark 4 and line a baking sheet with baking paper.

Roll out the dough on a lightly floured surface to a thickness of 5mm. Cut out 12 biscuits with a 5cm round cutter and transfer the biscuits to the baking sheet. Bake for 15 minutes until firm but still pale. Transfer to a wire rack. Chop the rose petals and dust them over the biscuits with more caster sugar while the biscuits are still warm.

To serve, sprinkle the demerara sugar over the snow and serve with the fennel and rosewater biscuits alongside.

A late summer crumble with pedro ximénez custard

I always think the best crumble of the year is the first after high summer's hot-pudding break, just as autumn beckons in the air. Late summer fruits make for wonderful crumble. I've gone for plums and blackberries here, but if they were still around, I'd add or replace those with any of the summer berries and currants. Then, as the seasons' produce changes, they'll give way to apples, pears, rhubarb…

I have been known to nestle some chocolate nibs in among the fruits or the crumble topping. Subliminally inspired, perhaps, by Market trader Humble Crumble, whose crumbles never fail to hit the sweet spot of nostalgia plus innovation. It's a winning combination as the queues for their crumbles will testify.

Serves 4–6

150g plain flour

80g cold butter, plus extra
    for greasing

50g ground almonds

75g demerara sugar

75g rolled oats

1 tablespoon anise seeds

750g plums

200g blackberries

1½ tablespoons light soft brown sugar

For the custard

500ml whole milk

1 vanilla pod

5 egg yolks

60g caster sugar

2 tablespoons pedro ximénez sherry

You will need a 1.5–2-litre capacity baking dish

First, the crumble topping. Put the flour into a mixing bowl, add the butter and use your fingers to rub both together until it feels like breadcrumbs. Mix in the ground almonds, demerara sugar, rolled oats and anise seeds, add a pinch of salt, then set aside.

Preheat the oven to 180C fan/200C/400F/gas mark 6. Grease your baking dish with the extra butter.

Remove the stones from the plums, cut the flesh into chunks however large you like your crumble fruit to be, and mix in the baking dish with the blackberries. Scatter over the soft brown sugar, then top with the crumble mix. Bake for 30–40 minutes, until bubbling and browned.

Meanwhile, make the custard. Pour the milk into a saucepan. Split the vanilla pod in half lengthways and scrape out its seeds. Add the seeds and pod to the milk, bring to a low simmer, then turn off the heat and set aside for 5 minutes to infuse.

Whisk the egg yolks and caster sugar together in a bowl. Discard the vanilla pod, then pour a little of the warm milk into the egg yolk mix and whisk to combine. Gradually add the rest of the milk, whisking continuously, then pour into a clean pan. Set that over a gentle heat and stir constantly for 8–10 minutes, taking care not to let the custard simmer at any point, until it begins to thicken and has the consistency of single cream - remember it will thicken a little more as it cools down. Whisk in the pedro ximénez sherry and serve with the crumble.

Any extra crumble topping freezes well and can be used straight from the freezer. It's often a good idea to intentionally make too much so you have crumble on stand by.

Pineapple and rum upside-down cake

Also known as pina colada cake and as fabulously retro as that the name suggests.

The sweetness of pineapple benefits from a bit of a char at the beginning, for caramelisation and colour, just as in the mackerel and pineapple recipe on page 183. But beyond the charring, the two recipes go in very different directions very quickly.

The cake becomes more of a pudding if served warm with the custard from the crumble on page 192 – using rum (more rum!) instead of that recipe's pedro ximénez sherry.

Makes 10–12 slices

1 pineapple (about 900g)

300g butter, at room temperature

210g soft light brown sugar

110g caster sugar

250g self-raising flour

1 teaspoon baking powder

4 medium eggs

75ml dark rum

30g icing sugar

2 tablespoons organic
　 desiccated coconut

You will need a 25cm or 26cm springform cake tin

Trim off the pineapple's top and bottom then slice the pineapple into rings about 1cm thick. Run a knife around the inside edge of each slice to remove the skin and 'eyes', then cut out the core. Now have a practice run at sitting the slices in the cake tin to get an idea of how you will be positioning them, and how you want to cut them to fit. Place a large frying pan or griddle pan over a high heat and let it get hot – don't add any oil – then char the pineapple pieces for about 2 minutes on each side until nicely browned. Work in batches if you need to. Set the pineapple aside.

Preheat the oven to 160C fan/180C/350F/gas mark 4.

Melt 50g of the butter and 100g of the soft light brown sugar in a small saucepan. Pour it over the base of the tin, swirl or brush round to cover and – working quickly, before the sugar has time to set – sit the pineapple slices in their pre-determined positions. Set aside.

Put the rest of the butter into a large mixing bowl. Add the remaining brown sugar and the caster sugar, and beat with a wooden spoon until lighter in colour and texture. Into another mixing bowl, sift the flour, baking powder, and a pinch of salt. Beat the eggs into the butter mix one at a time, adding a spoonful of the flour each time. Fold in the rest of the flour, adding just a splash of the rum if you need to loosen the mixture a little so that it drops smoothly off a spoon.

Spread the batter over the pineapple in the cake tin and bake for about 50 minutes until risen and just about firm to the touch. Remove from the oven and sit the tin on a wire rack. Run a knife around the edge to loosen the cake, then leave it for 5 minutes before turning out onto a board or plate and removing the cake base.

Drizzle 25ml of the rum over the cake, using a skewer to make holes for it to sink into. Heat the rest of the rum with the icing sugar in a small saucepan. Let it bubble to reduce to a syrup and pour that over the cake.

Decorate with desiccated coconut – half while the cake is still warm, half once it has cooled. The cake will keep in an airtight tin for up to 3 days.

Candied citrus

All those spectacular citrus fruits on pages 176–7 pack as much (perhaps even more) flavour into their peel as their flesh. Making candying their peels a great way of preserving all that fabulousness.

The oranges, lemons or bergamot in the recipe here could be swapped for yuzu or citron. If you want to candy pomelo, bear in mind that they are the largest of the citrus fruits so just one or two of those would be enough. (And / or you could always use the pomelo to make the cocktail bitters on page 126.)

Winter citrus appears on the stalls just in time to make this candied peel to use in your festive baking. Try rolling the candied peel in sugar or dipping into dark chocolate.

**Makes about 300g
(dried weight of peels)**

2 oranges

2 lemons

1 bergamot

900g granulated sugar

*You will need 1 x 300g jar, sterilised
(or 2 jars if storing in syrup)*

Quarter the fruit by slicing from top to bottom. Prise the peel away from the flesh – see below for ideas for using the fruit flesh.

Put the peels into a large pan, cover with cold water, bring to a rolling boil and bubble for 2 minutes. Drain in a colander, rinse out the pan and repeat this process a total of five times. It is important to keep rinsing the pan and changing the water to remove the peels' bitterness as well as to tenderise it.

Drain the peel one last time and leave it to cool for a few minutes. If there are pieces with excess white pith or bits of stringy fruit membrane still attached, they can be lifted off at this stage by gently running a teaspoon over the pith side of the peel.

Put 450ml water into a large pan and add the sugar. Heat until the sugar has dissolved and the syrup looks clear. Add the peel, bring to the boil, then reduce the heat and simmer gently for 1½ hours, stirring occasionally. The peel will become translucent and look almost like stained glass. Remove from the heat and leave it to cool in the syrup in the pan.

Transfer the peels and syrup to sterilised jars for storage, making sure each piece is submerged. The undried peel can be kept in its syrup for several months.

To dry the peel out before using it: lift each piece from the jar and run your fingers along its length to draw off excess syrup, then lay the pieces on a wire rack for at least a day at room temperature to completely dry out.

Once dried into candied peel, it can be stored for up to 8 weeks in an airtight container.

Don't waste the gorgeous fruit flesh. Use for salads and cakes, or juice it and freeze. Note that bergamot flesh / juice can be used as you would lemon.

Greengages in bay, cardamom and calvados

This recipe is very much in keeping with the philosophy behind all the fruiterers at the Market: buying fruits when in their peak season and preserving them to be able to enjoy later.

Bottling fruits in alcohol is a great way of doing exactly that, especially for the greengages, which aren't around for very long. You could do the same for other plums, or the mirabelles and rainier cherries included in our round-up of stone fruits on page 174. Pears are also good to bottle, but poach them first.

Enjoy the bottled fruits as a dessert or with ice cream – and remember, the fruit-suffused alcohol is a very delicious digestif.

Fills 1 x 1.5 litre jar

150g demerara sugar

12 green cardamom pods

1 teaspoon whole black peppercorns

2 bay leaves

750g greengages, without blemishes

750ml calvados

You will need a 1.5-litre storage jar, sterilised

First make the spiced syrup. Pour 350ml water into a large saucepan, add the sugar and heat gently until it has dissolved. Lightly crush the cardamom pods then add them to the pan along with the peppercorns and bay leaves. Rapidly boil the liquid in the pan for about 10 minutes until it has reduced to about 150ml, to make a rich syrup. Allow the syrup to cool to room temperature.

Prick each greengage two or three times with a skewer, then put them into the sterilised jar. Pour over half the calvados, then add the sugar syrup and all its spices to the jar and stir gently. Add more calvados until the greengages are submerged. Seal, label and date, and store somewhere cool and dark for 2 months before using. Shake occasionally and check that the greengages remain below the liquid line – add more calvados if you need to.

They'll keep somewhere cool and dark for up to 6 months.

Borough Market – The Knowledge

Drinks

Sweet wines

The simplest, most straight forward advice is so often the most useful when thinking about wine and food matching. Like this on sweet wines from Richard Cartwright, who runs Cartwright Brothers Vintners at the Market (and is the son of Martin Cartwright, company founder alongside his brother David).

'A good sweet wine – with its many styles from off-dry to intensely sweet – should have a nice balance between sweetness and acidity. When food pairing with a sweet wine, the wine should unite with the food or contrast and add something to the experience.'

Think about Sauternes or Monbazillac – sweet French wines whose characteristics of marmalade, honey, vanilla and lychee partner fantastically well with desserts that share some of those flavour profiles. Yet they are just as happy poured alongside fattier savoury dishes, where their acidity helpfully and deliciously cuts through the fat and the sweetness.

THE STORE CUPBOARD II

For decades, Colombian coffee farmers have been subjected to economic exploitation. Yet when it's properly, ethically supported, coffee farming offers a way for rural Colombians to earn an income from a regular crop and combat the turmoil brought about by a decades-long civil war. The mission of Eduardo Florez and The Colombian Coffee Company is to achieve just that.

How ethics and quality intersect

Eduardo Florez, The Colombian Coffee Company

Coffee is one the world's most volatile commodities, second only to oil. But, unlike oil, the volatility of coffee is borne by the growers, not the consumers. They receive the day's prices, which are determined by the futures market. At the moment, the price they're being paid for their coffee is almost the same as in 1983. Even fair trade schemes only offer a premium on top of the market price, but sometimes market prices are way below the production costs. Yet whenever the price of Colombian coffee is high, buyers will switch to sourcing coffee from elsewhere in the world.

That's one reason commercial coffee houses work with blends, rather than showcasing individual varieties. It's purely economics. That's why, even though demand is growing and Londoners are drinking coffee like crazy, what we see is profits for the coffee industry in this part of the world and poverty in coffee-growing communities. I believe that by increasing quality, farmers can escape this trap. For as long as they are producing coffee of poor quality, they will be price takers: commercial coffee buyers will buy their coffee, over-roast it and blend it to

mask imperfections. Coffee farmers get less money, and consumers get bad-quality coffee.

In Colombia, we only grow arabica coffee, and we have the largest year-round production in the world thanks to the country's geography and latitude Yet within 'arabica' there are 56 different single varieties, and Colombia is host to numerous microclimates, so much so that two farms 5km apart could produce the same variety of coffee with very different tasting notes. By showcasing individual varieties and creating a demand for them, we can encourage farmers to focus on quality rather than quantity.

Encouraging demand for more single varieties gives us the chance to have more interesting coffee notes. If coffee is good quality, it doesn't need to be blended, and it doesn't need to be darkly roasted. That dark, shiny look that beans often have is actually a sign that they've been over-roasted. Our coffee is only ever roasted lightly.

Education is key, both here and in Colombia. Most people in the UK don't understand that the coffee they're buying is a blend and that the monoculture farming that produces it is

"
Londoners drink coffee like crazy, but what you see is profits for the coffee industry and poverty in coffee-growing communities.

> "Most people don't know that the coffee they're buying is a blend and that the monoculture farming that produces it is terrible for the environment.

terrible for the environment. When you see photographs of coffee plantations where only coffee is being grown, you see how exposed the soil is to the sun, which causes it to erode quickly. This means farmers need expensive fertilisers, and it also means a loss of biodiversity.

The quality of the arabica coffee cherry is better if it is grown under shade. By cultivating trees, such as banana, guanábana and citrus, farmers can provide shade for the coffee plants and fruit to eat or sell. Having a variety of crops means the farmers are less exposed to the volatility of coffee prices; greater biodiversity means more flowers to attract more insects and birds. Leaves falling from the bigger trees to the floor generate a layer of natural organic fertiliser, so the farmers don't need to invest as much money in chemical fertilisers. It is a beautiful circle in which value is attached to things that are lost in a monoculture.

If coffee growers remain poor, the pickers they employ will make no effort to collect cherries that are in the best possible condition; they'll put anything in the basket, even if the fruit is rotten or green. Nature doesn't work to business timescales. An organic harvest can last more than the two days planned. The longer the pickers wait, the more ripe, red and round the cherries. If farmers receive more money for their coffee – and pay more to the cherry pickers – they can afford for the selection process to be better. The result is better coffee.

Again, it is a beautiful cycle – but it can only keep going if farmers produce high-quality coffee and buyers understand and value its quality. That is why, as well as paying above market prices, I teach farmers English business language and the vocabulary of coffee tasting and valuation so they can describe their coffee to potential buyers and get the best price for it. The farmers benefit, their communities benefit, but so too do the people who get to enjoy this amazing drink.

Five dried chillies

Piri piri

Character Sold at Spice Mountain, this small, fiery chilli packs a punch, particularly when crushed.

Uses Extensively used in African, Chinese and southeast Indian cuisines. Good for making chilli oils and sauces. A versatile all-purpose chilli.

Kashmiri

Character A mild chilli that imparts more of a warm glow than a fiery heat. Another from Spice Mountain.

Uses Popular in Indian curries like rogan josh, and favoured as much for its deep red colour as its flavour. Traditionally ground into a paste or fried quickly in a little oil and used as a garnish for dal.

Arbol

Character Strong but clean heat, with grassy notes.

Uses Another all-rounder from Shop Padre, used in Cajun, Mexican and Creole cuisines to turn up the heat of stews and casseroles and make fiery sauces.

Pasilla

Character Rich but sweetly tangy – the name comes from the Spanish for 'raisin' – with a medium heat.

Uses Sourced by Changarro, pasilla is a common component of Mexican salsas and adobo and mole sauces, as well as partnering well with fruit and red meat.

Chipotle

Character A smoky and savoury Mexican chilli, with a definite heat.

Uses Imported by Shop Padre and widely used in Mexican cuisine, the chipotle is a smoked jalapeno. Its thick flesh is best suited to slow-cooked soups and stews, which benefit from the smoky depth it brings.

Food & Forest was born out of founder Charles Tebbutt's determination to further the practice of agroforestry – combining trees with livestock or arable crops – and thereby prove its potential to solve some of our most pressing environmental challenges. The result is an array of extraordinary nuts sourced from some of the world's most pioneering farms.

Charles Tebbutt

Food & Forest

At Food & Forest, you make a point of identifying on the label the specific variety of the nut. Why is nut variety so significant?

For most people, a walnut is just a walnut – just like 10 years ago a cup of coffee was just a cup of coffee. What we're trying to do is create an awareness of the contrasts that exist between different varieties of nut. Showing people who come to the Market that there is as much diversity in nuts as there is in coffee or apples is the big thing for us; it is, if you are into such mumbo-jumbo, our USP.

So how much of a bearing does a nut's variety really have on its appearance, texture and taste?

Take walnuts, for example. There is a huge difference between the walnuts of Grenoble in France, which are derived from three varieties of walnut tree, and the walnuts of California, which are mostly Chandlers. The ones we source from Grenoble's Isère valley are mild and creamy, and lower in tannins, so don't have the bitterness you usually associate with walnuts. The varieties we grow in our own orchards here in the UK are different again. On just one site, we grow over 20 walnut varieties, all of which are strikingly different. The Broadview is the strongest in flavour, with a great crunch; the Rita has a pinkish hue to the shells and a sweet, crunchy kernel; the bright pink Red Danube is a real showstopper, as is the Germisare, which looks like a nuclear warhead. It's huge.

Other nuts are similarly varied. Our Italian hazelnuts are the large, globular Tonda Gentile variety from Piedmont, where they're so prized that their cultivation is protected in European law, just like champagne. They look and taste vastly different from the green, citrusy English cobnuts we grow on our farm, even though they're from the same family.

You are major proponents of agroforestry. Does this method of farming impact on nut flavour and size?

The merits of agroforestry are not really about flavour, they're about the environment, about soil health. By experimenting in our own orchard in Kent, what we've found is that the biggest influence on taste is not so much how the orchard is maintained but how the nuts are handled post-harvest – the way they're treated when we take them from a green nut to a final roasted product. Nuts are similar to coffee, tea and chocolate in that way: a lengthy post-harvest production method is required to produce something delicious. What we have succeeded in showing, however, is that a low-input organic farm is capable of turning out some very tasty nuts and a fairly decent yield.

Does the timing of the harvest influence the finished product?

Ideally, you want the nuts left on the tree for as long as possible; if you harvest them too early, they won't have developed the oil content, which is where the flavour comes from.

If you're able to increase the oil content, you'll have a really great product: one you can bake and cook with as well as enjoy raw or roasted. That's easier said than done in the UK, because of the squirrels!

Why are nuts produced by large-scale commercial producers often so much drier than those found on your stall?

Part of the post-harvest process involves drying out the nuts to preserve them. In order to increase their shelf-life, most walnuts you find in the shops have been dried out to around 7 per cent moisture. By contrast, the French walnuts we buy are about 12 per cent moisture, making them creamy and rich, but at greater risk of rancidity. That's why our French producers tend to keep them in their shells; it means they keep better for longer.

What is the significance of the nuts you sell being salted and flavoured by hand?

It gives us the freedom to use the best possible ingredients in any combinations we want. The limitation of doing this by machine is that it can only work with a powdered substance that can be sprayed onto the nuts, and sometimes requires the use of edible glues. For example, instead of powdered chilli and garlic powder, we use ancho chilli flakes and fresh garlic, which we blend into a paste before coating the nuts by hand. They are miles apart in flavour.

HOW TO... brew a cup of filter coffee

'At Monmouth, we use 22g coffee for one cup of filter. You need a medium grind. Ideally, you'd grind the beans just before making it, as fresher coffee is always better, but we'll grind the beans for you if you don't have a grinder and it'll be good for a while. Getting your water to the right temperature is important. Too cold, and you won't extract its full flavour; too hot, and you'll get bitter flavours. You want water that's just off the boil – about 93C – so if you've boiled the kettle, let it sit for a couple of minutes.'

AJ Kinnell, Monmouth Coffee Company

Stallholder Ratan Mondal is passionate about shoppers understanding more about the tea they buy. Spend any time at Tea2You and he'll engage you in conversation about the environmental benefits of drinking tea over coffee, why tea is good for you, and so much more.

Making a perfect cup of tea

Ratan is also determined that we should all be able to make tea at home that's every bit as good as the cups poured at Tea2You. This is how he makes their first flush Darjeeling – and how he'd like us all to do it too:

> Store your tea in a sealed packet kept in a cool dry place. A kitchen cupboard is fine – the fridge isn't. Allow a large half-teaspoon of tea leaves for each cup.

> Pour over freshly boiled water, then add just a little cold water to bring the temperature down to 80–90C and allow more oxygen into the leaves.

> Let the leaves infuse for 2–3 minutes, then pour. Ratan is adamant not to use a strainer – let the leaves 'play inside your cup'.

> The leaves can be used twice and then should head to the compost bin.

Five spice blends

Shichimi togarashi

'In Japan you'll find shichimi togarashi on every restaurant table,' says Magali Russie of Spice Mountain. 'It's made with black and white sesame seeds, orange peel, sancho peppercorns, a bit of seaweed, ginger and chilli. It's a coarse blend and fairly spicy, though there are citrusy notes from the orange peel and sweetness from the ginger – and the seaweed makes it a little bit salty too. There's a lovely balance in there.' Magali suggests using it as you would salt and pepper on fish, meat or vegetables, cooking with it in stir-fries, or mixing it with soy sauce and mirin to drizzle onto pan-fried aubergine.

Chinese five-spice

Although used in savoury dishes, Chinese five-spice is made of sweet spices: fennel, cinnamon, clove, black pepper and star anise, the last of which is really the star of the blend. 'It's delicious in stir-fries – you just need a bit of shrimp powder and some soy sauce for saltiness,' says Magali. 'It's also good in Asian-style soups, not a laksa, but a pho. It's also very popular as a rub or seasoning for meat.'

Za'atar

Za'atar is a staple in the Middle East, where it's eaten with bread and oil, sprinkled on yoghurt and eggs, or used as a rub for meat. 'Ours is made by a small women's cooperative in the north of Jordan, in an area called Ajlun, which is very fertile and lush,' says James Walters of Arabica. 'There, the ladies harvest thyme and sumac, which is a berry from a small shrub, and make za'atar with them. The thyme is sun-dried and massaged with olive oil, and the sumac has the stone removed before it's crushed, which is unusual these days – large-scale producers crush the stone too.'

Ras el hanout

Ras el hanout roughly translates to 'grocer's top shelf': a blend of the most premium spices. As with many spice blends, there are loads of regional variations, but the core spices are cumin, ginger, turmeric, cinnamon, black pepper, coriander seeds, allspice, nutmeg, cloves and sometimes chilli to varying degrees. 'Some regions add all sorts of weird and wonderful things, like rosebuds or long pepper,' says James. 'It's good for marinades, spicing roasted vegetables and soups, and, of course, most famously, lamb tagine. We make small batches regularly for maximum freshness and punch.'

Jerk seasoning

'In Jamaica, we grew up with jerk. Jerk pork was to be enjoyed on the side of the road, with friends and a bottle of beer,' says Dawn Smith of Pimento Hill (pictured opposite). Jerk is the cooking style; jerk spice is the marinade. Meat, heavily spiced with pimento, scotch bonnet chillies and other flavours thrown in for balance, is slow cooked in a 'drum pan' or in a makeshift pit covered with pimento wood and sheets of zinc. 'Our jerk seasoning, which uses Jamaican pimento berries straight from the island, will take you there, without the hassle of travelling. You can marinate pork, lamb, chicken, tofu and vegetables. You can mix in honey for a bit of sweet heat, add rosemary or thyme for flavour, or add it to butter to marinate seafood. You can do quite a lot with jerk, actually, except make rice...'.

The Store Cupboard II

Five salts

Fleur de sel de Camargue

The name translates from French as 'flower of salt' – an apt description for this prized salt, which forms as a wafer-thin crust on the surface of salt marshes. Fleur de sel de Camargue is harvested in the Camargue, Provence, by skilled people called *sauniers*. 'If you can describe any salt as sweet, then this is it,' says Amy Harrison of Le Marché du Quartier. Use as a finishing salt, rather than for cooking. 'Duck mousse on toast with a shaving of truffle and a little pinch of fleur de sel is divine,' says Amy.

Sel gris

Whereas fleur de sel is harvested from the top of salt marshes, sel gris is the heavy, wet salt harvested from the bottom. Like fleur de sel, it is neither processed, washed nor bleached, and is rich in trace minerals on account of both the seawater and the clay lining of the salt beds. 'It is powerfully salty,' says Amy, 'so you want to use it earlier in the cooking process. It's also still moist, as they put it straight into bags after harvesting.'

Pink Himalayan rock salt

'Don't be deceived by the delicacy of its pink colour', says Magali Russie of Spice Mountain. 'Himalayan rock salt is 'strong and salty, meaning you can use less of it'. Harvested in the Himalayan foothills, its colouring is the result of iron oxide and other trace minerals, which also serve to blunt the sharpness of sodium chloride and give it a cleaner, more rounded taste. Use as a finishing salt or in cooking.

Cornish smoked sea salt

Cornish Sea Salt Co., based at Pol Gwarra on the Cornish coast, combines ancient salt-harvesting techniques with modern science by using sea-derived electrolytes to create the right conditions for sea salt crystals to form, then harvesting them by hand. 'The salt is taken straight from the sea water, so it's got all the goodness in it,' says Richard Vines of Wild Beef. Some of this sea salt is smoked over cherry and apple wood, lending its fresh mineral flavour a subtle barbecue tang.

Celery salt

A fresh and slightly grassy salt made from a blend of sea salt and celery seeds. 'It's best known for being used in bloody marys,' says Magali, but its potential extends far beyond that. 'It's perfect for adding to soups and salads or as a seasoning for meat or fish before grilling or pan-frying.'

Moong dal dosa with tomato chutney, by Gaurav Gautam and Sandhya Aiyar of Horn OK Please

Head to Borough Market Kitchen's Horn OK Please and from the moment you place your order what you get is the theatre of street food. The dosas are freshly made in front of you. Every order is put together to be exactly what that customer wants. There's an energy and dedication to the whole experience, and that's before you've even tasted Gaurav Gautam and Sandhya Aiyar's incredible vegetarian Indian street food.

This recipe is a Horn OK Please staple. A breadth of store cupboard ingredients come together in the dosa batter flecked with cumin seeds, its filling of masala potatoes and the spiced chutney.

Serves 6

For the dosa batter

400g yellow split moong dal

200g basmati rice

1 teaspoon cumin seeds

½ teaspoon ground turmeric

½ teaspoon chilli powder

1 teaspoon salt

50g piece of fresh ginger

2 garlic cloves

Handful of coriander leaves

For the tomato chutney

1½ tablespoons pitted dates

1 red onion

300g cherry tomatoes

300g fresh plum tomatoes

80g piece of fresh ginger

5 garlic cloves

1 tablespoon sunflower oil

½ teaspoon black mustard seeds

½ teaspoon cumin seeds

4 whole dried Kashmiri chillies

Small handful of coriander

To make the dosa batter, mix the yellow split moong dal in a bowl with the rice, add the cumin seeds, turmeric, chilli powder and salt, mix well, cover with water and leave to soak for 2 hours. After 2 hours, drain off the water and put the mix in a blender with the ginger, peeled garlic cloves and coriander leaves. Add a cup of room-temperature water and blend to make a fairly thick, coarse batter.

To make the tomato chutney, start by soaking the dates in water for 30 minutes. Meanwhile peel and dice the red onion, chopping the tomatoes, and crush the ginger and garlic. Then heat the sunflower oil in a wide-based frying pan or saute pan over a medium heat, adding the mustard seeds and cooking for about a minute until they start to pop. Add the cumin seeds and Kashmiri chillies and saute for a minute until the aromas are released, taking care not to burn the chillies. Add the diced red onion to the pan with a pinch of salt and sweat for 5 minutes, until the onion becomes translucent but has not coloured. Add the crushed ginger and garlic, then the chopped coriander, turmeric and curry leaves and cook for 2–3 minutes over a gentle heat, stirring, until the raw aroma of the garlic and ginger has been cooked out. Add the tomatoes and cook over a low heat for 10–15 minutes, stirring occasionally and adding water if it starts to dry out. The mixture should be softened and thickened to a ketchup consistency. Take off the heat, place in a blender with the drained dates and lemon juice and pulse to a fine, even consistency, adding Himalayan salt to taste. The chutney will keep for up to 5 days in the fridge and can be eaten hot or cold.

To make the filling: wash the potatoes and cut into 1cm dice, leaving the skin on. Heat the oil in a deep heavy-based saucepan over a medium heat, add the mustard seeds and after a minute, once they start to crackle, reduce the heat and add the turmeric, chilli powder, salt and diced potatoes. Mix well, increase the heat to high and cook for 10 minutes,

Cont. overleaf

½ teaspoon ground turmeric

4 or 5 curry leaves

Juice of 1 lemon

Himalayan salt

**For the masala potatoes
(the dosa filling)**

1kg floury potatoes

150ml sunflower oil, plus extra
    for cooking the dosas

1 teaspoon black mustard seeds

1½ teaspoon ground turmeric

1 teaspoon chilli powder

1 teaspoon salt

1 tablespoon ground coriander

1 tablespoon amchoor
(mango powder)

stirring frequently. Once the potatoes have softened a little, cover the pan and continue to cook over a medium heat for 15 minutes. Keep stirring at regular intervals so they don't stick to the bottom of the pan. Once they have cooked to a soft mush, stir in the ground coriander, cover and cook for another 2 minutes, then switch off the heat and stir in the amchoor. Keep warm until you are ready to serve.

To make the moong dal dosa, place a large frying pan (about 24cm) over a medium heat, add a few drops of sunflower oil and spread it around the pan using a damp piece kitchen paper. When the pan is hot, take a ladleful of batter, pour it in the middle of the pan and spread it outwards in a circular motion using the bottom of the ladle, just like a thin crepe. Let the dosa cook for about a minute, and once the dosa is ready, add some of the warm masala potatoes and roll it up, then cut it in half and serve with the tomato chutney as a dip. Repeat with the rest of the dosa batter.

Broth of white beans and winter greens

This broth manages to be hearty and healthy, comforting and delicious all at the same time. It's also a perfect example of why having dried beans on standby is so useful. Only a relatively small amount of them is used here, so I'd always cook extra to freeze or whizz into a dip....

The broth is finished with a drizzle of herb oil of the kind often seen on market stalls and that, again, is a good store cupboard standby. Serve with chunks of crusty bread for dunking. You can make the dish meat-free if you opt to not include pancetta.

Serves 4–6

125g dried cannellini or borlotti beans

1 leek

2 tablespoons olive oil

70g diced smoked or unsmoked pancetta (optional)

1 bay leaf

1 sprig of thyme

100ml amontillado sherry

2 floury potatoes (about 400g in total)

500ml chicken or vegetable stock (bought or see pages 82 and 147)

100g winter greens (kale, cavolo nero or savoy cabbage)

1 tablespoon freshly grated parmesan

2 tablespoons herb oil

Cook the beans as described on page 221. Drain and set aside.

Trim the leek, remembering the ends can be kept and used for stock. Slice it in half lengthways and then into semi-circles the approximate width of a pound coin. Heat the oil in a large saucepan over a low heat, add the leek and cook gently until softening. If using the diced pancetta add it now and allow to cook for a further 5 minutes until just browning. Add the bay leaf and thyme, then pour in the sherry. Bubble for a minute on a higher heat, then turn the heat back down.

Peel or scrub the potatoes, as you prefer. Cut them into whatever size you would like them to be in your finished broth, and add to the pan. Pour in the stock and 700ml water (or use a total volume of 1.2 litres of vegetable stock). Season well and simmer for 10–15 minutes until the potatoes are tender.

While the broth is cooking, shred the greens of your choosing.

Find and discard the bay leaf and thyme sprig. Stir in the drained beans, shredded greens, and parmesan. Give it another 3 minutes over the heat for the greens to wilt, then check the seasoning and serve. Finish with a drizzle of herb oil.

(This broth is hardly hard work, but you could, of course, take the even less effortful route and swap the dried beans for a jar of pre-cooked cannellini or butter beans, see tip.)

Dried and pre-cooked beans can be used interchangeably in recipes. As a rough guide, their dried weight doubles once cooked, so 250g dried beans gives you approximately 500g cooked beans.

More ways with dried beans

Dried beans are bagfuls of culinary potential. There's a lot to be said for having jars of pre-cooked beans on stand-by, but the dried ones will stand you in enormous culinary stead too.

Shop

Older beans take longer to cook because they have dried out that bit more, and some will just never reach tenderness no matter how hard you try. The likely youth of the dried beans is certainly one of the reasons I tend to buy mine at the Market. As ever, ask – or see if the packet gives you a harvesting date. Anything more than two years is considered a little old.

Types of beans can so often be interchangeable in recipes. Here are a few particularly useful / interesting ones to look out for:

Flageolet beans: These are haricots harvested before they are fully ripe. Flageolets are small, with a lovely green colour, and good flavour. They cook a little quicker than most beans, so need less time to soak and simmer.

Chickpeas, aka garbanzo beans: Not all chickpeas are equal, and therefore not all hummus is either. The quality and flavour of the one definitely depends on the other. Imagine how good hummus will be made from chickpeas harvested every year at organic farms in Greece, then get yourself over to Oliveology and pick some up along with their sensational tahini.

Gigantes / butter beans / judion: Three names for one glorious bean. They have thin skin, a gorgeously soft texture, and the ability to both give and take on flavour.

Fava beans: The dried form of broad beans.

Cook

Soak your beans in water overnight, or for at least 8 hours.

As a rough guide for 500g dried beans:

- First rehydrate them by soaking them in lots of water. Adding 1 teaspoon of bicarbonate of soda to the water will help them soften.

- Drain the beans and rinse.

- Simmer them in about 1.5 litres of water, and again you can add a little bicarbonate of soda to reduce the cooking time. You could also add herbs or a chopped onion to the pot to enhance the flavour. Go steady with the salt – it helps to shorten the cooking time, but can also toughen the skin and result in the beans having a bit of a floury texture.

- It will take 45–60 minutes for the beans to tenderise, depending on type and age. (Note that if you have a pressure cooker, the beans will be tender in a fraction of the time.)

- Once tender, the beans are ready to drain and use, or freeze them to use later.

Use

- All beans can be whizzed into wonderful dips. Marry their flavours with any combination of fruit vinegars, garlic, herbs, nuts, anchovies, parmesan, oils...

- Make a bean mash, perhaps adding grated courgette or sweetcorn kernels. Take your pick of seasoning – from lime juice, to soy sauce, to sherry vinegar. Serve with meat or fish dishes. Soft gigantes (aka butter beans / judion beans) make for the best bean mashes.

- Use for soups and stews, like the broth on page 219 or the Slow-cooked cuttlefish and white beans on page 47.

- Fava beans are essential for ful medames.

- Beans taken out of the pot just before being fully tender can finish cooking around a lamb shank (or other meat joint) and / or root vegetables, and will take on lots of flavour.

These uses, of course, barely scratch the surface of bean potential.

Muhammara and griddled prawns

Walnuts are the flavour foundation for this delicious Levantine dip. Shop for the freshest walnuts you can, and think about how their variety affects texture, colour and flavour. Yes, varieties of walnuts. Read Charles Tebbutt of Food & Forest on page 209 and you, like me, may never think about nuts in quite the same way again.

Aleppo pepper rather than another chilli is important for the dip's mellow spicing, gentle sweetness and the Syrian connection it shares with the dip. You could, though, roast your own bell or romano peppers rather than using jarred. Three would be enough.

Muhammara makes a terrific flavour bed for griddled prawns – page 18 might help you decide which to use. The chickpea flatbreads on page 294 go very well alongside too.

Makes about 350g muhammara –
enough for 4 as a dip, or as a small
plate with the griddled prawns

For the muhammara

60g walnut halves

1 x 450g jar roasted red peppers
(300g drained weight)

1½ teaspoons smoked paprika

¾ teaspoon dried Aleppo
pepper flakes

2 tablespoons pomegranate molasses

20g breadcrumbs (optional)

4 sprigs of dill

For the griddled prawns

8 raw shell-on king prawns or 4 tiger
prawns (or for other shellfish
see page 18)

2 tablespoons rapeseed or olive oil

½ lime

To make the muhammara, lightly toast the walnut halves in a dry frying pan, then put them into a food processor with everything except one of the dill sprigs. Add a pinch of salt and blitz to a rough paste. The breadcrumbs (if you are using them) will thicken it up. Taste for seasoning, then set aside at room temperature for at least one hour for the flavours to develop.

It will keep in the fridge for up to 3 days. Serve with the griddled prawns below (or as a dip), with the fronds of the reserved dill sprig scattered over.

To make the griddled prawns

Brush the prawns with the oil. Get a griddle pan (or barbecue, or just a frying pan) very hot. Add the prawns in and cook until pink all over. How long this takes will depend on the size of your prawns. Serve – shells on or off, as you prefer – on top of or beside the muhammara, adding a squeeze of lime juice and a smattering of salt flakes.

The Store Cupboard II

Oregano-poached peaches, halloumi and hazelnuts

There are fresh herbs, there are dried herbs, and then there are frankly incredible dried herbs. Into that last camp fall dried herbs that are produced to exceptionally high standards and don't just harness the flavour of the starting point, but elevate it. Those are the only dried herbs really worth having in your store cupboard.

This recipe goes for poaching fresh peaches with dried oregano, which brings even more depth of flavour than fresh oregano would. Given the choice, I use one of the beautiful dried sprigs at Oliveology, but their ground oregano is lovely too. The poaching liquor is then reduced to a fragrantly sweet syrup for pouring over tender peach slices and fried halloumi, and finished with seasoned toasted nuts and mint. Perfect for a hot day.

Serves 2 as a main, 4 as a side or small plate

2 teaspoons dried oregano
   (or an Oliveology dried sprig)

1 tablespoon honey

1 orange

2 peaches

40g skinned whole hazelnuts

1 tablespoon fruity olive oil

6 sprigs of mint

225g halloumi

Pour 500ml water into a medium saucepan. Add the dried oregano (or oregano dried sprig), the honey and two broad strips of zest from the orange. Bring to the boil and, meanwhile, quarter and stone the peaches. Put them into the water, lower the heat to a simmer and sit a piece of baking paper on top. Simmer for 7–10 minutes until the peaches are fully tender. Use a slotted spoon to lift the peaches out and set aside. If their skins start to flake away as they cool, just peel them off.

Strain the poaching liquor, discard the oregano and orange peel, then pour the poaching liquor back into the saucepan. Don't worry if a few pieces of oregano are left in the liquid. Boil over a high heat for 10–15 minutes to reduce to a syrup – you are aiming for about 75ml syrup.

While the poaching liquor reduces, toss the hazelnuts in the olive oil along with some salt flakes and freshly ground black pepper. Set a small dry frying pan over a low heat, then add the seasoned nuts and stir for 3 minutes or until they are just getting nicely toasted. Transfer to a bowl. Once they have cooled, roughly chop with the leaves from the mint sprigs. Cut the poached peach quarters into slices about 1cm thick.

Once the syrup is almost sufficiently reduced, cut the halloumi into 1cm-thick slices. Set the same frying pan the nuts cooked in back onto the heat, then add the halloumi pieces turning each over after 2 minutes or so once they are browned. You might need to do this in two batches.

Serve either on individual plates or on a large platter. Sit the halloumi on first, then arrange the peach slices prettily on top, scatter over the seasoned nut and mint mixture, and finish by spooning over your oregano-infused peach syrup.

Walnut and pomegranate baby aubergines with saffron quinoa

Spelt, barley, buckwheat, quinoa – they're all brilliantly useful store-cupboard staples for whipping up all kinds of salads and platters. It's quinoa's turn here, with a mix of red and white giving the dish variety of colour and texture.

At least half of the ingredients here are store cupboard treasures of different kinds that you'll find yourself calling on time and again for all kinds of cooking. I know you might only be getting one preserved lemon out of the jar to use here, but the others will do you good service for marinades, tagines and in the quick Store cupboard suppers on page 119.

Serves 4 as a main or 8 as a side or small plate

160g white quinoa

160g red quinoa

1 red chilli

Pinch of saffron

2 garlic cloves

80g shelled walnuts

1½ tablespoons tomato puree

2½ tablespoons pomegranate molasses

8–12 baby aubergines, depending on size and shape (about 600g in total)

4 tablespoons olive oil

2 red onions

1 tablespoon black mustard seeds

1 teaspoon ras el hanout

1 orange

1 teaspoon rosewater

1 preserved lemon

50g dried apricots

Handful of fresh dill

6 sprigs of mint

Rinse and drain the quinoa. Bring a large saucepan of salted water to the boil. Add the whole chilli, saffron and drained quinoa, stir and cook uncovered over a medium heat for about 14 minutes until just about nuttily tender. Drain and set aside in a serving bowl.

Peel the garlic cloves and crush with the back of a heavy knife. Use a pestle and mortar to work the walnuts and garlic into a paste with some salt. Mix in the tomato puree and 1½ tablespoons of the pomegranate molasses. Season well. Slice through the aubergines as if quartering them lengthways, but taking care not to cut through the stem. Open each one up like a flower and stuff with the walnut mix.

Heat 2 tablespoons of the olive oil in a large frying pan over a medium–high heat, get it hot, then carefully sit the aubergines in the pan and cook for a couple of minutes until blistering. Turn them so they blister all over. Pour 2 tablespoons water into the pan, put a lid on and let the aubergines cook for 20 minutes.

While the aubergines cook in the pan, finish preparing the quinoa. Peel the red onions and slice into thin half-moons. Heat the remaining 2 tablespoons of olive oil in a saucepan over a medium heat and cook the onions until soft and taking on some colour. Stir in the mustard seeds and ras el hanout, finish with the juice of the orange and the rosewater, and then stir all that through the quinoa. Finely chop the preserved lemon, apricots, dill and mint and stir those through the quinoa, keeping back a little of the herbs for garnish.

When the aubergines are ready, carefully lift each one out and onto the quinoa. Pour over any juices or stuffing left in the pan, followed by the remaining tablespoon of pomegranate molasses. Scatter over the reserved herbs and serve.

Beef skirt with coffee and chilli dry rub

Shopping for cuts of beef skirt, flank or bavette can be a little confusing as the names are often used interchangeably. Just know they all come from the abdomen of the cow and are all very well suited to this method of cooking: fast and rare. The beef is given a rub of coffee, Urfa chilli and other spices. They are rubbed into the meat a couple of hours before cooking, enhancing the beef's flavour and giving a fabulously smoky crust at the end of its minimal cooking time.

Serves 6 as a main

About 1kg beef skirt

2 tablespoons ground coffee

1 tablespoon Urfa chilli flakes

1 teaspoon wild sumac

1 teaspoon ground cumin

1 tablespoon soft dark brown sugar

1 tablespoon rapeseed oil

Start the rub up to 4 hours before cooking, and not less than 30 minutes.

Cut away any visible pieces of fat from the beef and (unless your butcher has done this already) pull away the thin membrane stretched over the meat. You don't need to get every last bit off, but get what you can. Sit the meat on a large chopping board or plate.

Mix together in a bowl the coffee, chilli flakes, sumac, cumin and brown sugar. Rub half into one side of the meat, pressing it into the gorgeous folds and pleats that give this cut its name. Carefully turn the meat over and repeat on the other side. Set aside until needed – room temperature is fine unless your kitchen is very warm.

When it is time to cook, sit a large frying pan or griddle pan on the hob over a medium–high heat. Scatter salt flakes over the uppermost side of the beef. Add the oil to the pan and – only when it is very hot, almost smoking – sit the beef into the pan, salted side down. Cook for 3 minutes, salt the side that's now facing up, then turn the beef to cook that side for a further 3 minutes.

Lift the beef onto a chopping board, pour over any juices from the pan, cover loosely with foil and rest the meat for at least 5 minutes and up to 10. Then slice the rested meat into thin strips to serve it, taking care to cut across the grain, which means finding the direction the muscle fibres are going in and cutting perpendicular to those. The meat will be gorgeously pink and exceptionally tender.

There's no need to make a sauce with this – the beef rub brings all its own flavour. And it is plenty juicy enough too. As cooking the meat takes so little time, I'd suggest you get ahead with sides before cooking the meat and keep them warm until the beef is ready. There's at least 5 minutes of beef resting time for anything that needs finishing / fast cooking.

Almost the most important part of this recipe is its last instruction – to rest the meat, then slice it against the grain. That's how you ensure this hard-working cut from the cow's diaphragm muscles is tender on the plate.

The Store Cupboard II

Oat milk and rosewater rice pudding with toasted granola

I first came across baldo rice at The Turkish Deli and couldn't wait to get home to try it in rice pudding. Sure enough, being a short-grain rice, it makes brilliant rice pud. It's partnered here with oat milk rather than the more traditional dairy milk I grew up thinking was non-negotiable. There's no going back for me now, though – oat milk makes this not just creamy but oatily nutty too.

That nuttiness marries with the toasted granola topping. Toasting granola which has already been toasted in its making might seem odd, but it softens the granola up a little and releases more flavours. Chloë Stewart at nibs etc. gave me her approval to do it, so that's good enough for me.

Serves 4–6 for dessert, or perhaps as breakfast if you're up early enough to put it in the oven and leave it

150g baldo rice, or other
   short-grain rice

750ml–1 litre oat milk, plus a little
   extra to serve

45g caster sugar

1 teaspoon rosewater

Nutmeg, for grating

100–150g granola (25g per serving)

You will need a flameproof baking dish of approx. 1.2-litre capacity

Preheat the oven to 130C fan/150C/300F/gas mark 2.

Sit the baking dish on the hob over a medium heat and add all the ingredients except the nutmeg and granola, using just 750ml of the milk initially. Bring to a low simmer, then transfer to the oven.

After 30 minutes, take the dish out of the oven, give the rice a stir, then grate half of the whole nutmeg over the surface. Return the dish to the oven and bake for another 30 minutes. Check how it is going, and if it looks to be getting a little dry for your liking, use a spoon to ease away an edge and pour a little more milk in. Return to the oven for up to a further 30 minutes – it is ready when the rice is tender and the top nicely browned.

Remove from the oven and let the rice pudding cool a little before serving, giving you time to toast the granola. Set a small frying pan over a low–medium heat, add the granola and gently toss for just a minute or so to release even more of its flavour.

Serve the rice pudding warm with the granola, and extra milk on the side for those who like their rice pudding that bit looser.

Whisky mocha charlotte

Charlottes were a 19th-century showstopper of a dessert, and are just as full of wow now. In this one, savoiardi biscuits (aka ladyfingers or boudoir biscuits) are dipped in whisky, then used to encase richly smooth chocolate mousse with a hit of espresso.

The end result is stunning, much sturdier than it looks (or you might fear), and proves the worth once again of having in your cupboard the Italian deli staples of savoiardi biscuits, good chocolate and coffee.

Makes 8–10 slices

275g dark chocolate (70 per cent cocoa solids)

6 medium eggs or 5 large eggs

75g caster sugar

275ml double cream

75ml freshly made espresso

200g savoiardi biscuits (about 24)

100ml whisky

80g caster sugar

2 teaspoons icing sugar, to serve

You will need a deep 20cm springform cake tin

First, make the mousse. Break the chocolate into a heatproof bowl suspended over a pan of simmering water (make sure the bowl isn't touching the water), and let it melt. Once the chocolate has melted, take the bowl off the pan and set aside.

Separate the eggs, putting the whites into a scrupulously clean mixing bowl and the yolks into a saucepan. Add the sugar and cream to the yolks, then use a hand whisk to get them nicely mixed together. Sit the pan over a low heat and stir continuously with a wooden spoon until the mixture is thick enough to coat the back of the spoon. Take off the heat, then stir in the melted chocolate and freshly made espresso.

Whisk the egg whites to meringue-like stiff peaks, then use a metal spoon to fold them into the chocolate. Work gently, quickly and thoroughly to combine them without losing the air. Chill the mousse mix you've just made for about 30 minutes.

To build your charlotte: stand the savoiardi biscuits around the inside edge of the cake tin so you can gauge how many you need to line it. Trim off one curved tip from each biscuit to give you a flat edge. Keep the trimmings. Pour the whisky into a shallow bowl and, working one by one, dip the non-sugared side of the biscuit into it. Straight away stand it in the tin, flat end down, whisky-dipped side facing inwards. Go all round the tin without leaving gaps and making sure it looks neat. Use more biscuits to fill the base, again dipping them in whisky first. Cut the biscuits to cover the base as fully as you can.

Spoon half the mousse inside the ring of biscuits. Scatter over the pieces of biscuit you trimmed off, then top with the rest of the mousse. Chill for at least 6 hours.

To make your spun sugar decorations, put a large piece of baking paper on the worktop. Heat the caster sugar in a saucepan over a medium heat and watch – but don't stir – as it melts, then turns golden. Working quickly, use a spoon to dribble spirals or strands onto the baking paper. Leave to cool and after a couple of minutes you will be able to ease them off the paper with a knife.

To serve, sit the cake tin on whatever you will be serving the charlotte on. CAREFULLY release the springform and ease the tin up and away. Tie ribbon around the charlotte – for looks, but also to help relieve any nerves that it might collapse before reaching the table. Although honestly, this isn't as delicate as it appears.

Arrange your spun sugar decorations on top, sift over the icing sugar and either slice into it straight away or put it back into the fridge until needed (in which case add the sugar decorations and icing sugar just before serving).

The Store Cupboard II

Jasmine tea loaf with salted lime butter

This recipe risks the wrath of Ratan Mondal by requiring the straining of the tea. That's not what he does in his skills guide on page 211 and knowing just how deliciously he makes his Tea2You tea I will always follow his guidance for a cup of tea to drink. For a tea to bake with, however, straining is the way to go.

It is the choice of jasmine tea, with its Darjeeling green tea leaves scented by jasmine buds and flowers that elevates this loaf into something special. The fragrance and flavour connect with the musky sweetness of the dried fruit. Then it's all finished off with the zesty, salty kick of the lime butter on top.

Makes 1 loaf

100g dried figs

100g dates

50g dried apricots

50g raisins

1 teaspoon jasmine flower tea leaves

300ml just-boiled water

250g self-raising flour

70g soft dark brown sugar

1 teaspoon mixed spice

¼ teaspoon salt

1 egg

For the salted lime butter

125g unsalted butter, at room
    temperature, plus extra
    for greasing

1 lime

¼ teaspoon salt flakes

*You will need 1 loaf tin of approx.
19 x 9 x 6cm*

*This salted lime butter will keep
happily in the fridge for a few days
and is also good for cooking or
finishing fish and vegetables.*

Use scissors to finely cut up the figs, dates and apricots into a mixing bowl, discarding their stones and stalks as you go. Add the raisins. Make the tea by immersing the tea leaves in the water. Allow to brew for 4 minutes, then strain and pour over the fruit in the bowl. Stir, cover with a cloth and set aside overnight, or for at least 6 hours, for the dried fruit to absorb most of the tea.

Preheat the oven to 160C fan/180C/350F/gas mark 4.

Grease the base and sides of the loaf tin and line with baking paper. Mix the flour, sugar, mixed spice and salt into the fruit bowl. Beat the egg and add that too. Mix thoroughly and then spoon into the loaf tin. Spread evenly and bake for about 1 hour – it's ready when springy to the touch in the centre, and a skewer inserted into the middle comes out clean.

Remove from the oven and leave to cool for 10 minutes in the tin, then transfer to a wire rack and take out of the tin, removing the paper too. Give it just another 10 minutes or so before trying to slice into it. The warmer it is, the crumblier it will be (which isn't necessarily a bad thing).

To make the salted lime butter, mix the butter with the grated zest of the lime and most but not all of the salt. Squeeze the juice of just half the lime and mix that in too. Wrap, roll and chill for 30 minutes to firm up. Serve with the remaining salt flakes scattered over, ready to be spread onto slices of the loaf.

Borough Market – The Knowledge

Borough Market – The Knowledge

Pomegranate margarita

A classic margarita (one of the daisy style of cocktails on page 129) is made with orange liqueur, but here that is switched up for pomegranate liqueur and its extra depth of flavour. You could use any fruit liqueur you find or like, you could use tequila or mezcal, but one tweak you absolutely must not make is to skip the salting of the rim of the glass. It is essential to the margarita experience that your taste buds get that salty hit first – so why not have a little fun choosing which salt to use.

Himalayan pink brings a kitsch colour-match to the pomegranate liqueur. That's my choice here. But then fleur de sel has a classic edge, or perhaps go for a smoked salt... There are more salts and salty thoughts on page 214.

Serves 1

2 teaspoons Himalayan pink salt

1–2 limes, depending on their size and juiciness

50ml tequila

25ml pomegranate liqueur

Mint leaves, to serve

Lightly crush the salt using a pestle and mortar. Sit the salt in a shallow dish. Halve one lime and run the flesh-side of one half around the rim of your glass then turn the glass upside-down and sit it in the salt so the salt sticks to the rim. Put the glass into the fridge to chill while you carry on fixing the drink.

Squeeze the juice from the limes – you want to end up with 25ml. Put lots of ice into a cocktail shaker or measuring jug, pour over the lime juice, tequila and pomegranate liqueur. Shake or stir vigorously for a minute. Strain the drink into the chilled, salted glass and garnish with mint to serve.

Borough Market – The Knowledge

Drinks
Cider and perry

Nipping into The London Cider House for a glass of warming mulled cider is a winter ritual for many. In summer the stall beckons with the promise of something deeply refreshing. And year round it never fails to offer up a cornucopia of ciders and perries that go brilliantly with all kinds of foods.

Felix Nash of The Fine Cider Co. has worked with The London Cider House team for years. He is evangelical about how good cider and food can be together – with each sip of cider's inherent acidity acting as a cleanser for the palate.

As Felix says, a commercial cider might be only 35 per cent apple juice (the UK legal requirement). That's not really a whole lot of apple in your glass. To know what it is you are drinking, you need to look to one of the ever-increasing number of small producers who understand that provenance and production matter.

Felix and The London Cider House shared with me more thoughts on shopping for ciders and perries, and how to drink them:

Still / dry cider

Think of still ciders like wines, with apple variety and terroirs every bit as impactful as grapes are to wine. Herefordshire ciders, for example, are especially tannic and full-bodied. They're great with something similarly hefty (perhaps the beef skirt recipe on page 228 in this chapter), or pork dishes as a nod to the heritage of pigs being fed on apple pomace.

Serve at room temperature and their flavours will open up.

Ice cider

Most definitely a dessert cider but not just for serving with desserts. The mix of acidity and sweetness makes ice ciders terrific with savoury dishes too, and perhaps cheeses especially.

Not that ice ciders aren't for desserts. Chocolate and pastry make good alliances with ice ciders. A small glass alongside the Whisky mocha charlotte on page 232, for example, is a winning combination.

Sparkling cider

There's so much variety here, some being made in the traditional champagne method, others in the lower-intervention 'pet nat' style (see page 167). Think of sparkling ciders as being fruity alternatives for sparkling wines, with the breadth of possibilities – perhaps as a pre-dinner drink, for serving with fish or seafood, or using in cocktails.

Perry

Here it's the turn of pears rather than apples, with perries being that bit more delicate and citrusy on the palate. They'll often have notes of elderflower and grapefruit, and residual sweetness. They are excellent with anything in the fish or seafood line, goat's cheeses or salads. I'm definitely going to remember to seek out a perry next time I make the Oregano-poached peaches, halloumi and hazelnuts earlier in this chapter (page 224).

THE DAIRY

Hugh Padfield's great-grandparents established a traditional mixed farm in the foothills of the Cotswolds in 1914. In 1990, his father Graham decided to resurrect their tradition of cheesemaking, a tradition Graham, and now his son Hugh, have been building on to this day.

The craft of the cheese maturer

Hugh Padfield, Bath Soft Cheese Co

At the core of all good cheese is good-quality milk. Unlike intensive farming, which has such a huge negative impact on the animals and the land, the organic system we have here is one in which the cows are well looked after and can graze outside during the spring and summer. If cows are grazing on wildflowers and grasses, the milk they produce will be much creamier and more flavoursome than if they've been inside eating a maize mix. Our work as cheesemakers begins out there in the fields.

One of the things I'm always keen to point out is that while our milk here at Park Farm is pasteurised, our cheese is very much alive. Our pasteurisation process is very gentle – we only heat the milk to 63C, so it retains its true character. Also, our commitment to organic, pasture-based farming brings different flavours to our milk through the seasons.

This variability is part of what makes maturing a cheese such a complex challenge. There are so many variables: the milk, the starter cultures you add at the beginning of the cheesemaking process, and the temperature and humidity, which drive the development of the cheese. Subtle changes to these can make a tremendous difference, which the maturer needs to take into account for each cheese.

We source our starter cultures from small-scale producers here and in France. These bacteria digest the sugars in the milk, and in doing so they develop an array of flavours. What is fascinating is how the starter cultures interact with the naturally occurring moulds that grow on the cheese – something that is particularly noticeable with our soft cheese.

Bath Soft Cheese is salty and brittle when young, even when the mould has spread across the cheese like new snowfall. It takes a week for the mould to break down the paste, which encourages the bacterial soup inside to release its flavours. It's a lovely combination: the moulds introduce more garlicky, mushroomy flavours as they grow, which work perfectly with the lemony, chalky notes created by the starter culture and the curds. This will continue to change even after you've bought the cheese, getting stronger and more savoury in flavour. We have some customers who prefer to eat it the moment they buy it; others who keep it far beyond the suggested use-by date. It is absolutely a living thing.

"
Subtle changes to the milk, starter cultures and weather can make a tremendous difference, which the maturer needs to take into account.

> " The only way we can ever really know when a blue cheese is ready is by tasting it, which we do each Friday with a cheese iron.

A hard, aged cheese like our Wyfe of Bath works differently. Like a cheddar, it gets its flavour from the ageing process, which means we must work hard to minimise mould growth and encourage the cheese to dry out. Lots of hard cheeses are given an artificial rind to suppress mould growth, but we want to keep things as natural as possible, so instead we brush the cheeses regularly using a bespoke brushing machine. Our standard cheese is aged for four to six months; our extra-mature for over a year. The young cheese is very popular with children, as it's sweet and creamy with a bit of grassiness and hay, but the longer we age it, the stronger the fudgy, nutty flavours.

The maturing process for a blue cheese like our Bath Blue is particularly interesting. You have the starter culture, which gets the cheese going, as well as the penicillium roqueforti, which creates the blueing. The blue mould starts to grow five weeks into the make, after we pierce the cheese with needles, allowing air to enter. The curd is lemony and crumbly towards the centre, and softer and gooier towards the edge. Surrounding the cheese is a natural rind which develops of its own accord – a result of the yeasts, moulds and bacteria that live in the air, on the other cheeses, even on the skin of the cheesemaker. These bring a whole new range of biscuity, fungal flavours.

The development of the rind and the blue mould is affected by temperature and humidity, but it is also affected by the acidity of the curd, which can inhibit or accelerate the rate of growth. The only way we can really know when a blue cheese is ready is by tasting it, which we do each Friday with a cheese iron. Sometimes you can tell by picking it up and feeling the weight, but every so often we're surprised.

Unlike the Wyfe of Bath or the Bath Blue, the taste of the Merry Wyfe, our washed rind cheese, is dependent not on moulds or ageing, but on the rind. The rind is created not by a mould but by bacteria, known as B linens. This occurs in the surrounding environment, but we encourage its growth by washing the curds every day with salt water and my father's homemade cider, which provides nutrients on which the bacteria can grow. It's the rind that's responsible for that characteristically pungent aroma we associate with washed rind cheese. Over time – about 28 days – this rind develops a beautiful pinky-orange hue, which grows more and more vivid as it gets older; looking from the younger cheeses to the older cheeses in the maturing room is like watching the sun set.

Five butters

Cultured butter

The cultured butter at Northfield Farm is made in small batches by Grant Harrison at the Ampersand Dairy in Oxfordshire. 'Cream from the milk of Holstein and Jersey cows, Himalayan salt and lactic cultures. That's it,' says Dominic McCourt of Northfield Farm. Lactobacillus cultures are added to the cream and left to ferment before churning, lending the butter its rich, slightly tangy flavours and lengthy shelf life. After churning, the fermented cream is kneaded by hand with the salt before being shaped into fat pats.

Unpasteurised butter

The butter at Hook & Son is made from the cream of unpasteurised semi-skimmed milk, matured for between 24 and 48 hours before being churned. It's a sweet cream butter, so unlike cultured butter, no bacteria are added. 'Because it's raw, it develops a stronger, more savoury taste after a week or so,' says Stephen Hook. 'When it has that stronger flavour, it's delicious in mashed potatoes and scrambled eggs. If you prefer it mild, cut it into portions while it's still young and freeze them.'

Ghee

'Ghee is clarified butter: butter that has been heated until the moisture steams off and any impurities either come to the surface or sink to the bottom,' says Stephen of Hook & Son. The clear oil is poured through a muslin cloth and sealed in jars. Discerning customers buy their ghee in spring and summer. 'The best milk of the year is from April to June, which is when the grass is at its most luscious.' You won't find a 'use by' date on Stephen's ghee. 'We put the date it was produced. Ghee is over 99 per cent pure oil; nothing can survive in it, and it doesn't even need refrigerating.'

Mussels in lemongrass, galangal and turmeric broth, page 39.

Whey butter

Whey butter is 'a reflection of how, in dairy farms of yore, nothing went to waste during the cheesemaking process', says Bronwen Percival of Neal's Yard Dairy. Although most of the fat from the milk goes into the cheese, a small proportion will get lost in the whey. By collecting this 'whey cream' and churning it into butter, cheesemakers 'ensure they get every bit of yield out of the milk that they possibly can'. Neal's Yard Dairy sells two versions: clean, fresh Keen's Moorhayes butter from the makers of Keen's cheddar, and the more flavourful Appleby's whey butter from the makers of Appleby's Cheshire.

Flavoured butter

'Flavoured butter has long been a companion for filled pasta in northern Italy, as it adds to the flavour but doesn't overpower the filling,' says Giuseppe Palumbo at La Tua Pasta. When married with filled pasta, the starch from a splash of reserved pasta water combines with the fat from the butter, coating the pasta with a silky emulsion. 'The classic flavouring is sage, typically served with pumpkin- or spinach-filled pasta,' says Giuseppe. 'Lemon butter or chilli and garlic butter both go well with seafood fillings, and truffle is perfect with mushroom.'

For more flavoured butters to cook with, see miso butter (page 162), smoked garlic butter (page 150), and salted lime butter (page 234).

The Hook family own a small dairy farm in the Pevensey Levels, an area of permanent pasture teeming with rare species of flora and fauna. Father Stephen and son Phil farm organically, in harmony with the area's unique ecology, and produce raw milk: milk that has not been pasteurised.

Stephen Hook

Hook & Son

Why is the flavour of raw milk more pronounced than that of pasteurised milk?

By law, you can only buy raw milk if it comes from a single farm. That means you're getting the flavour of that farm, of what the cows have eaten. My cows are grass-fed. They roam on wild meadows, rushes and marshes and choose what they want to eat. If you're buying industrially produced pasteurised milk, it will have come from multiple cows from multiple herds. They will have been fed a specific diet to support high yields and productivity. All too often that diet is high in soy and grains and doesn't reflect the local area. Then pasteurisation kills off all the good bacteria in the milk and denatures the proteins. It ends up far removed from what it was intended to be.

Why does grass-feeding matter, beyond the benefits to flavour?

Grass is the planet's second biggest storer of carbon after the rainforests – and the UK has one of the best climates in the world for growing grass. Yet today we have a dairy industry that is increasingly dependent on soy, a lot of it grown in South America on farms that are contributing to deforestation. It's mad. Our cows graze on the very western edge of the Pevensey Levels. This means we're producing food on marginal land, which is a very good thing. It's not cheap – we cannot produce large quantities efficiently by farming the way we do – but it's a quality product, so people buy it for its taste and don't waste it like they might with cheaper food.

Your milk has a cream line, which is rare to see. Why is that?

A cream line only exists when the milk is not homogenised. Homogenisation is a process in which the fat globules are smashed up to create an even suspension throughout the milk. When milk always came in glass bottles, people loved the cream line, but the switch to plastic bottles meant that the cream formed a plug in the top and in the handle and people didn't like it any more. The only way to deal with that was to homogenise it. The fact that younger generations find a cream line weird or gross when they see one is evidence of just how much we've lost our way with milk.

How can you be sure that raw milk is free from bad bacteria?

Pathogenic bacteria are not particularly competitive. If they land on pasteurised milk, in which all other bacteria have been killed, they can grow exponentially, as they can feed on the sugars and nutrients without any competition. But if they land on raw milk, they'll be in trouble. Lactobacillus – the good bacteria found in raw milk – is an incredibly competitive bacteria that digests lactose and multiplies rapidly. If I were an E coli bacterium landing in a herd of Lactobacillus, I wouldn't stand a chance.

A few years ago, as an experiment, I put 200 litres of milk into a stainless-steel tank, uninsulated. I left it in the cow yard from April to October, with the cows walking past twice a day.

In October I sent a sample to the lab; it was clean as a whistle. Perfectly fine. It's not surprising: people used to keep fresh meat in raw milk to preserve it. The cream would form a seal, the good bacteria would repel pathogenic bacteria, and the build-up of lactic acid would sour the milk and act as a critical control, preventing bacterial growth.

How should raw milk be kept?

You need to get it into the fridge as quickly as possible and then make sure it's kept nice and cold – below 4C. If you've bought more milk than you'll be able to use within three or four days, the best thing is to freeze the surplus. Freezing doesn't affect the milk quality. If the milk does start to sour, don't throw it away, whatever you do, as there are loads of ways you can use it. Sour milk is good for baking, for marinades, or for making your own soft cheese.

Bay and cardamom raw milk pannacotta, page 269.

Five cheeses

Kilmora

Country Ireland
Milk Cow's milk (pasteurised)

Character A Swiss-style cheese with a waxed rind and a pliable, pleasantly elastic texture, sold at Heritage Cheese. Reminiscent of Emmental in style and taste, with fine holes and a gently sweet and nutty texture.

Paski Sir

Country Croatia
Milk Sheep's milk (pasteurised)

Character Taste Croatia's signature product is a hard cheese with a natural rind. It is made on the island of Pag, where the aromatic herbs and sea-salt-flecked grasses lend the sheep's milk a distinctly complex and fragrant flavour.

Basajo

Country Italy
Milk Sheep's milk (unpasteurised)

Character From L'Ubriaco –
Drunk Cheese, this soft blue
cheese is embalmed in sweet
passito wine, lending it a richly
honeyed flavour that gives way
to a creamy, salty, mildly blue
body. It comes crowned with
wine-soaked raisins.

Finn

Country England
Milk Cow's milk (unpasteurised)

Character Made in Herefordshire
and sold by Trethowan Brothers,
this bloomy-rind soft cheese is
infused with a little extra cream
to create the richest of textures.
The slightly tangy, lactic taste
contrasts with the creamy body,
and becomes increasingly nutty
as it matures.

Belper Knolle

Country Switzerland
Milk Cow's milk (unpasteurised)

Character A hard cheese
infused with garlic and
Himalayan salt and coated
with a fine dusting of black
pepper. Sourced by Jumi
Cheese, it has intense herbal
flavours, a melt-in-the-mouth
texture and an intensely
peppery finish.

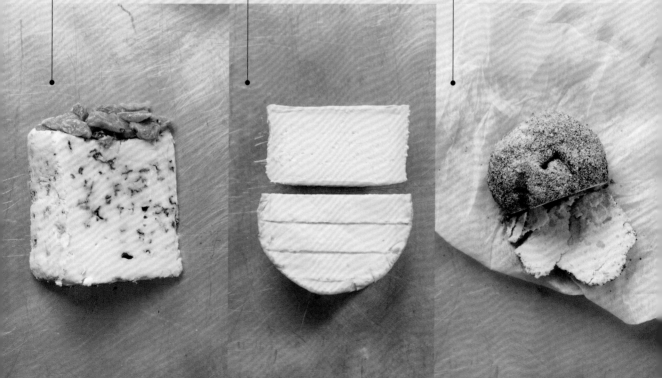

Cauliflower, parmesan and cauliflower leaf soup

This bowlful of goodness makes the most of every bit of a cauliflower's beauty – its florets and stalk cooking with the largest of the leaves to make the base of a soup that is given extra depth with three layers of parmesan. First, a parmesan rind is cooked with the soup to give it an umami-filled bed. (Optional only in case you might not have one. The moral is to always keep the rinds from your parmesan for things like this.) Then there's grated parmesan blended in with the soup, and more added just before serving.

The soup is finished off with an elegant charring of the smallest cauliflower leaves and a drizzle from a bottle of herb oil.

Serves 4–6

1 cauliflower with leaves
(about 800g)

2 leeks

1 celery stick

2 tablespoons olive oil, plus
extra for charring

20g butter

3 garlic cloves

2 bay leaves or sage leaves

1½ teaspoons ground cumin

80g parmesan, plus (optional)
parmesan rind

1 litre chicken or vegetable stock
(bought or see pages 82 and 147)

Herb oil, to serve

Trim the leaves off the cauliflower and set aside. If your cauliflower has a very gnarly end to its stalk, cut off and discard that, then chop the rest of the cauliflower florets and stalk into chunks. Set aside.

Divide the cauliflower leaves into small delicate ones and larger tougher ones. The smaller ones will be used to garnish the soup so, ideally, you'd have one of those for each serving. Finely chop the larger leaves. Trim the leeks (remembering you might want to use the trimmings for stock) and thinly slice along with the celery.

Heat the 2 tablespoons olive oil and the butter in a large saucepan over a medium heat. Add the chopped cauliflower leaves, celery, leeks and some salt. Put the lid on and cook, stirring occasionally, until the vegetables are soft but not colouring. Peel and crush the garlic cloves and stir into the pan along with the bay or sage leaves, and cook for a further 5 minutes. Add the cumin and stir for about 30 seconds to release its flavour, then add the chopped cauliflower florets and stalks, the parmesan rind (if using), and pour over the stock. Stir and simmer with the lid on for about 20 minutes until the cauliflower is thoroughly tender.

Remove the bay leaves / sage and the parmesan rind. Grate the parmesan, stir 60g of it into the soup and blend. Make it as smooth or chunky as you prefer. Check the seasoning. Up to this stage can be done ahead of time and the soup frozen / reheated as needed.

When you're ready to serve, set a small frying pan over a medium–high heat, add a splash of olive oil and, when it's hot, sit the reserved small cauliflower leaves in the pan. Give them a minute or so each side to crisp up and char. Ladle the hot soup into bowls, scatter over the reserved parmesan and sit a charred cauliflower leaf on each serving. Finish with black pepper and a drizzle of herb oil.

HOW TO... choose parmesan by age

'The minimum age of Parmigiano Reggiano is 12 months, when it has a simple flavour with strong notes of milk and butter. The taste of parmesan gets stronger as it gets older:

18 months: ideal for salads and aperitifs, combined with dried fruit or fresh pears.

24 months: perfect for tasting with balsamic vinegar, but also for grating on pasta and risotto.

30 months: pair with a flavoured honey or jams.

36 months: has a strong flavour. Perfect to be served at the end of a meal.

From 48 months onwards: the consistency of Parmigiano Reggiano becomes more crumbly and grainy, the taste is defined and acquires clear, but never spicy notes, and the aroma becomes explosive.'

Ewa Weremij, Bianca Mora

Borough Market – The Knowledge

Three-cheese bourek with honey and nigella seeds, by Philip Juma of JUMA Kitchen

Self-taught British-Iraqi chef Philip Juma is on a mission to spread awareness of – and appetite for – Iraqi cuisine. If the lunchtime queues at his stall in Borough Market Kitchen are anything to go by, it's going pretty well.

They are queuing for the kubba (stuffed dumplings), for charcoal-cooked kebabs on freshly baked tanoor breads that soak up all the juices… and for the love that Philip and his team put into everything they do.

These bourek are compelling to eat. It's perhaps just as well that Philip says they can be frozen once rolled and then fried straight from the freezer, making them a terrific make-ahead treat.

Makes about 30 bourek

300g halloumi

100g feta, drained

100g ricotta

1 teaspoon ground cinnamon

1 packet filo pastry (Philip likes to use a 470g pack of Au Ble d'Or filo)

About 100ml sunflower oil, for frying

To serve

2 tablespoons honey

1 tablespoon nigella seeds

Crumble the halloumi and feta into a bowl. You are looking for a fine crumb that is easy to roll in the filo. Add the ricotta and cinnamon and mix well.

Prepare the filo by laying it out flat. Cut the pastry in half lengthways and put one pile on top of the other. Cover with a damp tea towel to avoid the pastry drying out and becoming hard to manage.

Take one rectangle-shaped pastry sheet and trim off the excess so it looks like a square, then turn the square so one corner is facing you (like a diamond shape). Take a tablespoon of the cheese mix and place at the bottom of the filo sheet (above the corner). Shape the mix horizontally and then take the bottom corner and wrap it over the cheese mix. Roll again, then fold over each side. Roll once more, which should leave you with 5cm border of filo. Brush this border with water, then complete the bourek by rolling it on the dampened side so it's sealed. You should have a cigar shape. Set aside on greaseproof paper. Repeat with the rest of the filo pastry and filling.

Once all the bourek are rolled, allow them to air-dry on the paper for 5 minutes. You can freeze any that you don't wish to eat straight away (they fry perfectly from frozen, too).

Heat the oil in a small frying pan – you want enough oil so the boureks will be half-covered when you add them. It's important to shallow-fry (not deep-fry) the bourek, as they will have a more golden colour. When the oil is hot enough that you hear some sizzle, add the bourek in batches of 4–6 at a time so as not to overcrowd the pan and fry for about 8 minutes, turning them so they fry evenly, until crisp and golden.

Remove from the oil and drain on kitchen paper. Repeat with the remaining bourek. Drizzle with honey and sprinkle with the nigella seeds.

Vegan blue cheese, mango and watercress salad

The brevity of this recipe should be a clue to how very quick and easy this salad is to prepare. It's just the thing for high summer, when spending too long in a hot kitchen can start to feel like disproportionate effort.

Juicy mango brings its refreshing flavour sunshine, partnered here with a vegan blue cheese such as Palace Culture's Sacré Bleu. It's the creation of Mirko Parmigiani who ferments his nut-based cheeses over in Bermondsey, barely a leg-stretch away from his stall at the Market. Mirko's focus is absolutely on the health and sustainability impacts of his cheeses, but also just as much on the pleasure of eating. The ingredients are nut milk, salt and fermenting cultures. That's it, nothing more – resulting in a blue cheese that is gorgeously salty, tangy and with a rounded taste.

Serves 4 as a light main or 6 as a small plate

1 mango

180g vegan blue cheese
(or swap for non-vegan
blue cheese)

125g watercress

3 tablespoons walnut oil

3 tablespoons sherry vinegar

¼ teaspoon wild sumac

Cut through the mango on either side of its stone. Score the flesh in a 1cm square lattice (down to but not through the skin), then push the skin so the flesh lattice pops. Use a knife to cut the pieces away from the skin. Cut the rest of the flesh around the stone into 1cm cubes.

Cut or crumble the cheese into similar-sized pieces to the mango.

Sit the watercress in a serving bowl or on individual plates. Arrange the mango and cheese over and amongst the leaves.

Whisk together the oil, vinegar and sumac with a good pinch of salt. Pour the dressing over the salad, finish with a grinding of black pepper and serve straight away.

Tartiflette

Reblochon cheese is the traditional choice for this dish, coming from the same region of France where tartiflette has for years been warming up skiers. (I can vouch for it doing the same job at the end of a day in the Market's crisp cold.) Head to Mons Cheesemongers and they'll be able to tell you all about reblochon's 13th-century origins and what makes this soft cheese made from the milk of three Alpine breeds of cow so very special.

Resist any temptation to add other things into this. Get really good ingredients and let them sing out on their own. That includes waxy potatoes that will hold their shape, and smoked pork belly of the calibre found at The French Comte, where pork bellies are cured over pine, spruce and juniper for 2–3 weeks into the French equivalent of Italian pancetta.

Serves 3 – which also means 2 very hungry people, or 4 who are taking it a bit easier

600g waxy potatoes

140g smoked pork belly slices or lardons

1 onion

Splash of rapeseed oil (optional)

150ml white wine

100ml double cream

½ reblochon (about 250g)

Nutmeg, for grating

You will need a baking dish of approx. 1.5-litre capacity

Cook the potatoes in salted boiling water for 12–15 minutes until just about cooked. Drain and set aside. (You could do this ahead of time, or while you are doing the steps below.)

Cut the pork belly into small chunks if not using lardons. Set a large frying pan over a medium heat and, when it is hot, add the pork. Fry for a couple of minutes to start to release its fats, using that time to peel and slice the onion into thin half moons. Add the onion to the frying pan and stir. Add a splash of oil if you think it needs extra fat to prevent sticking. Cook until the onion is softening and starting to colour, by which time the pork should be crisping up nicely. Pour in the wine and let it bubble for a couple of minutes to reduce by about half. Turn off the heat and stir in half the cream. Season, being especially generous with the pepper and remembering the pork will be quite salty on its own.

When the cooked potatoes are cool enough to handle, slice them into rounds about 1cm thick. Cut the cheese into squares about 1.5cm, keeping the rind on.

Up to this stage can be done an hour or so ahead of when you want to bake your tartiflette; just keep the elements separate.

Preheat the oven to 190C fan/210C/410F/gas mark 6.

Lay half of the potato rounds in the baking dish, then cover with half the pork and onion mix. Next comes half the cheese, then repeat the layers, finishing with cheese on top and the remaining cream. Sit the dish on a baking tray to catch any bubbling-over cheese and bake for 25–30 minutes until hot, bubbling and golden.

When you take the tartiflette out of the oven give it a good grating of nutmeg before serving. Glasses of crisp white wine always go well alongside, as does a crisp salad with sharp vinaigrette.

Loaf-baked whole cheese with girolles

Camembert is really just one of many soft cheeses that would work well for this. I try not to get too caught up on marching to the Market with a specific cheese in mind, but prefer to talk to the stallholders about what they have and what might suit what I want to do with it. For this, I'd be just as happy with a vacherin Mont d'Or or Époisses. Whatever cheese you choose nestles within a whole loaf and is then baked for tearing and sharing, its flavours layered up with garlic, mushrooms, honey and wine.

Serves 3–4 as a main or 6 as part of a feast

1 round baking cheese such as camembert (about 250–300g)

1 round sourdough or cob loaf

1 garlic clove

30g butter

25g small girolle mushrooms

½ teaspoon herbes de Provence

2 teaspoons honey

50ml white wine or vermouth

Preheat the oven to 170C fan/190C/375F/gas mark 5.

Cut the top rind off the cheese. Then cut the top off the loaf and pull out enough of the crumb inside that the cheese can sit comfortably in the loaf.

Peel the garlic and cut into slivers. Melt the butter in a small saucepan over a low–medium heat. Cook the mushrooms until just softening, then add the garlic slivers and stir in the herbes de Provence. Take off the heat and stir in the honey and the wine. Mix well and season lightly.

Sit the loaf on a large piece of foil on a baking tray. Spoon the mushroom mix over the top of the cheese, then spoon the rest of the juices over, allowing some to go over the outside of the bread too. Push at the garlic pieces so they sink into the cheese a little. Wrap loosely in the foil and bake for 20 minutes. Increase the oven temperature to 190C fan/210C/410F/gas mark 6, open the parcel up just enough to reveal the cheese, and return to the oven for another 5 minutes to finish off.

Cut or tear the loaf into wedges and serve immediately while the cheese is still meltingly hot.

There are plenty of things you can do with the bread left over from this recipe. Blitz into crumbs and freeze, then think about making:

- *Borough queen of puddings, page 296.*
- *Pear and ginger treacle tart, page 298.*
- *Damson ripple sourdough ice cream, page 302.*

Cheese board accompaniments

Deciding what to serve with your cheeses can be as confusing – and exciting – as choosing the cheeses themselves. It's all about balance, and given that the cheeses tend to bring umami and salty profiles, you are relying on the accompaniments for complementing with sweet, sour and even bitter elements.

Two important things to bear in mind:

- The accompaniments need to let the cheese(s) shine. They are the support act, not the main event.
- You don't necessarily need to have everything on your cheeseboard. Just pick a few things to do well.

And a third thing, perhaps most important: ask the cheesemonger what they'd recommend on the side.

Honey

Or rather, honeycomb. As Samantha Wallace of From Field and Flower explains, 'Honeycomb is what the bees use to store honey, and it is only made at a certain stage of the hive's cycle. Its taste and texture varies according to the type of honey. Mostly, the style we sell is delicate and soft, with myriad floral undertones. It's heaven on a cheeseboard with saltier cheeses like parmesan. I wouldn't bother pairing with a blue – it's too light, and won't cut through – but a mild, lactic goat's cheese would work well.'

Otherwise, look out for honeys made close to where cheeses are produced as they will share flavour profiles of the terroir.

Fruits

Think seasonally: seasonal cheeses deserve seasonal fresh fruits alongside. That might mean figs and pears in the autumn and winter; peaches and plums in the summer.

Think flavour: blue cheeses, especially something like a gorgonzola, can be quite salty. Head towards the ultra-sweetness of figs for balancing contrast.

Think cleanser: crisp apple can be especially useful for cheeseboards with quite a range of cheeses. A quick bite can reset the palate brilliantly.

HOW TO... store cheese

'How you store your cheese really depends on how often you shop for cheese, or rather how quickly you consume it. Personally, I'd rather people buy less cheese more often, as that's the best way of maintaining quality. When that's not possible, you have to consider the moisture content of the cheese. The moister it is, the faster it will ripen, so the more slowing down it will need. Wrap it in wax or greaseproof paper – if you're going to a reputable cheesemonger, they'll present it in suitable paper – and put it in the vegetable drawer of the fridge, which is protected from draughts. This will prevent it from drying out. Hard and blue cheeses can be kept out of the fridge if the temperature is below 18C. Make sure to take it out of the fridge a couple of hours before serving so it can acclimatise. When cheese is a little warmer, the texture is looser and you get more flavour flooding your senses.'

Dominic Coyte, Borough Cheese Company

Moving away from fresh fruits, look out for fruit pastes. Membrillo quince paste is the classic, and while manchego is its most traditional partner, you'll find it goes well with lots of different styles. The Neal's Yard Dairy quince paste is especially lovely for being made with the whole fruit (rather than just the juice) and that means more intense flavour and a jammy texture. Damson paste (also Neal's Yard Dairy) offers a particularly British take on the membrillo classic.

Chutneys

Chutneys bring cheeses all the sweetness of fruits and fruit pastes, but give a helpful undertone of sourness too. A couple of contrasting chutney styles is a good idea: something on the sweet side like a plum chutney, a mellow caramelised onion, then perhaps a sharp rhubarb.

Quick pickles

Remembering that chutneys are basically fruits with a vinegar / acidic hit you could take things a step further with a quick-pickle of pear slices or blackberries. Another great way to cleanse the palate between cheeses.

Nuts

Walnuts and pecans are lovely with cheeses. You can do no wrong by heading to Food & Forest, telling them about the cheeses you've chosen, and taking their steer.

As suggested by Chloë Stewart of nibs etc.: a clustery, nutty granola can be good on a cheeseboard too.

Bread

Over to Olivier Favrel of Olivier's Bakery on choosing bread to balance and complement your cheeses:

'The important considerations when choosing bread as an accompaniment are taste and texture. You don't want a hard cheese with a hard bread, and you don't want soft cheese with soft bread. Our caramelised walnut bread is a bit sweet and works well with hard cheeses, and even blue cheese like stilton, because the flavours are balanced – but I wouldn't put it with something soft and creamy like a brie.'

Crackers and oatcakes

Remembering that the quest is for complementary balance, the crackers and oatcakes that tend to work best on a cheeseboard are the ones that bring some flavour but don't overwhelm, and which have interesting texture. There are plenty of interesting types to buy at the cheesemongers.

HOW TO... serve cheese

'When cutting cheese, ideally you want to present a cross-section of the whole, showing both the rind and the paste in appropriate proportions. If people can see the rind, they can see it's a handmade product. More importantly, the taste of the cheese varies from the rind to the centre. In general, the centre is brighter and more acidic, while towards the rind you get the effect of the mould ripening, which creates more savoury flavours. If someone just cuts the nib off the end, not only do they shatter the look of the cheese, they miss out on the opportunity to taste through this range of flavour profiles. When it comes to softer cheeses these differences are less pronounced, although in almost all instances you should leave the rind on. It has its own flavours – sometimes the best flavours – and is always good to eat.'

Jason Hinds, Neal's Yard Dairy

Borough Market – The Knowledge

Buttermilk crumpets

Buttermilk makes for crumpets that are extra fluffy and with lovely flavour. Note, though, that this does need to be 'proper' buttermilk that's the by-product of churning butter, rather than a commercial approximation. I can't tell you how excited I was when I first saw that Northfield Farm had started stocking it. Regular dairy milk will work for these too, though.

Let your culinary imagination run free when it comes to toppings. Perhaps 'nduja and honey, honey-glazed bacon, nutmeg syrup, or – tastiest of all? – lots of the best butter you can lay your hands on.

Makes about 12 crumpets

400ml buttermilk

200g strong white flour

100g plain flour

1 teaspoon caster sugar

1 teaspoon fine salt

7g sachet fast-action yeast

½ teaspoon bicarbonate of soda

Butter, for greasing

2 tablespoons rapeseed oil

Whatever toppings you want, to serve

You will need 4 x 9cm crumpet rings (or biscuit cutters)

Combine the buttermilk, flours, sugar, salt and yeast in a large mixing bowl. Cover the bowl with a tea towel and set aside somewhere warm for 1 hour, to allow it to froth up (you might have to leave it a little longer if it's cooler).

Mix the bicarbonate of soda with 100ml water in a small bowl then stir it into the crumpet mix. Set aside again for 30 minutes, by which time you should see lots of bubbles on the surface.

Grease the crumpet rings with butter. Pour a little rapeseed oil into a large frying pan over a medium heat then, when it is hot, sit the crumpet rings in. Spoon some of the crumpet mix into the rings, filling each ring just slightly more than halfway. Leave the crumpets to cook for 10–15 minutes, depending on the heat of the pan and the depth of your crumpets – the trick is to cook them through without burning the base. I tend to start them on a medium heat then turn the heat down. When the crumpets are ready to turn, they should be nearly dry on top, with lots of burst bubbles.

Use tongs to lift off the crumpet rings, and a palette knife to flip the crumpets over. Give them just a minute to brown on the other side, then transfer to a wire rack to cool, bubble side up. (If the rings won't lift off, just turn the whole thing over.)

Repeat for the rest of the mixture, taking care to re-grease the rings and pan as you go along.

Store the cool crumpets in an airtight container until you want to toast them and top with whatever you fancy. They'll keep for up to 3 days.

Labneh with watermelon, honey and mint

I like to serve this as part of a medley of salads on a hot day. Or – noting that it is really on the cusp of savoury or sweet – lean into the sweetness and hold back a little on the salt: as a dessert it is especially appreciated by anyone without a super-sweet tooth.

Making your labneh is simplicity itself – it is, after all, just strained yoghurt – and a lovely thing to do, so long as you start at least six hours before wanting to eat it. Actually, every part of this recipe can be made ahead of time, chilled, then quickly assembled for serving at room temperature.

Serves 6 as part of a sharing feast

500g labneh made from 900g thick Greek yoghurt (see box)

About 800g watermelon

2 tablespoons olive oil

½ orange

1 teaspoon wild sumac

2 tablespoons wild thyme honey

Handful of mint

Spoon the labneh into a large serving bowl.

Trim the ends of the watermelon and cut the fruit into triangles about 1cm thick. Mix the olive oil with the juice from the orange, half the sumac and a good pinch of salt. Get a griddle pan (or barbecue) good and hot, brush the watermelon pieces with the dressing and sit the pieces in a single layer in the pan (or on the grill). If using a griddle pan you will probably need to do this in two batches. Turn them over after a couple of minutes, when nicely charred underneath. Let the other side char, then lift the slices out to cool.

Add any juices from the pan to your leftover oil, orange and sumac dressing. Whisk in the honey and the rest of the sumac. Add more salt.

Sit the watermelon pieces on the labneh and pour over the dressing. Chop the mint and scatter over, then finish with a grinding of black pepper.

MAKE YOUR OWN LABNEH

For 500g labneh, start with 900g thick Greek yoghurt. Mix the yoghurt with 1 teaspoon of salt, then spoon into a sieve lined with a double layer of muslin (cheesecloth). Tie its ends together and sit in the sieve in the fridge over a bowl for 6–12 hours to strain. The longer you leave it, the thicker your labneh will be.

A few ways with butter sauces

It will come as little surprise that the better and more flavoursome the butter you start with, the better and more flavoursome your sauces will be.

These are simple sauces – don't be put off by any intimidating names. With just a modicum of skill and some good ingredients (and a little know-how on how to fix them if they should go wrong), they can lift all kinds of dishes.

125g unsalted butter

2 egg yolks

2 teaspoons lemon juice

Hollandaise

Set a heatproof bowl over a pan of gently simmering water. Put the butter in the bowl, let it melt, then set aside. When making the hollandaise you want to work with warm – not hot – melted butter.

Set another heatproof bowl over the pan of simmering water. Add the yolks, lemon juice and 1 tablespoon of warm water with a pinch of salt and whisk together. Keeping the heat under the pan very low, whisk in the butter, going slowly and in stages. You are aiming for a thick emulsion. Taste and season.

Top tips:

- Keep the heat low and the base of the whisking bowl away from the water's surface to prevent curdling or splitting.

- If your hollandaise threatens to split, whisk in an ice cube for a miracle rescue.

- Freshly made hollandaise will be fine for up to an hour kept in the bowl over the water but off the heat. Just cover it.

Options:

- Add a pinch of cayenne, a little Tabasco, or sriracha; or chopped herbs, such as dill and mint.

- Whisk in the grated zest and juice of a blood or Seville orange (to make sauce maltaise) and serve with asparagus, purple sprouting broccoli, or fish.

- Before starting, take a small pan and put into it 1 very finely chopped small shallot, 50ml tarragon vinegar (or white wine vinegar) and 2 tablespoons water. Reduce over a low-medium heat until you have just about 1 tablespoon of liquid. Strain and use that liquid in the hollandaise recipe instead of the lemon juice. Finish with chopped tarragon and you've just made bearnaise sauce, which will be outstanding with meats, fish or vegetables.

Borough Market – The Knowledge

Bechamel

The base of a bechamel is its 'roux' – the term for cooking off flour with fat. Melt 30g butter in a heavy-based saucepan over a low–medium heat, then add 30g plain flour and stir for a minute or two until it becomes thickly glossy and turning light brown. That's your roux ready for whisking in 500ml or so of milk, bit by bit. Keep stirring, let it bubble gently for a couple of minutes to cook the flour, and it will thicken to something glorious. All ready for you to add seasonings of grated cheese, chopped herbs, cloves, nutmeg, etc; and serve with fish, meat, or over a whole roasted cauliflower.

Top tips:

· To avoid a lumpy bechamel, don't add the milk all in one go.

· Be patient! The bechamel is only ready when it coats the back of a wooden spoon, leaving a gap when you draw a finger through it. If you aren't sure if it's ready, it probably isn't.

· Using a deep, heavy-based saucepan will ensure even distribution of heat as you make the sauce and prevent burning or curdling.

Veloute

Similar to a bechamel, but you cook the roux until it is lightly golden before adding stock instead of milk. Go for chicken, beef or vegetable stock, as suits whatever you are serving it with. Again, stir in seasonings at the end. Some chopped mushrooms can be great in a veloute. The sauce in the Fishmonger's pie on page 42 is a sort of bechamel / veloute cross as it uses the stock from poaching the fish and milk as well.

A gluten-free variation:

Something similar to a veloute can be made without flour, by just using heat to reduce and therefore thicken the sauce. Melt a knob of butter, add stock, simmer to reduce, then finish with a little cream and whatever flavourings you fancy. Useful for those avoiding gluten.

More ways with butter sauces

· A knob of butter whisked into gravies and deglazed pan juices will make them that bit richer.

· Brown butter on its own makes for a simple sauce: melt butter in a small saucepan over a low heat – choose a pan with a pale interior if you have it, so it's easier to see the colour changing. Swirl the pan occasionally and see the butter turning from golden and frothy to turning amber. At that point take it off the heat and go no further or the butter solids will burn.

· Flavoured butters – like the miso butter on page 162, and the smoked garlic butter on page 150 – are useful to have in the fridge or freezer. Just a slice on top of cooked meat, fish or vegetables will melt to a puddle of deliciousness. Think about making butters with surplus herbs and anchovies, or perhaps edible flowers like nasturtiums.

Bay and cardamom raw milk pannacotta

These pannacottas are gorgeously light, not too sweet (thanks to their subtle herb and spice), and have just the right amount of wobble. The key ingredients are the milk and cream – the better and more flavoursome these are, the better the pannacotta will be too.

That's the reason for specifying raw milk here. As Stephen Hook of Hook & Son explains on page 247, raw milk retains more flavour of the pasture the cows have grazed upon – which in his case includes wild meadows, rushes and marshes on the western edge of the Pevensey Levels in East Sussex. And why wouldn't we want milk that speaks of the land it comes from?

Serves 4

125ml raw whole milk

375ml double cream

80g caster sugar

½ vanilla pod

4 bay leaves

6g gelatine leaves

Vegetable oil, for greasing

Edible flowers and unwaxed lemon
    zest to garnish

For the cardamom syrup

6 green cardamom pods

60g granulated sugar

*You will need 4 small, round
espresso cups*

Put the milk, cream and caster sugar into a medium saucepan. Split the vanilla pod down its length, scrape out the seeds, then add the seeds and the pod to the pan along with the bay leaves. Set over a low heat so the sugar dissolves, then let it simmer gently for 3 minutes. Take off the heat and set aside for 1 hour to let the vanilla and bay infuse the milk and cream.

Strain the milk / cream mixture through a sieve into another pan. Immerse the gelatine leaves in a bowl of very cold water and leave for 5 minutes until they become soft and floppy. Squeeze out the excess water from the gelatine then add to the infused milk and cream. Stir over a very low heat until the gelatine has fully dissolved, then take off the heat.

Grease the espresso cups with vegetable oil. Divide the pannacotta mix evenly between them, cover with non-PVC cling film and chill overnight or for at least 4 hours.

To make cardamom syrup for pouring over the finished pannacottas, crush the cardamom pods and put them into a small pan along with the granulated sugar and 60ml water. Heat until the sugar dissolves, then leave to cool and strain.

To serve, briefly dip the base of each espresso cup in a bowl of just-boiled water and turn out onto small plates or bowls for serving. Use a sharp knife to prise the pannacottas away from the cups if necessary. Pour a little of the cardamom syrup over each, then decorate with edible flowers and lemon zest.

Ginger and pink peppercorn baked cheesecake

A glorious marriage of cream-cheese mascarpone with whey-cheese ricotta. The ricotta giving a pleasing, slightly grainy texture, which works as a nice contrast to those super-smooth cheesecakes made with all cream cheese.

A cheesecake will always be rich and sweet – otherwise really, what's the point? – but this one achieves cut-through with stem ginger baked into the crust, more ginger over the top via the sweet syrup from its jar, and then crushed pink peppercorns.

Serves 12

For the base

225g rye digestive biscuits

1 tablespoon caster sugar

85g butter, plus extra for greasing

3 pieces of stem ginger

For the filling

500g ricotta

250g mascarpone

4 eggs

1 tablespoon cornflour

125g caster sugar

½ teaspoon vanilla extract

To serve

Stem ginger syrup

1 tablespoon pink peppercorns

You will need a 23cm springform cake tin

Rye digestives are often sold at the cheesemonger's, and at the Market you'll also find them at The Cinnamon Tree Bakery. They give extra flavour depth and go well with the ginger, but ordinary digestives will do too – as would gluten-free ones.

Preheat the oven to 160C fan/180C/350F/gas mark 4.

Use a little of the extra butter to grease the base of the tin, then sit a large piece of baking paper over the base and clip the springform ring over it, neatly trapping the paper.

First make the base. Put the biscuits in a mixing bowl and crush with the end of a rolling pin. Stir in the sugar and a pinch of salt. Melt the butter in a small saucepan over a low heat and add that too. Then finely chop the stem ginger and mix everything together well. Press the mix into the base of the lined tin, getting it as even as you can. Bake the crust for 10 minutes, then set aside to cool.

Reduce the oven temperature to 120C fan/140C/275F/gas mark 1.

As the base cools, prepare the cheesecake filling. Beat the cheeses together in a large mixing bowl. Separate the eggs into two mixing bowls, ensuring the one for the whites is spotlessly clean. Beat the yolks and add them to the cheeses along with the cornflour, sugar and vanilla extract. Mix thoroughly but gently. Whisk the egg whites to stiff meringue-like peaks, then fold them, again, gently but thoroughly, into the cheese mixture. Use the rest of the extra butter to grease the sides of the cooled tin, then spoon the filling over the biscuit crust, levelling the top.

Bake for about 1 hour 20 minutes, checking at the hour point to see how near it is to being ready – which is when the outside edge is pretty set but the middle still has a definite wobble. When it is done, turn off the oven and let the cheesecake cool in the oven for an hour with the door wedged partially open with a wooden spoon. Then run a spatula around the outside of the cake and let it finish cooling out of the oven before chilling for at least 4 hours. Up to this stage can be done a couple of days before eating.

To serve, release the cheesecake from the tin and drizzle syrup from the stem ginger jar over the top. Lightly crush the pink peppercorns using a pestle and mortar, then scatter them over as prettily as you like.

MAKE YOUR OWN STEM GINGER

Making your own stem ginger is a great way to preserve surplus root ginger. Freeze 200g of fresh root ginger overnight. Let it sit out of the freezer for ten minutes before peeling. Cut into 2cm pieces, put into a medium saucepan with 800ml water, put a lid on the pan and gently simmer for about 1 hour or until tender. Lift out the ginger with a slotted spoon. Pour the cooking liquor into a measuring jug and return 200ml of it to the pan with 200g granulated or caster sugar. Heat to dissolve the sugar. Simmer the ginger in the syrup for 5 minutes then transfer to a sterilised jar. The ginger should be submerged. If it isn't, just make more simple syrup with any leftover water from cooking the ginger. The stem ginger will keep for up to 2 months in the fridge.

Borough Market – The Knowledge

Rhubarb and sweet vermouth fool

This recipe for poaching rhubarb in vermouth allows the stalks to benefit from all the botanicals of roots, flowers, herbs and spices that the vermouth freely offers up. After just a few minutes you have rhubarb pieces that are tender and taste like the best possible version of themselves. The poaching liquid then gets reduced down to a headily flavoured bubblegum-pink syrup that is stirred with the fruit through a fool of yoghurt and cream.

Any dish like this, where the dairy is front and centre is simply going to taste better if you can shop for the best possible versions. Go for cream and yoghurt that you and the farmer are proud of.

Serves 4

300g forced rhubarb, the pinkest
    stalks you can find

300ml sweet red vermouth

1½ tablespoons caster sugar

1 star anise

200ml double cream

150g Greek yoghurt

1 orange

Wash the rhubarb, cut off its tough ends but do not peel. Cut into pieces about 2.5cm long. Put the vermouth and sugar into a saucepan and heat just until the sugar has dissolved. Add the rhubarb and the star anise, put on the lid and let it bubble gently for 5 minutes. Check after 3 minutes – you are aiming for tender pieces of rhubarb that are just about beginning to lose their shape, but not collapsing completely. Use a slotted spoon to carefully lift the rhubarb out of the pan and onto a plate or board to cool. Discard the star anise then rapidly boil the vermouth poaching juices to reduce them down to 1–2 tablespoons of bright pink syrup. Remove from the heat and chill until needed.

To make the fool, whisk the cream in a bowl until it holds firm peaks. Carefully fold in the yoghurt. Finely grate the zest of the orange and ripple it through the dairy, along with the cooled poached rhubarb and its syrup. Spoon into bowls or glasses for serving, and chill until it's time to dive in.

To use any leftover poached rhubarb and its syrup:
- *Amp up a slice of sponge cake or Madeira loaf with a few pieces of poached rhubarb and the vermouth syrup drizzled over the sponge to soak in.*
- *Serve the poached fruit with some top-notch vanilla (or bay leaf) ice cream and the syrup poured over.*
- *Add to granola, or even to the rice pudding and granola recipe on page 230.*
- *The syrup can be used in cocktails.*

Dark rum egg nog

Egg nog is one of the most indulgently decadent and delicious of all traditional festive drinks. The addition at the end of whipped-up egg whites is what gives this its wonderful light frothiness.

It's a recipe I've done before for demonstrations in the middle of the Market when crowds of shoppers gather nearer and nearer the closer you get to having something finished to share round, and also for the Borough Market Cookbook Club's Christmas parties. There's almost as much pleasure to be had in converting people to the deliciousness of this, as drinking it yourself. Shaking off egg nog preconceptions, one elegant glass at a time.

Serves 4

2 eggs

80g caster sugar

200ml chilled single cream

200ml chilled whole milk

200ml dark rum (see note)

8 dashes of orange cocktail bitters, or the pomelo bitters on page 126

Nutmeg, for grating

4 whole star anise or sprigs of thyme

Separate the egg whites and the yolks into two clean large mixing bowls. Divide the sugar evenly between the bowls. Whisk the yolks and sugar until thick; then whisk into that the cream, milk and dark rum. Add the dashes of orange bitters. Transfer to a serving bowl.

Now for the egg whites. Whisk them with the sugar until they form meringue-like stiff peaks, then gently but thoroughly fold the stiff whites into the bowl containing the cream and rum etc. Ladle into glasses, finishing each one with a grating of fresh nutmeg and a star anise or thyme sprig.

Your choice of rum ideally needs to be not just dark but also interesting. East London Liquor Co.'s Rarer Rum is definitely both things, being made in Guyana from demerara sugar cane that brings its caramel notes. It is aged in former bourbon casks (and it's worth noting that bourbon would be a good swap for the rum in this recipe, as would whisky).

The Dairy

Borough Market – The Knowledge

Drinks

Jura wine

The Jura region in eastern France is known for both its glorious cheeses and wines, making it little surprise at all that they go exceptionally well together and that bottles of Jura's traditional yet idiosyncratic wines can be found at The French Comté right alongside Jura's comté and gruyère cheeses.

The wines of the region make a good match not just for those, but for lots of creamy, strong-flavoured cheeses and dishes that embrace garlic, herbs, bacon and mushrooms. Look out for these Juras:

Vin jaune: bone-dry white wine that is aged under a layer of yeast. Its intense, golden colour brings notes of hazelnut, almond and fresh mushrooms. Heaven with just a simple cheese and bread combination.

Vin de paille: a deliciously sweet white wine that would be a good fit for a sweeter cheese recipe. I'll be pouring a glass to serve with the Rye, ginger and pink peppercorn baked cheesecake on page 270.

Poulsard: on first look these could be taken as a rosé wine but don't be fooled. Poulsard is a red grape that produces white juice and is made into very pale red wine. Typically fruity and refreshing, it's good for mild cheeses.

POTATO &
ROSEMARY
SOURDOUGH

BREAD AHEAD
SPECIAL

£3.50

ALLERGENS. GLUTEN

SLEEPER
TIN

BREAD AHEAD,
SPECIAL

£4.50

ALLERGENS. GLUTEN

WHOL
SOUR
SM

TRAD

£3

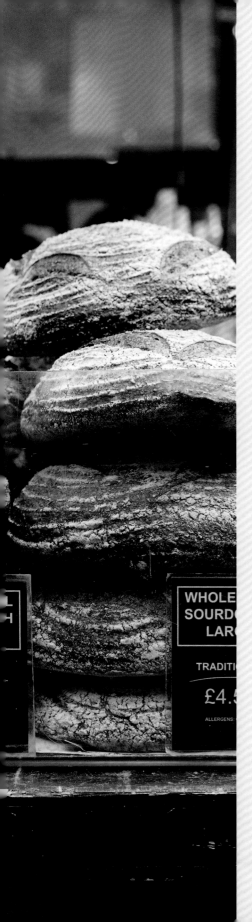

THE BAKERY

ESTABLISHED
1756

**BOROUGH
MARKET**

Olivier Favrel was just 13 years old when he started his career as a pastry chef in Brittany. Today, he brings more than three decades of baking experience to bear on the bread and pastries he produces for his Borough Market stall, marrying the rich culinary heritage of his native France with British organic grains.

The secrets of better bread

Olivier Favrel, Olivier's Bakery

You cannot accelerate. You cannot cut corners. You can only follow the process until it is ready. Bread is the food of life, and it's a living thing, which is why the relationship between bread and baker is so important. You can't start it and then do something else; you have to stay with it, feel it, observe to see how it reacts, and adjust your methods accordingly. An unhappy baker, a distracted baker, can't make good bread.

Good bread begins with the raw ingredient, which is good flour. We use organic British flour from Shipton Mill in Gloucestershire. Organic means no pesticides or chemical fertilisers have been used on the wheat, which means the grain is stronger and more deeply rooted in the soil, as it isn't dependent on chemicals to grow and fight against the weather. This results in more nutrients and more flavour. Yet organic grain is not fully consistent. It changes according to the weather and the soil, so every week we need to think: how does this flour work?

This is good for us, because to do the same thing every week would be boring. We don't want to just push a button on a machine filled with pre-mix; there is no

care there. We have to adapt the quantities, the speed of mixing, the time, the temperature of fermentation and baking. Flour itself doesn't taste of much; it is the water and salt and the way you use the flour that brings flavour to it. Time is the most important ingredient.

Most industrially made bread is rushed, which means adding stabilisers, soya and preservatives to speed up the process. Reducing the mixing time to seven or eight minutes, which is standard in most factories, results in much stronger chains of gluten, which are harder for your body to break down and digest. We spend around half an hour mixing, then each bread will spend four to six hours fermenting, then another two to three hours fermenting once it's been shaped. If it's not ready, it's not rushed.

Another thing that creates flavour is the crust. Some people think a thin crust is a sign of better bread – but a thick crust will keep the inside of the bread softer for longer. We create ours by opening a damper on the oven during the final minutes of the cooking time, which allows the humidity in the chamber to escape and the

> We don't want to just push a button on a machine filled with pre-mix; there is no care there.

> "The relationship between bread and baker is so important. An unhappy baker, a distracted baker, can't make good bread.

sugars in the bread to caramelise, creating more flavour in both the crumb and the crust.

I didn't go into baking to get rich. I am not looking to steal money from people. Our bread is priced well for what it is: made by hand, over the course of 12 hours, by skilled, experienced bakers. A loaf of our bread will feed you for a week. It will keep your family full.

Mediterranean vegetable picnic loaf, page 292.
Damson ripple sourdough ice cream, page 302.

Five
pastry types

Shortcrust

A good pastry for beginners, shortcrust is quite simply fat – butter or lard – rubbed into plain flour and bound with ice-cold water. Quiches, tarts and pies all draw upon shortcrust, which, as the name suggests, should be crusty rather than flaky, although it shouldn't be dry. One of its key advantages is that, because it's more forgiving than some other forms of pastry, it's much easier to experiment with different types of flour, such as spelt, einkorn and rye.

Pear and ginger treacle tart, page 298.

Suet

Another easy win, although less versatile than shortcrust and far less common than it used to be. Flour, salt and shredded beef suet are mixed together using the blade of a knife, then pulled together with water into a smooth elastic dough. The flavour is light but rich, making it a perfect foil for the rich fillings of hearty dishes, such as steak and kidney pudding and Sussex pond pudding – a classic dessert packed with lemon, butter and sugar.

Puff

'The key to good puff pastry is temperature,' says Victor Arias of Comptoir Gourmand. 'You must ensure you're working quickly to keep the butter cold. If the butter gets too warm, there will be no puff in your pastry and it will not hold its shape.' He recommends keeping your hands cool by running them under cold water before drying them thoroughly. The aim, at the end of a lengthy process of rolling and folding, is to have layers upon layer of thin dough and butter. 'Finally, make sure the oven is at 200C. This is very important, as the oven needs to be hot enough to create the steam that will cause your pastry to puff up.'

Choux

'As a chef intern, aged 16, Jonathan was asked to fill and glaze eclairs on his very first day,' says Bianka Ozsvath, who founded Taste of Joy with pastry chef Jonathan Georgery. From that day forth, Jonathan has been looking to elevate choux pastry – the delicate, puffy dough used for eclairs and puffs – as well as lesser-known patisserie like the St Honoré and the religieuse. 'Choux pastry is a super-light pastry overall. That's what makes it stand out,' Bianka continues, 'and it's incredibly versatile, so you can play with it and use your creativity endlessly.'

Hot water crust

Hot water crust pastry is easily shaped, thanks to the high proportion of water present, so it's a favourite among the makers of intricately decorated wellingtons and pies. Unlike most other pastry styles, hot water crust demands that the fat be hot rather than chilled when added to the dry ingredients.

Deep celeriac, potato and gruyère pie, page 288.

The origins of Karaway Bakery lie in the Baltics, where rye bread has been a staple for centuries. It is this rich baking tradition that the bakery's founder Nadia draws upon in her loaves, cakes and biscuits.

Nadia Gencas

Karaway Bakery

What is rye flour?

Rye flour is a dark, nutty flour milled from rye kernels, also known as rye berries. Baking with rye was once widespread in the UK, but it's now more commonly associated with Germany, Scandinavia and the Baltic countries, which is where we source our flour from. The heritage and rich baking traditions of the Baltics mean there are many varieties of rye bread based on different techniques and ingredients, each with its own characteristic taste profile and texture.

Is rye bread always sour and dense?

Like wheat flour, the characteristics of different rye flours are determined by how much of the kernel – the endosperm, bran and germ – is present. The greater the proportion of rye kernel, the darker the flour, and the stronger the flavour and density of the final loaf. Rye does have a strength of flavour that wheat doesn't have, and if wholegrain rye flour is used in a simple sourdough, the bread will be sour and dense. We do sell these firmer versions, and some people do really love them, but a lot of our breads are mellow, moist and soft. Customers tell us they can't believe that it's rye bread.

What techniques do you use to make those breads less dense and sour?

One of our signature techniques, which derives from the Baltics, is the scalding process. This takes place pre-fermentation: we scald the rye flour with boiling water, which breaks up the gluten, making it more digestible. Then, during the bread dough resting stage, the natural sugars develop, contributing to the sweeter, mellower flavours of the bread. By keeping the moisture in, the scalding process also extends the shelf-life of the bread – bread made with scalded flour will stay softer and fresher for longer. The fermentation process is also important: each type of loaf has its own sourdough starter and goes through a three- or four-stage natural fermentation process, taking up to 48 hours.

What do you use to flavour your loaves?

We use four or five different rye flours, milled to different textures, as well as other flours like wheat or spelt that we can add to the rye. Some loaves contain malted grains, roasted and ground to different levels, lending a particular colouring and aroma. We might also add seeds, nuts, sprouting grains, fruit and spices. Caraway, for example, is particularly popular in the Baltics, and we use loads in our breads, sometimes in unusual combinations: our fruity rye has prunes, apricots, raisins and caraway seeds, which gives it a bit of a kick and rounds out the flavours. Another Baltic classic is the borodinsky bread, which is very fragrant and infused with coriander seeds. Then there is a bread with six different types of nuts, which when you cut it looks like a biscotti.

How have you incorporated rye into your sweet bakes?

The main reason we decided to experiment with using rye flour in sweet bakes was health: rye contains more fibre than modern refined wheat and has a different type of gluten, which people with mild gluten intolerances are less likely to react to. In the process of developing them, we found we were creating some really nice-tasting bakes, such as our carrot, rye and caraway cake, which won a Great Taste Award. The technical challenge with rye is that, because it has less gluten, it doesn't create a good rise. It works well with biscuits and denser products, but when we create muffins and cakes, we combine rye with spelt to give it a lift and a more open texture.

Pear and ginger treacle tart, page 298.

Although no single alternative will ever fully replace wheat flour, there is an alchemy to creating flavoursome, gluten free bakes using a combination of different grains. The best ingredients are those with structural protein that can work in a similar way to gluten by binding the mix together.

Five gluten free grains

Caroline Aherne, The Free From Bakehouse

Sorghum

An important flour for gluten-free baking on account of its high protein and fibre content, and its sweet flavour. When mixed with a couple of other flours, sorghum is particularly good for light bakes.

Teff

Used in Ethiopian cuisine to make injera, the country's staple flatbread, teff is available in dark and light versions. The light version is good in cakes, such as victoria sponges. The dark version works in crackers, biscuits and pastry.

Rice flours

Brown rice flour, which is bland and has a slightly gritty texture, is a staple base flour. White rice flour has higher levels of starch and works extremely well in flour mixes, as it not only aids the binding process but also holds in moisture.

Buckwheat

Buckwheat isn't actually wheat – it comes from the rhubarb family. It has a nutty, slightly bitter flavour and a high protein content. In France, it's popular in savoury pancakes called galettes, and in biscuits. Make sure you're buying certified gluten-free buckwheat.

Oat flour

Oat flour is a great source of protein and fibre. When fine, it adds a softness to bread dough; when not so fine, it produces a really good texture in biscuits. Look for certified gluten-free oat flour or else buy porridge or whole oats that you can grind yourself.

Five Turkish sweets

Graham Teale,
The Turkish Deli

Turkish delight

Turkish delight is all about texture. It shouldn't be chewy, and it shouldn't stick to your teeth, which is the most common complaint when it's mass produced. The traditional recipe involves boiling sugar, corn starch and water for two hours, adding flavourings such as rosewater, pistachio and cherry, then leaving it to set for 24 hours before slicing it on marble slabs.

Baklava

Fine filo pastry layered with ground nuts and either butter or olive oil. The rule in Turkey is that the filo pastry, known as 'yukfa', must be so fine that you can read the Qur'an through it. You have to work very quickly as you layer it with the nut mixture, before cooking it. Immediately after cooking, a sugar syrup is poured over the top.

Helva

Making helva involves weaving the fibres of sugar and tahini together rather than kneading them, which means that while the result looks fudgy, the texture is very light and fibrous, even if the flavour is incredibly rich.

Cezerye

A sweet made with caramelised carrots, shredded coconut and roasted nuts. With much of its sweetness coming from the carrot, cezerye has a less sugary flavour than Turkish delight and a texture more akin to dried fruit. In Turkey it's sometimes set in large blocks, which are sliced in a similar fashion to a doner kebab, but that's hard to manage in a British climate.

Pestil

Molasses boiled down into a fruit leather-like gum. Our pestil hails from an area of Turkey famed for its vineyards, where making sweets from grape molasses reduces the waste generated by viticulture. In other areas, pestil is made with apricots – it depends which fruit is most abundant. The sheets of pestil are often rolled up and stuffed with ground nuts and sugar.

Deep celeriac, potato and gruyère pie

This is a tall, standing-proud pie made with hot water pastry, which is not only delicious but so easy to work with. Forget everything you know about keeping things cool to work with pastry – the onus here is on working with this pastry while it is still hot. Or at least warm.

Classic hot water pastry, like Paul Hartland of Mrs King's Pork Pies makes for his pork pies, contains lard. This is in part for the connection between the meat and the fat of the same animal, but also for the remarkable flavour and texture the lard gives. The recipe here has measurements for using butter or lard. The measurements are different as butter contains more water.

The meat-free filling is deeply flavoursome, given a double-umami lift from fresh wild mushrooms and dried porcini. It can be made a day ahead of baking the pie and chilled until needed.

Serves 6–8 as a main

25g dried porcini

250ml boiling water

1 small celeriac (about 650g)

800g potatoes

2 onions

60g butter

1 tablespoon olive oil or rapeseed oil

1 sprig of rosemary

80g mixed mushrooms of your choosing

1 apple

250g creme fraiche

80g gruyère

For the pastry

350g plain flour, plus extra for dusting

250g strong white flour

2 teaspoons fine salt

220g butter (or 200g lard)

1 egg

You will need a deep 22cm springform cake tin

Sit the dried porcini in a heatproof bowl and cover with the boiling water. Set aside.

Cut off the gnarly top and bottom of your celeriac. Peel, halve and cut it into slices about 1cm thick. Put the celeriac slices in a saucepan of boiling salted water and cook for 15–20 minutes until just tender. Peel the potatoes, cut into slices about 1.5cm thick and simmer in a separate pan of boiling salted water until tender. Drain the vegetables when ready and set aside, seasoning them while they're still warm.

Peel and finely chop the onions. Heat the butter and oil in a large saucepan over a medium heat, then add the onions and cook until just softening. Chop the rosemary leaves and add those too. When the onions are soft, add the mushrooms, roughly chopping them if large. Lift the now-rehydrated porcini out of the water (keep the water), roughly chop them, and add to the pan too. Cook for 5 minutes, then pour in the porcini soaking water. Mix and remove from the heat.

Peel, quarter and core the apple, dice, then add to the pan of mushrooms. Now cut the cooked celeriac and potato slices into roughly 1cm cubes (you don't need to be too precise about it), add to the onion / mushroom pan, stir in the creme fraiche and season generously with salt and freshly ground pepper. Your filling is now almost ready – carry straight on or keep it in the fridge for up to a day, making sure you return the filling to room temperature before building your pie.

Borough Market – The Knowledge

To build your pie

Grate the gruyère and keep back for adding to the filling.

Preheat the oven to 170C fan/190C/375F/gas mark 5 with a large baking tray inside to get hot. Use just a little of the butter (or lard) to grease the base and sides of your tin.

To make the pastry, sift the flours and salt into a large mixing bowl, making a well in the middle. Cut the butter (or lard) into pieces into a saucepan and add 180ml water (or 200ml if using lard). Place over a medium heat and as soon as it is bubbling fast, pour the fat / water mix into the flour bowl. Stir together using a wooden spoon to form a dough and then use your hands. It won't need much kneading.

Separate off two-thirds of the dough. Roll it out on a lightly-floured worktop to a thickness of about 4mm and cut out a circle that covers the base of the tin. Lift the dough over and into the base. If it can go a little way up the sides of the tin then all to the good. Use more dough to roll pieces for the sides of the pie. This pastry is incredibly amenable to patching up and pressing pieces together. When you have the base and sides done, spoon in about a third of the filling mix, then scatter over half the grated gruyère. Repeat with another third of filling, the rest of the cheese, and finally the last of the celeriac / potato mix.

Take most of the remaining pastry and roll out to form a lid. Lift it onto the pie and bring the side pastry up and over the edges and press together, so you are building your pie to sit inside and below the top of the tin. Crimp as prettily as you can or want to.

The last of the pastry can be used to make decorations. I like to make stars or leaves and cut them out with biscuit cutters before pressing them on top.

Push the handle of a wooden spoon through the centre of the pie's lid to make a steam hole. Beat the egg with a little water and brush over the pastry. Then put your beautiful pie into the oven, sitting it on the hot baking tray. Bake for 45 minutes, then lift the pie out and gently release and remove the springform ring. Return the pie to the oven for 15–20 minutes so that the pastry sides can brown a little too. It is ready when the pastry is beautifully golden on top.

Let the pie sit out of the oven for 5–10 minutes before slicing. It is a pie best eaten while still warm. Some sort of greens alongside are a very good idea.

Mediterranean vegetable picnic loaf

Chargrilled vegetables layered inside a loaf along with fresh herbs and capers make the perfect addition to a summer's picnic – not least as it's so easy to transport. The vibrant colours as you slice into it are their own blast of sunshine.

You need to choose a loaf that can take the juices of the vegetables without becoming soggy. A good sourdough is perfect. You could add slices of mozzarella or burrata tucked in among the vegetables too. If I have a jar of the pickled chillies on page 107 in the fridge, I like to slice and add one of those as I layer it all up.

Serves 6 as a lunch or part of a picnic feast

1 small red or orange pepper

1 small yellow pepper

1 courgette

1 fennel bulb

125ml olive oil

2 teaspoons red wine vinegar

1 garlic clove

1 tablespoon fresh oregano leaves

2 teaspoons capers

2 sprigs of mint

1 small round sourdough loaf

6 basil leaves

Quarter and deseed the peppers; slice the courgette on the diagonal into rounds about 5mm thick; cut the top and bottom off the fennel, discard its outer layer then slice about 5mm thick. Toss all the vegetables in a bowl with 4 tablespoons of the olive oil and season.

Get a grill or griddle pan very hot over a high heat and lay the vegetables out in a single layer. Cook them until lightly charred and tender on both sides, keeping an eye on them as the different vegetables will be done at different times. You might need to do this in two batches, depending on the size of your pan.

While the vegetables are cooking, mix 2 tablespoons of the olive oil and all the red wine vinegar in another large bowl. Peel the garlic and cut into slivers then mix into the dressing with the oregano and season with salt and pepper. As the vegetables are done put them into that bowl too and toss. Set aside to marinate.

Rinse, pat dry and chop the capers. Finely chop the mint leaves.

Cut the top off the sourdough loaf about a third of the way down. Remove the inner breadcrumbs from the loaf's base and sides, leaving a lining of a few centimetres. Keep what you take out for use as breadcrumbs (see page 256).

Drain away any excess oil in the vegetable bowl (you could keep it to use for dressings or cooking), then begin to stuff the loaf. Use half the peppers to line the base, then layer up with the slices of courgette, fennel, basil, chopped capers and mint, finishing with peppers on the top. Keep seasoning as you go. Press down to fit in as much as you can.

Brush the remaining tablespoon of olive oil on the underside of the loaf's 'lid'. Press it down on top of the filled loaf, then wrap it all up tightly in non-PVC cling film. Sit the wrapped loaf on a tray, put another tray on top and weight it down with tins of food or cookbooks. Leave for a couple of hours or overnight in the fridge.

To serve, just unwrap the loaf and slice it into wedges.

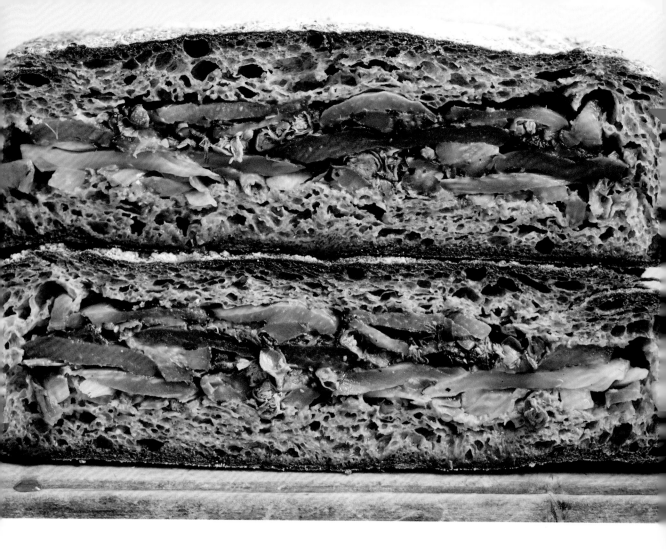

HOW TO... store bread

'To be honest, good bread doesn't keep that well. It's not designed to keep well. The real answers are to bake or buy smaller loaves more often, and to use older bread to make croutons, bruschetta, panzanella or breadcrumbs. That's far better than trying to disguise the flavour of old, musty bread.

The best way to store fresh bread that you're going to eat over a short period of time – three days, maximum – is in a bread bin, with a wooden lid to allow it to breathe. Bread also keeps very well in the freezer, if you pre-slice it for toasting later. Don't put bread in the fridge. It'll simply dry out – and besides, it's weird. It's like wearing odd socks – you just don't do it.'

Matthew Jones, Bread Ahead Bakery & School

Chickpea flatbreads with za'atar

Chickpea flour – also known as gram flour, or farina di cerci when I pick up a bag at Gastronomica – has a slightly nutty element to it that makes these light flatbreads especially moreish. In Nice you might see them as socca, and in Genoa as farinata. Call them what you will, they're a superb base for dips, olives, cheeses, and the muhammara on page 222.

They partner well with charcuterie too. Perhaps something like the Dorset air-dried ham produced by Capreolus, where the rare-breed pigs have their diet supplemented with milk whey in the same way as happens for traditional Parma ham. Or the lean intensity of bresaola at Alpine Deli, made by marinating silverside of beef in alpine spices before gently smoking it over beech and air-drying for three months.

Serves 4 people (3 pieces each)

150g chickpea flour

¾ teaspoon fine salt

150ml olive oil

1 tablespoon za'atar

Whisk together the flour, salt and 2 tablespoons of the olive oil in a large mixing bowl. Add 275–300ml cold water – just enough to achieve a batter with the consistency of double cream. Cover and set aside at room temperature for 2 hours.

Preheat the oven to 200C fan/220C/425F/gas mark 7.

Choose a large ovenproof frying pan and set that on the hob over a medium heat with 2 tablespoons of the oil. When it is hot, pour in half the batter and – as you would if making a crepe pancake – move the pan around so the batter reaches the edges. Let it cook for about 3 minutes, until turning golden on the underside, then put the pan into the oven for about 10 minutes. It's ready when the surface is crisped but the middle is still soft.

Turn the flatbread out so the side that had contact with the base of the pan is uppermost. Drizzle over 1 tablespoon or so of the olive oil, then scatter over half of the za'atar and some salt. Slice into 6 and serve while still hot.

Re-oil the pan before repeating with the remaining batter.

Spiced shortbread tails

These are shortbreads given golden colour from their gentle spicing and the inclusion of unrefined caster sugar. So much more interesting than the plain, pale shortbreads we're all used to.

Two main things to know to get these right:

- Don't overwork the dough. As soon as it comes together, it is ready to roll.
- Like all biscuits, these will carry on cooking in their own heat once out of the oven, so take them out while they are still slightly soft.

Bake in a fluted tart tin for extra prettiness.

Makes 8 pieces

80g golden (unrefined) caster sugar

160g salted butter, at room
  temperature

185g plain flour

60g fine semolina or ground rice

¼ teaspoon each ground cinnamon,
  ground cloves and mixed spice

1 tablespoon granulated sugar

*You will need a 22cm loose-bottomed
tart tin*

Line your tin with baking paper.

Use a wooden spoon to beat the sugar and butter in a large mixing bowl until soft. Sift in the flour, semolina or ground rice, and the spices. Mix by hand to form a dough but take care not to overmix. Using your hand will help you gauge as soon as the mixture holds together – that's when it is ready to roll.

Roll out the dough on a large piece of baking paper to a thickness of about 1cm, using your tart tin as guide to size. Sit the paper-lined side of the tin's base directly on top of the dough. Trim off any excess dough (you could bake those trimmings separately as a cook's perk), then quickly but carefully flip the rolling paper, dough and tin base over in one movement. Peel off the large sheet of rolling paper and sit the dough and base in the tart tin. Don't worry if any small pieces crumble away, you can just patch them back on.

Use a sharp knife to score 8 even portions, then use the prongs of a fork to prick a pretty pattern. Chill for 30 minutes.

Preheat the oven to 140C fan/160C/325F/gas mark 3.

Bake your shortbread for 35–40 minutes. It is ready when the edges are just about starting to crisp and it's still slightly soft to the touch. With the shortbread still in its tin, cut through the slice marks you made earlier and go back over your forked pattern. Sprinkle over the granulated sugar.

Ease the base and shortbread out of the tin and carefully transfer each slice onto a wire rack to cool and harden. The shortbread tails will keep well in an airtight tin for a few days.

Borough queen of puddings

Imagine toffee-coloured meringue billowing above a layer of sweet fruit and a base of soft custardy 'sponge', with a hint of orange and cinnamon. And what you have is this take on old-school queen of puddings.

The muscovado sugar in the meringue is what makes it deep in colour and flavour. Brown sugars can be switched into the sugar quotient in any meringue-making, but are perhaps most welcome in dishes like this where the meringue is served hot from the oven, it's texture pillowy with the Italian meringue process (see below).

You could use whatever jam you have got excited by on a market stall or have to hand, and switch up the accompanying flavourings accordingly. This is, of course, another great use for your freezer-bag of breadcrumbs.

Serves 6

125g breadcrumbs

1 orange

150g caster sugar

1 teaspoon ground cinnamon

500ml whole milk

4 medium eggs

½ teaspoon vanilla extract

250–300g plum jam

80g dark muscovado sugar

Cream, to serve

*You will need a baking dish
of approx. 1.5-litre capacity*

*This recipe uses extra-airy
Italian meringue. The roulade
on page 300 is French meringue
(and you could use that simpler
technique here in this recipe).
The other meringue style is
Swiss meringue, where the whites
and sugar are heated together
in a double boiler to 71C and
then whisked.*

Mix the breadcrumbs in a bowl with the finely grated zest of the orange, 50g of the caster sugar and the cinnamon. Set aside in the baking dish.

Preheat the oven to 160C fan/180C/350F/gas mark 4.

Heat the milk in a saucepan over a medium heat until just simmering. Use that time to separate the eggs, putting the whites into a scrupulously clean mixing bowl and the yolks into another bowl. Whisk the yolks until thick and lighter in colour, then whisk the scalded milk into them, going slowly so as not to scramble them. Add the vanilla extract, then pour the mixture over the breadcrumbs in the dish, mixing well and spreading out in an even layer.

Bake the base layer for about 20 minutes until just about firm. Remove from the oven and let it cool, then spoon the jam over the base and spread it out evenly. Set aside while you make the topping.

Mix the muscovado sugar and the rest of the caster sugar in a pan with 75ml water and heat until it reaches 118C on a thermometer. Whisk the egg whites as the syrup heats, taking them just to the point of forming stiff peaks, then very slowly pour in the hot syrup as you continue to whisk. Whisk at the highest speed until the mixture has cooled down to room temperature, then lightly spoon the meringue mixture over the jam.

Bake in the oven for 10-15 minutes until the meringue is just crisping up.

Let it sit out of the oven for 5 minutes before serving, with cream on the side.

Pear and ginger treacle tart

Treacle tart filling (which traditionally doesn't actually contain treacle, but uses golden syrup instead) is here made with a combination of rye breadcrumbs and white breadcrumbs. The presence of the rye gives the filling a lovely flavour and I think helps with the texture too. Use all white breadcrumbs if that is what you have, but perhaps not all rye – you need the balance, ideally.

Serves 8

For the pastry

225g plain flour, plus extra for dusting

25g ground almonds

50g icing sugar

150g cold butter, plus an extra knob
for greasing

1 egg yolk

1 tablespoon cold milk (optional)

For the filling

1 x 454g tin golden syrup

90g rye breadcrumbs

80g white breadcrumbs

1 unwaxed lemon

2 teaspoons ground ginger

1 egg

For the poached pears

200g caster sugar, plus 1 tablespoon
for sprinkling

3 ripe pears

½ lemon

1 cinnamon stick, broken in half

3 cloves

1 star anise

*You will need a 22–23cm fluted,
loose-bottomed tart tin*

First, make the pastry. Sift into a large mixing bowl the flour, almonds and icing sugar. Dice the butter and rub it into the flour mix using your fingertips until it looks like breadcrumbs. Beat the egg yolk, add that and bring it together into a smooth dough. You might need to add a little cold milk to help it come together, but add as little as you can get away with. Shape into a disc, wrap and chill for 1 hour.

While the pastry is chilling, prepare the treacle tart filling. Gently heat the syrup in a large pan over a low heat. Take it off the heat and stir in the breadcrumbs, zest and juice of the lemon, and the ginger. Beat the egg until frothy and fold that in too.

To poach the pears, choose a saucepan that will hold the pears snugly. First put the caster sugar and 500ml water in it and bring to the boil. Peel the pears, halve and core them, then rub them with the cut side of the lemon half and slide them into the water. Add the cinnamon stick, cloves, star anise and juice from the half lemon. Simmer with a lid on over a low–medium heat for 20 minutes, or until the pears are tender, then take them out of the pan to cool.

Preheat the oven to 170C fan/200C/400F/gas mark 6 and lightly grease the base and sides of the tart tin.

Roll out the pastry on a lightly floured surface until it is large enough to line your tin. Carefully lift the pastry over the rolling pin and transfer to the tart tin. Gently press the pastry into the fluted sides. Let the pastry overhang, as it will shrink as it cooks. Chill for 20 minutes.

Prick the base of the chilled pastry case a few times with a fork. Line with baking paper and fill with rice, dried beans or baking beans. Bake in the oven for 15 minutes, remove the paper and beans, then return to the oven for another 5 minutes. Transfer to a wire rack to cool and trim the pastry edges. While it's cooling, slice the poached pears into lengths about 1cm thick.

Spread the filling mixture inside the tart case. Arrange the pears on top and sprinkle a little caster sugar over. Bake for about 45 minutes, checking after 30 minutes. If the pastry is getting a bit dark, cover the pastry edges with foil. You want the treacle centre to be lightly browned and starting to firm up.

Remove from the oven and let the tart cool in its tin on a wire rack before removing it from the tin to serve with cream or ice cream.

Any good in-season pears are fabulous here. But if while out shopping you happen to see the distinctive Crassane pears they would be exceptionally good. They are harvested in the late autumn when not yet ripe, then stored for several months with their stalks dipped in red wax to prevent moisture loss. By December they are soft and juicy, with a remarkable smell and taste. (You can see them on page 258 amongst the cheeseboard accompaniments.)

Cherry meringue roulade

See the stacks of beautiful meringues over at Comptoir Gourmand and you'll want to know their head chef Victor Arias's advice on making the best meringues – crispy outside and gooey inside:

'Use the freshest eggs you can get your hands on. The egg whites must be at room temperature to achieve the lightest meringue, as it creates the biggest volume and they will whip faster than cold eggs. Always start to whip slowly and gradually increase the speed. This goes for using an electric or hand-held whisk. Our top tip is always leave meringues in the oven (turned off) once cooked, to stop them from cracking.'

Here the meringue is wrapped around cherries that have macerated in sweet vermouth and lavender for a fruitily musky hit amongst the sweet meringue and cream. Sheer decadence and elegance.

Serves 6

4 large egg whites, at room
    temperature

200g caster sugar

1 teaspoon vanilla extract

1 teaspoon white wine vinegar

1 teaspoon cornflour

2 tablespoons icing sugar

400ml double cream

75g dark chocolate,
    broken into pieces

For the cherry filling

250g fresh cherries

250ml sweet vermouth

½ teaspoon dried lavender

1 teaspoon cornflour

You will need a 23 x 32cm baking tray

Preheat the oven to 170C fan/190C/375F/gas mark 5. Grease the baking tray, then line it with baking paper that comes 1cm higher than the sides.

Whisk the egg whites in a large, very clean mixing bowl until stiff. Add 1 tablespoon of the caster sugar, whisk again, then add the rest of the sugar in stages, whisking constantly until the mixture forms stiff peaks. Then, very carefully, fold in the vanilla extract, vinegar and cornflour. Spoon the meringue mix onto the prepared tray and loosely spread it to the edges with the back of a spoon. Put it into the oven, straight away turning the temperature down to 130C fan/150C/300F/gas mark 2. Bake for 30 minutes, by which time the meringue should have a bit of a crust and feel firm to the touch. Turn the oven off and leave the meringue inside to cool.

While the meringue is baking, halve and stone the cherries. Put them into a saucepan along with the vermouth and lavender and simmer for 10 minutes over a low–medium heat. Mix the cornflour with 2 teaspoons cold water, then add it to the pan of cherries and simmer for another couple of minutes so that the juices thicken. Set aside to cool.

To build your roulade. Sift half the icing sugar over a large piece of baking paper. Carefully turn the meringue onto it, then peel off the paper the meringue cooked on. Whip the double cream in a bowl with the rest of the icing sugar. Spread the cream over the meringue, leaving a border around the edge of 2cm or so. Spoon the cooled cherries and their sauce over the cream.

Roll up the roulade starting from one of its short edges – go as tightly as you can, using the paper to help you. Carefully transfer to a serving plate and chill for at least 30 minutes.

Break the chocolate into a heatproof bowl suspended over a pan of simmering water (making sure the water doesn't touch the bottom of the bowl). Once the chocolate has melted, take the bowl off the pan and let it cool for just 10 seconds as you take the roulade out of the fridge. Use a fork to drizzle the melted chocolate over the roulade, then return it to the fridge to carry on firming up.

Slice to serve.

Damson ripple sourdough ice cream

You know that feeling when you have just one last piece of a sourdough loaf left? Perhaps it has gone just a bit too hard that even a thick spreading of butter can't rescue it. You know you don't want to waste it – especially once you've read Olivier Favrel of Olivier's Bakery on page 280 explaining how much love and care goes into making really good bread. That's when you need a recipe like this up your sleeve.

Using sourdough is a twist on the classic brown bread ice cream. Small pieces of bread are caramelised to nuggets of sweetness that give texture to the ice cream with its tart damson ripple.

Makes about 1 litre

10 egg yolks

170g caster sugar

700ml whole milk

300ml double cream

2 vanilla pods

100g sourdough bread

20g unsalted butter

75g demerara or soft light brown sugar

350g damsons

1½ teaspoons icing sugar

Beat the egg yolks and sugar together in a large mixing bowl until they become lighter in texture and colour.

Pour the milk and cream into a large saucepan. Split the vanilla pods lengthways, scrape out the seeds, and add the pods and seeds to the milk. Place over a low–medium heat and heat until almost boiling (if you have a cooking thermometer, it should read about 80C). Whisk the hot milk into the sugared eggs, adding it a little at a time so as to not scramble the yolks.

Pour it all back into the saucepan and stir continuously over a low heat until you have a custard that is thick enough to coat the back of a wooden spoon. Remove from the heat and pour it – pods and all – into a bowl or large jug. Cover and leave to cool, then chill in the fridge overnight or for at least 4 hours.

For the sourdough crumbs: preheat the oven to 170C fan/190C/375F/gas mark 5 and line a large baking tray with baking paper. Tear or blend the sourdough into crumbs. You are after a mix of crumb sizes, none bigger than a small pea. Melt the butter in a large frying pan over a low heat, stir in the breadcrumbs, then stir in the demerara or soft light brown sugar. Keep stirring until every piece of bread is coated. Spread out evenly on the lined baking tray and bake in the oven for 12–15 minutes, stirring occasionally. They are ready when on their way to a deep brown colour. Remove from the oven and set aside to cool.

To make the ripple, put the damsons into a medium saucepan with 4 tablespoons water, then cover and cook over a low–medium heat for 10 minutes until the fruit is collapsing. Push it all through a sieve into a bowl, getting as much out of the fruit as you possibly can. Don't forget to scrape off and use the puree coating the underside of the sieve. Stir through the icing sugar and chill.

Remove the vanilla pods from the chilled custard, then churn in an ice cream machine according to the manufacturer's instructions. When it's almost ready, add the baked sourdough crumbs to the mix. Once fully churned, spoon about a third into whatever you'll be freezing the ice cream in and spoon over about a third of the damson puree. Ripple it through with a cocktail stick or skewer. Repeat with the rest of the ice cream and the puree. Freeze until ready to serve.

Brown butter victoria sponge with orange and saffron curd

This is a very grown-up victoria sponge, made slightly addictive by browning the butter for the sponge to give it an almost fudge-like character. The sandwich layers are filled with a fresh but quite intense curd to make a tall, impressive cake for any occasion.

Serves 8–10

4 eggs

250–270g unsalted butter, plus extra
    for greasing

250–270g golden caster sugar

250–270g self-raising flour

1 teaspoon vanilla extract

1 tablespoon cold milk (optional)

225ml double cream

For the orange and saffron curd

Pinch of saffron threads

3 oranges

70g caster sugar

2 whole eggs, plus 2 yolks (4 eggs)

70g unsalted butter

*You will need 2 x 20cm sandwich
cake tins*

Begin by weighing the eggs in their shells – their weight determines the weights of butter, sugar and flour you will use. They all need to be equal.

To brown the butter, put it into a small saucepan over a low heat – choose a pan with a pale interior if you have it, so it's easier to see the colour changing. Swirl the pan occasionally and in about 5 minutes you'll see it start to transform from golden and frothy to amber. At that point remove it from the heat and go no further or it will burn. Pour into a heatproof bowl and chill for 30–45 minutes or long enough for the butter to firm up again to the consistency of the softened butter you'd usually use for a sponge cake recipe.

Preheat the oven to 160C fan/180C/350F/gas mark 4. Lightly grease the base and sides of both cake tins and line their bases with baking parchment.

Beat the browned butter in a mixing bowl with a wooden spoon until creamy, then beat in the sugar until light and fluffy. Beat in the eggs one at a time, with an accompanying tablespoon of the flour to prevent curdling. Beat in the vanilla extract, sift in the rest of the flour, then fold it gently into the mix so as not to lose all the lightness you've been beating in. You want a mixture that drops easily off the spoon – if it feels a bit thick, you could add a little milk.

Divide the mixture evenly between the lined tins, weighing them if you want to make sure you have the same amount in each. Use a knife to level out the mixture and bake for 25–30 minutes, until a skewer inserted into the centre of each cake comes out clean. Remove from the oven and let the cakes cool in their tins for a couple of minutes, then turn out onto a wire rack to cool completely. Turn the oven down to 110 C fan/130C/250F/gas mark ½.

While the cakes are baking, make the curd. Put the saffron in a small bowl, pour over 1½ teaspoons hot water and set aside. Use a vegetable peeler to remove the peel from one of the oranges, taking as little of the white pith as possible, and set aside for decoration. Squeeze the juice from all the oranges – you need 150ml. Mix the caster sugar and the whole eggs and yolks in a bowl. Stir in the orange juice, saffron and its infusing water, and a pinch of salt. Melt the butter over a very low heat in a medium saucepan, then stir the orange / egg mix into the melted butter and keep stirring continuously over a low heat for 10–12 minutes until it thickens. Pour it into a heatproof bowl and chill for 1 hour or so to thicken up.

Line a baking tray with baking paper. Slice the reserved orange peel into strips roughly 2mm-thick, scatter onto the tray and bake in the cooled oven for 20 minutes until dried and curling. Remove from the oven and set aside to cool. Whisk the double cream until thick, gently ripple through three-quarters of the curd, then chill until you need it, so it stays firm.

Use your most impartial eye to choose which is the better-looking sponge and that will be your top layer. Sit the base layer on a plate, flattest side down. Spoon on two-thirds of the cream and curd filling, then sit your top layer on top, flattest side facing up. Spread the remaining curd-rippled cream on the top, then spoon the remaining curd over. Scatter over the dried orange peel to decorate.

The Bakery

Orange blossom doughnuts

The Bread Ahead Bakery doughnuts at the Market are iconic, legendary and incomparable. They are also pretty big. Eating one is a challenge I can't say I haven't succeeded at, but sometimes the kind of doughnut I want to make and eat is something a little smaller. So these fluffy rounds of doughnut are only a little bigger than bite-sized, with a hint of orange blossom worked into the dough.

They are ideal for dipping. That's where having a jar of Porteña dulce de leche in the cupboard pays dividends. Or I might make some rich chocolate sauce as in the recipe below. Go wherever your doughnut inclinations take you.

Makes 12 doughnuts

20g unsalted butter, at room temperature

75ml whole milk

210g strong white flour, plus extra for dusting

7g sachet fast-action yeast

½ teaspoon fine salt

25g caster sugar, plus 3 tablespoons extra for finishing

1 egg

1½ tablespoons orange blossom water

1 litre sunflower oil or other deep-frying oil

Cut the butter into small pieces into a small bowl. Gently warm the milk in a small saucepan until almost boiling (about 80C), then pour it over the butter to melt it. Set aside.

Put the flour, yeast, salt and caster sugar into a large mixing bowl. Beat the egg and add that too, along with the orange blossom water. Add the slightly cooled butter and milk mixture and start to bring it all into a dough with your hands. Knead on a lightly floured surface for 10 minutes, or until smooth and springy. Shape the dough into a large ball, put it in a bowl, cover with a tea towel and leave somewhere warm for about 1 hour to double in size.

Shape the risen dough into 12 equal balls, about 30g each. Sit them on a lightly floured tray somewhere warm for 30 minutes to rise a little more.

Spoon the extra caster sugar into a shallow bowl. Pour the oil into a large deep saucepan – the oil should come about a third of the way up the pan. Heat to 160C, then use a slotted spoon to slide the dough balls into the hot oil. Don't crowd the pan – just fry three or four at a time. Fry them for 2–3 minutes until the undersides become golden brown, then flip over with a spoon or fork and fry for another few minutes. Lift out with the slotted spoon, drain briefly on kitchen paper, then roll in the caster sugar.

Serve your doughnuts with a dipping sauce of your choosing.

With a cup of rich chocolate

Break 200g of dark chocolate into a heatproof bowl sitting over a pan of simmering water (making sure the water doesn't touch the bowl). As the chocolate starts to melt, whisk in 200ml whole milk and 2 teaspoons of cornflour. Keep whisking for about 5 minutes to thicken. Pour into a bowl for dunking the doughnuts into.

Drinks

Sherries

There's a style of sherry for pretty much every dish you might care to serve a glass with. Starting at one end with bone dry styles and running a spectrum that takes us all the way to sweet sherries that can be a dessert in their own right.

The shelves at Brindisa and Bedales of Borough cover them all, so to help you choose what's what and what to serve them with:

Fino / manzanilla

The driest of the sherry styles are the fino and manzanilla. They can be salty, lemony and just glorious with anything in the salty, fried line of things.

Amontillado

This is where things move up a gear in flavour. As Mario Sposito of Bedales of Borough explains, Amontillado is 'a richer, darker and more complex sherry style. Amontillado ages under flor for a period of time and then is refortified to age oxidatively until bottling. This style of sherry offers a wide range of flavours, from biscuit and bread to walnuts and caramel.' Amontillados can be dry or sweet, with food matchings similarly varied.

Oloroso

All deep and nutty and just delicious. Back to Mario for the technical steer: 'Oloroso sherry ages in contact with oxygen and over time takes a brown colour and develops notes of dried fruit and walnuts.' Serve with hearty meat dishes or note that its deep nuttiness can stand up to desserts too.

Pedro ximénez

At the sweetest end of the sherry spectrum is pedro ximénez – often shortened to just PX. Smooth, dark and raisiny with notes of dried fruit, coffee and liquorice. For dessert you may well decide you need little more, but if you do want to put it with foods think depth and dark chocolate. Or the classic serve of pedro ximénez poured over vanilla ice-cream.

Dietary matrix (brackets signify an option)

THE FISHMONGERS	VEGAN	VEGETARIAN	GLUTEN FREE	DAIRY FREE	NUT FREE	PAGE
Sardines with fennel, capers and mint			x	x	x	29
Bourbon and coriander seed gravadlax			x	x	x	30
Arbroath smokie croquetas					x	33
The whole crab – crab toasts with crab and vegetable broth			(x)	(x)	x	34
Deep-fried oysters with horseradish sauce, quick-pickled ginger and spring onion					x	36
Mussels in lemongrass, galangal and turmeric broth				(x)	x	39
Scallop and bacon bap				x	x	40
Fishmonger's pie with fish crackling					x	42
Bream fillets with buttered cobnuts and mixed beans			x			45
Slow-cooked cuttlefish and white beans			x	x	x	47
One-tin herb-stuffed fish on roasted vegetables			x	x	x	48
Roasted cod's head with clams and seaweed			x		x	50
THE BUTCHERS						
Game terrine with fennel, apple and radish remoulade				(x)	x	67
Rabbit ragu pappardelle			x		x	70
Pork cochinita pibil tacos with black beans and x ni pek onions			x	x	x	72
Venison steak with samphire			x		x	75
Pork tomahawk			x	x	x	76
Black pudding, cavolo nero, potato and egg breakfast pan			x		x	79
Stuffed hogget with spelt and chard				x		84
Oxtail with herbed suet dumplings and blackberry-braised shallots					x	88
Beef, leek and ale pie			(x)		x	90
THE STORE CUPBOARD I						
Pickled habanero and serrano chillies with lemongrass	x		x	x	x	107
Hot anchovy and garlic sauce for roasted purple sprouting broccoli and walnuts			x			109
Nicoise bundles			x	x	x	110
Truffled lentils with radicchio and carrots	x		x	x	x	112
Baked gammon with Market preserve glaze			x	x	x	113

	VEGAN	VEGETARIAN	GLUTEN FREE	DAIRY FREE	NUT FREE	PAGE
Partridges in sloe gin with creamed Jerusalem artichokes			x		x	116
Chestnut honey and rosemary ice cream			x		x	120
Salted nut butter millionaires						122
Chocolate olive oil cake with figs and hazelnuts						125
Pomelo cocktail bitters		x	x	x	x	126
THE GREENGROCERS						
Tomatoes fermented with celery and lime leaves	x		x	x	x	142
Watercress soup with lemon and thyme breadcrumbs		x			x	144
Asparagus with quail's eggs and shaved truffle		x	x	x	x	147
Globe courgettes with wild mushrooms and nuts	x	(x)		x		148
Parsnip gnocchi and smoked garlic butter with crisped sage leaves		x			x	150
Grilled sweetcorn cobs with toasted coconut, lime and Urfa chilli	x		x	x	x	152
Black rice and feta-stuffed chard with spiced yoghurt		x	x		x	154
Charred hispi cabbage with bottarga cream sauce			x		x	157
Shaved kohlrabi, chickpeas and little gem salad	x		x	x	x	158
Warm borlotti bean and pea salad	x		x	x	x	160
Mixed root hasselbacks with miso butter	(x)	x	(x)	x	x	162
THE FRUITERERS						
Blood orange, watermelon radish and purple kale salad	x		x	x	x	180
Charred pineapple and soused mackerel with cucumber and mint			x	x	x	183
Hot and sour green papaya curry with prawns			(x)	x	x	184
Roast duck legs with spiced quince and charred sprout tops			x	x	x	186
Fig and liquorice sorbet	(x)		x	x	x	189
Apple snow with fennel and rosewater biscuits					x	190
A late summer crumble with pedro ximénez custard						192
Pineapple and rum upside-down cake					x	194
Candied citrus	x		x	x	x	195
Greengages in bay, cardamom and calvados	x		x	x	x	197
THE STORE CUPBOARD II						
Moong dal dosa with tomato chutney	x		x	x	x	215
Broth of white beans and winter greens		(x)	x		x	219
Muhammara and griddled prawns	(x)		(x)	x	(x)	222

Dietary matrix *continued*

	VEGAN	VEGETARIAN	GLUTEN FREE	DAIRY FREE	NUT FREE	PAGE
Oregano-poached peaches, halloumi and hazelnuts		x	x			224
Walnut and pomegranate baby aubergines with saffron quinoa	x		x	x		226
Beef skirt with coffee and chilli dry rub			x	x	x	228
Oat milk and rosewater rice pudding with toasted granola	x		x	x		230
Whisky mocha charlotte		x			x	232
Jasmine tea loaf with salted lime butter				(x)	x	234
Pomegranate margarita	x	x	x	x	x	237
THE DAIRY						
Cauliflower, parmesan and cauliflower leaf soup		(x)	x		x	250
Three-cheese bourek with honey and nigella seeds		x			x	253
Vegan blue cheese, mango and watercress salad	x		x	x		254
Tartiflette			x		x	255
Loaf-baked whole cheese with girolles		x			x	256
Buttermilk crumpets		x			x	263
Labneh with watermelon, honey and mint		x	x		x	264
Bay and cardamom raw milk pannacotta			x		x	269
Ginger and pink peppercorn baked cheesecake			(x)		x	270
Rhubarb and sweet vermouth fool			x		x	273
Dark rum egg nog			x		x	274
THE BAKERY						
Deep celeriac, potato and gruyère pie		x			x	288
Mediterranean vegetable picnic loaf	x			x	x	292
Chickpea flatbreads with za'atar	x		x	x	x	294
Spiced shortbread tails					x	295
Borough queen of puddings					x	296
Pear and ginger treacle tart					x	298
Cherry meringue roulade			x		x	300
Damson ripple sourdough ice cream					x	302
Brown butter victoria sponge with orange and saffron curd					x	304
Orange blossom doughnuts					x	306

Index

Metric / Imperial conversion chart

All equivalents are rounded, for practical convenience.

WEIGHT

25g	1 oz
50g	2 oz
100g	3½ oz
150g	5 oz
200g	7 oz
250g	9 oz
300g	10 oz
400g	14 oz
500g	1 lb 2 oz
1kg	2 lb 4oz

LENGTH

1cm	½ inch
2.5cm	1 inch
20cm	8 inches
25cm	10 inches
30cm	12 inches

OVEN TEMPERATURES

Celsius	Fahrenheit
140	275
150	300
160	325
180	350
190	375
200	400
220	425
230	450

VOLUME (LIQUIDS)

5ml		1 tsp
15ml		1 tbsp
30ml	1 fl oz	⅛ cup
60ml	2 fl oz	¼ cup
75ml		⅓ cup
120ml	4 fl oz	½ cup
150ml	5 fl oz	⅔ cup
175ml		¾ cup
250ml	8 fl oz	1 cup
1 litre	1 quart	4 cups

VOLUME (dry ingredients – an approximate guide)

Butter	1 cup (2 sticks) = 225g
Rolled oats	1 cup = 100g
Fine powders (eg flour)	1 cup = 125g
Breadcrumbs (fresh)	1 cup = 50g
Breadcrumbs (dried)	1 cup = 125g
Nuts (eg almonds)	1 cup = 125g
Seeds (eg chia)	1 cup = 160g
Dried fruit (eg raisins)	1 cup = 150g
Dried legumes (large, eg chickpeas)	1 cup = 170g
Grains, granular goods and small dried legumes (eg rice, quinoa, sugar, lentils)	1 cup = 200g
Grated cheese	1 cup = 100g

Biographies

Borough Market

Borough Market has existed in one form or another for over 1,000 years and has been trading from its current site since 1756. Despite its venerable status, it is as influential today as it has ever been. Run by a charitable trust, the Market's mission is to provide exceptional food in a manner that works for the benefit of the community: for shoppers, traders, neighbours, and all the other people whose lives it might affect. This means selecting traders not just for the quality of their food but for their approach to sustainability and traceability and their commitment to suppliers and staff. It means working hard to minimise the Market's environmental impact and keep food waste to a minimum. It means tapping into the traders' knowledge of food and cookery to provide education and inspiration, in everything from a regular schools programme to this beautiful cookbook.

Visit our website and social media to discover more about our traders:

www.boroughmarket.org.uk
@boroughmarket

Angela Clutton

Angela Clutton is a cook, presenter and award-winning food-writer.

Her debut book, *The Vinegar Cupboard*, won the Jane Grigson Trust Award, was shortlisted for the André Simon Food and Drink Awards; won two awards at the Guild of Food Writers Awards; and won 'Debut Cookery Book' at the Fortnum & Mason Food and Drink Awards. Angela has been the Co-director of the British Library Food Season since 2020, curating and presenting talks and events across food issues, culture and writing. She has written for a wide range of national publications and broadcast work includes the Channel 5 'Inside...' series.

Angela's long-standing relationship with Borough Market spans writing features, developing recipes, and live cooking demonstrations. She presents the Market's Borough Talks podcast series, and is host of the Borough Market Cookbook Club.

www.angelaclutton.com
@angela_clutton

Acknowledgements

Borough Market would like to thank:

The many traders who contributed their insights to this book and the dozens of others who share their knowledge with such generosity of spirit every day of the week. They are the Market.

The Hodder & Stoughton editorial team of Liz Gough, Issy Gonzalez-Prendergast and Liv Nightingall for another pleasurable instalment in a long and fruitful collaboration.

The food and photography team of Kim Lightbody, Kitty Coles and Tabitha Hawkins, whose vision sings from these pages, and the designer Dave Brown who brought our book together so beautifully.

Clare Finney, a brilliant food writer, for her obduracy in corralling dozens of busy traders to talk to her and her skill in recording and shaping their expertise for the Knowledge sections of this book.

Claire Ford for managing a large, complex project with such rigour and poise, and Mark Riddaway for being a sounding board and well of good sense.

Wine expert Jane Parkinson for her invaluable guidance, Justin Kowbel of Borough Kitchen for his generous loan of beautiful homewares, and Sharon Crane of The Gated Garden for gracing our tables with posies.

Fiona Smith, Emma Knight, Sahina Bibi and Alice Morley for bringing the book to the public's attention.

Our agent Zoe Ross for her invaluable support.

The many recipe testers who gave up their time to eat and assess.

The trustees who shape the Market's evolution, and the dynamic, hard-working staff and executive team, particularly Kate Howell, who has driven this collaboration from the start.

Finally, the amazing Angela Clutton – not just for her beautiful writing and recipes, or for being such a committed and energetic partner in this project, but for her extraordinary contribution over many years to the Borough Market community.

Angela Clutton would like to thank:

First and foremost, my thanks to Kate Howell and Claire Ford – two titans of the Market. Kate, thank you for inviting me to work on this project. Claire, thank you for steering it all so brilliantly. I could not have wished for a better teammate.

Clare Finney – such skilful wrangling of the traders and their knowledge! Mark Riddaway– you are a bit of a hero. Jane Parkinson – brilliant steers on the wines.

My thanks too to everyone at Hodder – Liz Gough, Issy Gonzalez-Prendergast and Liv Nightingall on the editorial side; Emma Knight, Sahina Bibi and Alice Morley for getting the word out about it all. Fiona Smith – always a joy! And Dave Brown, what a job you did wrestling all these different elements into a beautiful, dynamic book.

Kitty Coles and Florence Blair for working so bloody hard on the shoot days to make all the food look so wonderful. And Tabitha Hawkins for the gorgeous propping. Kim Lightbody – I think your photography is absolutely stunning.

Sabhbh Curran, my lovely agent – thank you for always being there with an ear, advice and support. I commend your instinct for timing arrivals at shoot days for just the right moment food is being served!

My James. Indefatigable in your support – even, or especially, when I was losing my mind a little in the thick of recipe developing. Marie and Ernie Clutton too, for helping out on the recipe tasting.

Lastly, my love and thanks to everyone at the Market: traders, trustees, staff, Cookbook Club-ers, shoppers... Borough Market is a place of community, and that community provides the heartbeat of this book.